Transformation, Development, and Regionalization in Greater Asia | 13

The Series

Transformation, Development, and Regionalization in Greater Asia

is edited by

Prof. Dr. Christoph Schuck
Department of Philosophy and Political Science
TU Dortmund University, Germany

Matthias Heise, M.A.,
Department of Philosophy and Political Science
TU Dortmund University, Germany

Aknolt Kristian Pakpahan

The Development of Business Clusters in Indonesia

The Cases of Cibaduyut and Plered, West Java

Nomos

BLOOMSBURY

Japan Indonesia Presidential Scholarship of the World Bank funded by a grant from the Government of Japan.

Parahyangan Catholic University, Bandung, Indonesia.

Die Deutsche Nationalbibliothek lists this publication in the Deutsche Nationalbibliografie; detailed bibliographic data is available in the Internet at http://dnb.d-nb.de

a.t.: Dortmund, TU, Diss., 2014

ISBN:	HB (Nomos)	978-3-8487-0694-5
	ePDF (Nomos)	978-3-8452-4905-6

British Library Cataloguing-in-Publication Data
A catalogue record for this book is available from the British Library.

ISBN:	HB (Bloomsbury):	978-1-4742-2499-4
	ePDF (Bloomsbury):	978-1-4742-2498-7
	ePub (Bloomsbury):	978-1-4742-2497-0

Library of Congress Cataloging-in-Publication Data
Pakpahan, Aknolt Kristian
The Development of Business Clusters in Indonesia
The Cases of Cibaduyut and Plered, West Java
Aknolt Kristian Pakpahan
259 p.
Includes bibliographic references.

ISBN	978-1-4742-2499-4	(hardcover Bloomsbury)
ISBN	978-1-4742-2498-7	(ebook (pdf) Bloomsbury)
ISBN	978-1-4742-2497-0	(ebook (epub) Bloomsbury)

1. Edition 2014

Acknowledgements

The writing of this dissertation has been one of the most important academic challenges I have ever had to face. I would like to express my greatest appreciation to Prof. Dr. Christoph Schuck and Prof. Dr. Bob S. Hadiwinata, my research supervisors, for their excellent guidance, enthusiastic encouragement, and useful critiques of this research work.

My candidature was made possible with the funding from the Japan Indonesia Presidential Scholarship Program (JIPS) of the World Bank and funded by a grant from the government of Japan. I must thank Ms. Danielle Carbonneau, Ms. Marie des Neiges Grossas, and Ms. Karim Gigler who fully assisted me during my study in Dortmund, Germany.

The significant support in focusing this work comes from colleagues at the Department of Philosophy and Political Science of TU Dortmund University, especially Kathrin Rucktäschel, Matthias Heise, Adrianus Harsawaskita, Julia Dumin, and Katharina Vitt. I must thank colleagues from the Department of International Relations of Parahyangan Catholic University especially Dr. Mangadar Situmorang, Dr. Yulius P. Hermawan, Dr. I. Nyoman Sudira, and Dr. Andreas H. Pareira for supporting and motivating me during my study. Mostly I am really grateful to Dr. Pius Sugeng Prasetyo and Dr. Sylvia Yazid who motivated me to finalize my dissertation during their short stay in Dortmund. My gratitude is also extended to Albert Triwibowo for the friendship and discussions to sharpen the focus of this research. For generously giving their time for both formal and informal meetings, I thank Abdul Nizar and his staff at the UPTD Litbang Keramik Plered and Wawan Dharmawan and his staff at Instalasi Pengembangan Industri Kecil Menengah Persepatuan Kota Bandung. Also, I would like to thank Giandi Kartasasmita, Cantika Paramitha Rustandi, Lukas Ronggur Tambunan, Atty Juliani, Rabby Putraditama, Adipurno Widi Putranto, and Marendra Cahya Sadikin for assisting me in conducting field research in Indonesia.

Last but not least, I would like to express a great amount of gratitude to my wife, Durienzia Wulanputri Supit, without whom this effort would have been worth nothing. Her love, support, patience, and belief in me allowed me to remain focused. I also would like to express my appreciation to my son, Andrew Tizi Landros Pakpahan for his unending support. He was always there cheering me up through the good and bad times. For my family, I am really sorry for the time we spent apart. Therefore, this dissertation is dedicated to them, Enzi and Andrew.

Contents

List of Tables and Figures

TABLES

FIGURES

Glossary of Terms

APACI	*Asosiasi Pengusaha Cibaduyut,* Businessmen Association of Cibaduyut
APSC	*Asosiasi Pengusaha Sepatu Cibaduyut*, Association of Shoe Businessmen in Cibaduyut
ATK	*Akademi Teknologi Kulit*, Leather Technology Academy
Bappeda	*Badan Perencana Pembangunan Daerah*, Regional Body for Planning and Development
Bappenas	*Badan Perencanaan Nasional*, National Planning Agency
BBKKP	*Balai Besar Kulit, Karet, dan Plastik*, Center for Leather, Rubber, and Plastics
BDS	Business Development Service
BDS-P	Business Development Services-Provider
BIPIK	*Pembinaan dan Pengembangan Industri Kecil*, small industrial development program
BKPM	*Badan Koordinasi Penanaman Modal*, Indonesia Investment Coordinating Board
BPP	*Balai Penelitian Perkebunan*, Plantation Research Institute
BPPT	*Badan Pengkajian dan Penerapan Teknologi,* Agency for the Assessment and Application of Technology
BPS	*Badan Pusat Statistik*, central bureau of statistics, Statistics Indonesia
BPS-KPKM	*Badan Pengembangan Sumber Daya Koperasi dan Pengusaha Kecil dan Menengah,* Agency for Developing Cooperatives Resources and Small and Medium-sized Entrepreneurs
BPPKU	*Badan Promosi dan Pengelola Keterkaitan Usaha,* Promotion Agency and Business Linkages
BSN	*Badan Standardisasi Nasional*, National Standardization Agency of Indonesia
BUMN	*Badan Usaha Milik Negara,* state-owned enterprises (SOEs)
CSF	common service facilities
CSR	Corporate Social Responsilibity
EOI	export-oriented industrialization
FKPSC	*Forum Komunikasi Pengusaha Sepatu Cibaduyut*, Communication Forum for Shoe Businessmen in Cibaduyut
GDP	Gross Domestic Product
GRDP	Gross Regional Domestic Product

IPR	intellectual property rights
IPTN	Industri Pesawat Terbang Nurtanio (Nusantara)
ISI	import substitution industrialization
K3	*Komite Kesehatan Kerja*, Working Health Committee
KADIN	*Kamar Dagang dan Industri*, Indonesian Chamber of Commerce and Industry
KIK	*Kredit Investasi Kecil*, small investment credit
KMKP	*Kredit Modal Kerja Permanen*, working capital credit
KSM	Kelompok Swadaya Mandiri
KUR	*Kredit Usaha Rakyat*, people-based small business loans
LIPI	*Lembaga Ilmu Pengetahuan Indonesia*, Indonesian Institute of Sciences
LEs	large enterprises
LIK	*Lingkungan Industri Kecil*, small-scale industry area
LP3ES	*Lembaga Penelitian Pendidikan Penerangan Ekonomi dan Sosial*, Institute for Social and Economic Research, Education and Information
MoU	Memorandum of Understanding
OVOP	One Village One Product
PCD	partnership and community development
PIK	Pemukiman/Perkampungan Industri Kecil, small industry estates
Posyantek	*Pos Pelayanan Teknologi Tepat Guna*, appropriate technology service center
PRA	Participation Rural Appraisal
SAKASAKTI	*Satu Kabupaten/Kota, Satu Kompetensi Inti*, one regency/city, one core competence
Senbik	*Sentra Bisnis UKM*, SMEs' business center
SMEs	small and medium-sized enterprises
SMIs	small and medium-sized industries
SNI	*Standar Nasional Indonesia*, national product standards
TNC	transnational corporation
UPL	*Unit Pelayanan Langsung*, direct service unit
UPT	*Unit Pelayanan Teknis*, technical service unit
UPTD	*Unit Pelayanan Teknis Daerah*, regional/local technical service unit
Wartek	*Warung Teknologi Tepat Guna*, appropriate technology outlet
ZOPP	*Zielorientierte Projektplanung*, Goal-Oriented Project Planning

1. Introduction

1.1 Background

This research examines the governmental roles in developing business clusters, and in the implementation of business clusters to promote economic development in Indonesia, the regional economic development in West Java in general, and to increase the competitiveness of the industry as well as to create a strong industrial structure in particular. The implementation of the concept of business clusters has attracted many researchers for many decades. The interest of winning tight world competition by having specialization has pushed many governments to find strategies to promote their economic policies. The climate of tight world competition has been a major reason for countries to develop their specializations as well as to increase their competitiveness. Here, countries have tried to put more attention on the economic development in their regions including cities and regencies. Many strategies and models have been introduced to boost up the economic development process. Before the 1990s, the approach to increase regional economic development depended on external factors (forces outside the region).[1] What is meant by an external factor is a situation in which a country depends heavily on its export-led industries. The principle of selling more exported goods abroad and buying less imported goods leads to a policy created by a country to give a series of incentives to local firms. This can be understood as a tool to protect local firms from outside firms producing similar goods, and also as a tool to reduce the cost of production so that the products of firms having these incentives will be cheaper than those of their competitors in global markets. Therefore, besides having advantages of winning the competition – in form of prices –, these firms could also contribute to the stimulation of the domestic economy by providing jobs. Another advantage of providing incentives is that this strategy will attract outside (or large) firms to open production facilities because the incentive package helps them reducing the cost of production.

---

1 Cf. Primont/Domazlicky 2008.

However, this strategy washed-out in the early 1990s when countries faced competition with each other due to economic liberalization. Countries tried to attract firms by offering their location advantages such as the proximity to raw materials and cheap labor in order to reduce the cost of production. The need to focus on increasing a nation's competitiveness is more important than offering a series of incentives to firms. The tight global competition has forced nations to find a suitable strategy. The concept of cluster is seen as the answer. The cluster analysis introduced by Michael Porter has attracted government leaders, economists, academicians, and business actors to learn more on how this analysis could help countries and/or firms winning the tight global competition. The idea is to create *co-opetition* (cooperation and competition) simultaneously among firms so that this action will push a firm to improve and innovate. Huggins/Izushi (2011) stated that Porter's Diamond framework (the cluster) has influenced many governments and scientists to apply this concept in order to create their regional economic development policy.[2] Placing enterprises (in this case small and medium-sized enterprises/SMEs) into one location or region gives many advantages because business rivalry and business networks have been proved effective to increase the competitiveness of SMEs.[3] Recent economic climate is dominated by competitions among not only countries but firms (even small firms). Many studies or reports found that cluster plays an important role in promoting regional economic development as seen in Isbasoiu (2007),[4] Sigurdson (2004),[5] Kuah (2002),[6] and Feldman et al. (2005).[7] Hence, it cannot be denied, as Porter found out that regional economic development is influenced by the strength of local clusters.[8]

In Indonesia, the interest to accomplish its national goal of achieving a just and prosperous society as mandated in the 1945 Constitution has led the government to devise economic policies in order to achieve this goal. Such policies include the industrial policy and policies on developing and

2 Cf. Huggins/Izushi 2011, p. 2.
3 See Porter 2008, pp. 194-200.
4 See Isbasoiu 2006.
5 See Sigurdson 2004.
6 See Kuah 2002.
7 See Feldman et al. 2005.
8 Cf. Porter 2003, p. 571.

empowering SMEs/small and medium-sized industries (SMIs).[9] The main goal of the industrial policy in Indonesia is to improve the competitiveness of the industry and strengthen the industrial structure to support Indonesia's national economic development goals which are to improve household incomes, to promote job creation, and to alleviate poverty.[10] In order to build a strong industrial structure, the government also focuses on the development of other economic units such as SMEs/SMIs as driving forces of economic development.[11] The main reason to focus on the development of SMEs/SMIs is because the existence of SMEs/SMIs remained stable even during the economic crisis in 1997. Looking at the objectives of Indonesia's national industrial policy, it is not surprising that the government encourages the implementation of the business cluster concept for the creation of a strong industrial structure. In order to develop a business cluster in Indonesia, the government has issued many regulations. *First*, in order to develop (and empower) SMEs as a driving force in a business cluster, the government has issued Law No. 20/2008 on Small and Medium-sized Enterprises (SMEs).[12] This law regulates several issues that are related to the development and empowerment of SMEs. In this law, the development of SMEs is defined as an effort made by the (central) government, the local governments, businesses, and communities to develop SMEs through mentoring assistance and strengthening assistance to develop and enhance the capability and competitiveness of SMEs.[13] The empowerment of SMEs is defined as an effort that is done by the (central) government, the local governments, businesses, and communities as they work together in increasing the economic environment and the development of SMEs so that they can grow into independent and strong businesses.[14] *Second*, to build a strong industrial structure, the government has issued Regulation of the President of the Republic of Indonesia No. 28/2008 on the National Industrial Policy.[15] In this regulation, the purpose

9 For the purpose of this paper, SMEs shall refer to micro, small, and medium-sized enterprises while SMIs shall refer to micro, small, and medium-sized industries.

10 See Regulation of the President of the Republic of Indonesia No. 28/2008 and Law No. 20/2008.

11 The definition of SMEs and SMIs will be explained in Chapter 2 – Theoretical Framework.

12 See Law No. 20/2008.

13 Cf. Article 1 Paragraph 10 of Law No. 20/2008.

14 Cf. Article 1 Paragraph 8 of Law No. 20/2008 on SMEs.

15 See Regulation of the President of the Republic of Indonesia No. 28/2008.

of the national industrial policy is to improve the competitiveness of the industry. In supporting this objective, the ministry in charge of and responsible for the field of industry prepares and establishes a road map of the priority industrial cluster development including the industrial manufacturing base, the agro-based industry, the transportation industry, and the electronics and telemetric industry.[16] They are also to support industries such as creative industries and the creative industries in particular SMIs.[17] In addition to those priority industries, the Ministry of Industry also prepares and establishes a road map of provincial industrial development and a guide road map of industrial districts and the municipality's development.[18]

There have been much research and many studies on the theory and the concepts of business clusters.[19] At the same time, many researchers have conducted research on the impacts on implementing business clusters.[20] Most of the researches focused on the national level, while only few researches focused on the micro level i.e. rural areas. In Indonesia, there are a handful of studies on the impact of clustering on firms in rural areas in which Tambunan (2009) and Sandee et al. (2000) have previously conducted research on the micro level.[21] Therefore, it is still necessary to conduct research on the implementation of the concept of business clusters in rural areas in Indonesia. Based on that reason, the research will focus on, *firstly*, the role of the Indonesian government in developing business clusters in Indonesia, *secondly*, the implementation of business cluster in rural areas in the Province of West Java, taking the case of footwear industrial cluster and (decorative) ceramic industrial cluster, *thirdly*, factors that impede the implementation of business cluster concept in Indonesia by analyzing the two clusters above and, *finally*, the researcher takes a case study of the two locations to contribute to Porter's diamond theory. The main aim of this research is to offer a contribution to implementing the concept

16 Cf. Article 2 of Regulation of the President of the Republic of Indonesia No. 28/2008.
17 Cf. Article 2 of Regulation of the President of the Republic of Indonesia No. 28/2008.
18 Cf. Article 6 of Regulation of the President of the Republic of Indonesia No. 28/2008.
19 See for example Porter 2008, Perry 2005, Fujita et al. 2001.
20 See for example Baptista/Swann 1998, Feser et al. 2008, Boari 2001, Tambunan 2005.
21 See Tambunan 2009a, Sandee et al. 2000.

of business clusters in other countries/regions that have similar characteristics (regarding both the political system as well as economics) like the two industrial clusters mentioned above.

1.2 Research Questions

This research focuses on the governmental roles in developing business clusters and the implementation of business clusters in Indonesia using two research sites, the footwear industrial cluster in Cibaduyut and the decorative ceramic industrial cluster in Plered. Porter's diamond theory will be used as the basis to conduct the analysis of the contribution of these two research sites to Porter's diamond theory. Therefore, the following questions will be researched and answered:

1. What is the role of the Indonesian government in developing business clusters in Cibaduyut and Plered, West Java?
2. How is the concept of business clusters reflected in contemporary regional economic development in the Cibaduyut Footwear Industrial Cluster in Cibaduyut and the Plered Decorative Ceramic Industrial Cluster in Plered? What are problems faced by business actors (including SMEs/SMIs) in the two locations as a case of study that impede the implementation of business cluster concept in Indonesia?
3. Are there any other factors that influence the implementation of business clusters in the two locations? How can the implementation of business clusters in the two locations contribute to Porter's diamond theory especially in understanding the implementation of business clusters in Indonesia?

The main argument in this research is that the implementation of business clusters can benefit a nation in terms of new innovations, higher productivity, which leads to higher wages, low production cost, wider employment opportunities, and the fostering of regional development. Here, the Indonesian government plays a dominant role in developing business clusters in Indonesia. As mentioned earlier, the government tries to increase the competitiveness of SMEs/SMIs by promoting and developing business clusters especially in the two locations as the case study above. Many programs and activities are created, planned, and implemented to develop a successful cluster. However, looking at the current performance of

SMEs/SMIs in both locations, there are other factors that must be considered in order to maximize the performance of clusters in the two locations.

1.3 Research Methodology

1.3.1 Type of Research

This study uses qualitative research methods. David Silverman states that there is no standard definition of qualitative research. As Silverman says: "[...this is because] 'qualitative research' covers a wide range of different activities".[22] This is similar to what Uwe Flick defined as qualitative research stating it: "[...] is intended to approach the world 'out there' and to understand, describe, and sometimes explain social phenomena 'from the inside'[...]".[23] On the other hand, John W. Creswell defines qualitative research as follows:

> "Qualitative research begins with assumptions and the use of interpretive/theoretical frameworks that inform the study of research problems addressing the meaning individuals or groups ascribe to a social or human problem."[24]

He then added another definition: "A qualitative study is defined as an inquiry process of understanding a social or human problem, based on building a complex, holistic picture, formed with words, reporting detailed views of informants, and conducted in a natural setting."[25]

To understand qualitative research, we can see the inherent characteristics of this type of research. Corbin and Strauss mentioned that qualitative research typically has the following characteristics:[26]

1. A humanistic bent
2. Curiosity
3. Creativity and imagination
4. A sense of logic
5. The ability to recognize diversity as well as regularity

---

22 Silverman 2001, p. 25.
23 Flick 2007, p. x.
24 Creswell 2013, p. 44.
25 Creswell 1994, pp. 1-2.
26 Corbin/Strauss 2008, p. 13.

6. A willingness to take risks
7. The ability to live with ambiguity
8. The ability to work through problems in the field
9. An acceptance of the self as a research instrument
10. Trust in the self and the ability to see value in the work that is produced.

Moreover, Corbin and Strauss stated that "[a] qualitative analysis is a process of examining and interpreting data in order to elicit meaning, gain understanding, and develop empirical knowledge".[27]

Since there is no standard approach for conducting qualitative research, the researcher will explore the research by focusing on all business actors involved for this research. To help the researcher identify actors, statements from Thomas R. Black are considered important. According to Black (2002), social science research involves an investigation on all aspects of human activity and interactivity.[28] Thus, all actors involved in the business clusters such as individuals, SMEs, the business cluster itself, research centers, universities, associations, and government institutions will be subjects of this research.

1.3.2 Data Collection and Respondents

To help collect and analyze data, this research will use several techniques. Uwe Flick mentioned three strategies to collect data: (a) by going into individuals' or groups' experiences, (b) by observing interactions and communications of the people/groups, and (c) by examining documents.[29] John W. Creswell also stresses the importance of applying such strategies. He defines the characteristics of a qualitative researcher as: (a) a natural setting, where the researcher should collect data in the research site(s) by conducting communication and interviews with the people/groups and (b) the researcher being a key instrument, meaning that the researchers themselves should collect data by doing observations and analyzing documents.[30]

27 Corbin/Strauss 2008, p. 1.
28 Cf. Black 2002, p. 1.
29 Cf. Flick 2007, p. x.
30 Cf. Creswell 2013, p. 45.

In order to collect data on this research, the researcher will conduct those three strategies:

a. Conducting and recording interviews with owners and employees of SMEs at the Cibaduyut Footwear Industrial Cluster and the Plered Decorative Ceramic Industrial Cluster. This will be completed as well with interviews with the government officials in charge of the two clusters. There are two technical services units in these two locations: the Office for Developing the Small and Medium-sized Shoe Industry in Cibaduyut and the Plered Ceramic Technical Services Unit. Not only that, the researcher also plans to interview experts and academicians who are experienced with this issue.
b. Conducting observations in the two sites to provide the researcher with direct experience and first-hand information. This observation is also conducted to cross-check data and information gathered and collected from other sources.
c. Analyzing documents that are collected from sources like: related ministries (in this case: the Ministry of Cooperatives and SMEs and the Ministry of Industry), the office of Statistics Indonesia (Badan Pusat Statistik, BPS) the office of West Java Statistics, the government of the West Java Province, the West Java Office of Cooperatives and SMEs, the West Java Office of Industry and Trade, the city of Bandung, the regency of Purwakarta, the Office for Developing the Small and Medium-sized Shoe Industry in Cibaduyut, and the Plered Ceramic Technical Services Unit.

These three strategies will be used to find answers to and to conduct analysis on the research questions.

1.3.3 Research Locations

There are two business clusters that will be used as a case study for this research. They are the Cibaduyut Footwear Industrial Cluster in Cibaduyut and the Plered Decorative Ceramic Industrial Cluster in Plered. Both are located in the province of West Java. The selection of these two sites is done with the following considerations: *First*, the location of the two clusters is not far from the city of Bandung so that the interview process and observations at the site are easier to conduct in order to complete the research process. In addition, the researcher is familiar with both locations since the researcher has spent almost twenty years studying and living in this area. *Second*, these two industrial clusters have been formed since the 1900s in the form of a *sentra*[31] before being formalized into industrial clusters in 2009. Both clusters are not (totally) new clusters. The two clusters have been operating long before they were declared industrial (business) clusters. Hence, these two locations are relevant for the assessment of the business cluster concept of this research. *Third*, the government and the Ministry of Industry have chosen these two sites to be developed into (dynamic/working) clusters by issuing Regulation of the President of the Republic of Indonesia No. 28/2008 on the National Industrial Policy, which served as the basis of the issuance of Regulation of the Minister of Industry of the Republic of Indonesia No. 110/M-IND/PER/10/2009 on the Roadmap of the Development of the Footwear Industrial Cluster and Regulation of Minister of Industry of the Republic of Indonesia No. 135/M-IND/PER/10/2009 on the Roadmap of the Development of Pottery and Decorative Ceramic Industrial Cluster. Therefore, the relevance of these two locations for the topic of this research is related.

Moreover, another consideration is related to what John W. Creswell mentioned about choosing a research site in order to ease the collection of data. Creswell emphasizes two things related to a research site. *First*, there must be permission from the authorities to be able to conduct research at the site. *Second*, it must be assured that there are individuals who will help at the study site with gathering the necessary data and information.[32] He also stresses the importance of data collecting that takes into consideration the entry and access required to collect data.[33] For this research it is the access to related organizations such as governmental offices or individuals at the site that have participated actively in the study. Before submitting the proposal of this research, the researcher has made a preliminary approach to the business owners and government agencies at the two research sites. The reason is not only to introduce the researcher but also to ask permission and assistance in order to conduct research at the location.

31 Martin Perry (2005) defines *sentra* (business center) as a collection of at least 20 similar enterprises (usually SMEs) that are located in the same area.

32 Cf. Creswell 2013, p. 151.

33 Cf. Creswell 2013, pp. 171-75.

1.4 Chapter Plan

This research will be structured into seven chapters. The first chapter is an introduction of the research. This is inspired by the scarcity of research and study on this topic in Indonesia. Even though many scholars and academicians wrote about SMEs/SMIs and their performance, research on a specific region, especially on the implementation of the business cluster concept, is limited. The researcher hopes that this research can contribute to the development and empowerment of SMEs/SMIs in the business cluster and serve as a reference for those interested in doing research on similar topics in different locations.

Chapter 2 discusses the concept business cluster in its theoretical and conceptual framework. It includes the role of the state in developing its economy and the policy on cluster development in Indonesia. *First*, an explanation of what is defined as SMEs/SMIs in Indonesia based on the official definition by the government. *Second,* an explanation of the concept of business clusters and the advantages for nation-states of implementing this concept in order to promote regional economic development. Here, the literature on business clusters and their relations to regional economic development will be explored. The *third* part discusses the role of the state in economic development. The *last* part discusses policies in developing clusters in Indonesia.

Chapter 3 gives a description of the role of the central government to promote the development and empowerment of SMEs/SMIs in Indonesia. This chapter describes policies of promoting the concept of business clusters to accomplish economic development goals. This will be followed by profiling the two ministries that are responsible for developing and empowering SMEs/SMIs, which are the Ministry of Cooperatives and SMEs and the Ministry of Industry. Here, the researcher will explain the relations among laws, regulations, and other minister decrees on developing and empowering SMEs/SMIs in Indonesia.

Chapter 4 describes the role of the local governments, in this case the Government of the West Java Province in developing and empowering SMEs/SMIs in order to promote regional economic development. This chapter will also cover the role of two local agencies, the Office of Cooperatives and SMEs and the Office of Industry and Trade in creating programs to develop and empower SMEs/SMIs in West Java.

Chapter 5 gives a description of the two research sites as a case of study of this research. This includes policies from responsible government agencies to develop business clusters in the area, the historical background of the two research sites, and the analysis of problems and challenges faced by SMEs/SMIs in these two locations.

Chapter 6 discusses the challenges with the implementation of Porter's diamond theory (the concept of business clusters) in the two research sites and gives a contribution to this theory using the Indonesian context (in this case looking at and analyzing research findings).

The last chapter, Chapter 7, concludes this research by providing research findings, limitations of the research, and recommendation.

2. Theoretical Framework

As mentioned in the introduction, this chapter will discuss the concept of business clusters in a theoretical and conceptual framework. This chapter will be divided into three parts. The *first* part will give the definition of a business cluster as well as the definition and identifying criteria of SMEs and SMIs in Indonesia. The *second* part will discuss business clusters in a conceptual framework such as types, characteristics, factors on cluster development, and the advantages of a cluster. The *last* part will discuss the role of the state in economic development. The reasons for overviewing the concept of business clusters in both theoretical and conceptual frameworks are: (a) to discuss the implementation of business clusters in relation to the national industrial policy and to policies to develop and empower SMEs and (b) to understand the complexity of implementing such a concept using the Indonesian context (in this case the two research locations).

2.1 Definitions

It is important to define some important concepts in this research especially to discuss the definition and criteria of SMEs/SMIs using the Indonesian version. Another definition presented in this section is that of the (business) cluster.

2.1.1 Small and Medium-sized Enterprises (SMEs) and Small and Medium-sized Industries (SMIs)

Currently, there are many definitions about SMEs created by different agencies. Many government administrations have developed definitions of SMEs based on their criteria in order to differentiate them from larger industries. The differentiation usually lies in terms of the number of employees and annual total sales. The definition is important for the government to give attention to maintaining the existence of SMEs as a backbone of its economic activities. The European Commission for instance, based on Article 2 of the Annex of EU Recommendation No. 2003/361/EC, defined SMEs as an enterprise having employees fewer than 250 persons and having an annual turnover not exceeding EUR 50 million.[34] Moreover, the European Commission then divides this type of enterprise into three categories: micro, small, and medium enterprise.[35] The table below shows the differentiation of those categories.

Table 2.1: Definition of SMEs in Europe

Enterprise/Category	Employees	Annual Turnover (in million EUR)
Medium-sized	< 250	< 50
Small	< 50	< 10
Micro	< 10	< 2

Source: Modified from European Commission (n.d.), p. 14

In the United States of America, the definition of SMEs focuses on the number of employees and annual firm revenue.[36] Here SMEs are classified as enterprises that have employees fewer than 500 workers and earn less than USD 250,000 in annual revenue.[37] As a consequence, there is no generally accepted definition worldwide.

In Indonesia, there is also no commonly accepted definition of SMEs. Here, the definition of SMEs in Indonesia is based on different criteria, namely the number of employees, assets (excluding land and buildings/production facilities), and annual total sales. The Ministry of Cooperatives and SMEs for example, refers to Law No. 28/2008 to define SMEs. Law No. 20/2008 on Small and Medium-sized Enterprises (SMEs) uses only total asset (net worth) and annual sales as a basis to define SMEs. According to this law, the definition of SMEs is divided into three categories of enterprises: micro, small, and medium-sized enterprises.[38] *First*, a micro enterprise is a productive enterprise that is owned by individuals and/or private entities and meets the criteria as set in this law.[39] *Second*, a

34 Cf. European Commission (n.d.), p. 5.
35 Please note that this definition took effect on January 1, 2005 as stated in European Commission (n.d.).
36 Cf. United States International Trade Commission 2010, p. 2.
37 Cf. United States International Trade Commission 2010, pp. 1-4.
38 See Law No. 20/2008.
39 Cf. Article 1 Paragraph 1 of Law No. 20/2008.

small enterprise is a productive enterprise which is managed by an individual or business entity that is not a subsidiary or branch company that is owned, controlled, or being a part (either directly or indirectly) of medium or large businesses that meet the criteria as defined in this law.[40] *Third*, a medium-sized enterprise is a productive enterprise which is undertaken by individuals or entities that are not subsidiaries or branch companies that are owned, controlled, or being a part (either directly or indirectly) of small or large businesses that meet the criteria as stipulated in this law.[41] However, this definition is not enough to define SMEs. To differentiate SMEs, the researcher uses the criteria of SMEs as stipulated in the above-mentioned law. The criteria of micro enterprises are: (a) an asset (net worth) that does not exceed IDR 50 million excluding land and buildings and (b) annual sales of IDR 300 million.[42] The criteria of small enterprise are: (a) an asset (net worth) of more than IDR 50 million up to at most IDR 500 million excluding land and buildings and (b) annual sales of more than IDR 300 million up to IDR 2.5 billion.[43] The criteria of medium-sized enterprise are: (a) a net worth of more than IDR 500 million up to at most IDR 10 billion excluding land and buildings and (b) annual sales of more than IDR 2.5 billion up to IDR 50 billion.[44]

On the other hand, Statistics Indonesia (known as BPS, central bureau of statistics, a non-departmental government institution) uses the number of employees as a basis to determine SMEs. According to the BPS, SMEs can be defined as enterprises having fewer employees than 100 persons.[45] The BPS then divides these enterprises into (a) micro enterprises that have less than 5 employees, (b) small enterprises that have 5-19 employees, and (c) medium enterprises that have 20-99 workers.[46]

In short, the definition of SMEs in Indonesia is divided into three size-classes: micro enterprises (having an asset not exceeding IDR 50 million and annual total sales of IDR 300 million), small enterprises (having a number of employees less than 19 persons with an asset not exceeding IDR 500 million and annual total sales of IDR 2.5 billion), and medium-sized enterprises (having a number of employees less than 100 persons

---

40 Cf. Article 1 Paragraph 2 of Law No. 20/2008.
41 Cf. Article 1 Paragraph 3 of Law No. 20/2008.
42 Cf. Article 6 Paragraph 1 of Law No. 20/2008.
43 Cf. Article 6 Paragraph 2 of Law No. 20/2008.
44 Cf. Article 6 Paragraph 3 of Law No. 20/2008.
45 Cf. Tambunan 2008a, p. 148.
46 Cf. Tambunan 2008a, p. 148, Marijan 2007, p. 109.

with an asset not exceeding IDR 10 billion and annual total sales of IDR 50 billion). The following table provides an overview of these criteria.

Table 2.2: Definition of Indonesian SMEs

Criteria	Micro Enterprise	Small Enterprise	Medium Enterprise
Number of employees	< 5	5-19	20-99
Total asset	< IDR 50 million	< IDR 500 million	< IDR 10 billion
Annual total sales	< IDR 300 million	< IDR 2.5 billion	< IDR 50 billion

Therefore, an enterprise can be categorized as an SME if it meets any of the definitions above.

In this study, the economic activities that occur in a business cluster also involve SMIs. The definition of SMIs can be found in Regulation of the Minister of Industry No. 98/M-IND/PER/12/2011 that states that SMIs can be divided into two groups.[47] *First*, the small-sized industry can be defined as an industrial company with a total investment value up to IDR 500 million excluding land and buildings.[48] *Second*, the medium-sized industry can be defined as an industrial company with a total investment value of more than IDR 500 million up to IDR 10 billion excluding land and buildings.[49]

At first, there is no differentiation between the definition of SMEs and SMIs as mentioned above. What distinguishes SMEs and SMIs is the scope of their business activities. According to Law No. 5/1984, industry is an economic activity that processes raw materials, materials, semi-finished goods, and/or finished goods to create a new product with a higher value for its use, including the activities of the design and engineering industry.[50] Meanwhile, the scope of business activities of SMEs is not

47 See Regulation of the Minister of Industry No. 98/M-IND/PER/12/2011.

48 Cf. Article 1 Paragraph 2 of Regulation of the Minister of Industry No. 98/M-IND/PER/12/2011.

49 Cf. Article 1 Paragraph 3 of Regulation of the Minister of Industry No. 98/M-IND/PER/12/2011.

50 Cf. Article 1 Paragraph 2 of Law No. 5/1984.

clearly defined in any regulations. Simply, SMEs are defined as enterprises/companies that conduct business in accordance with the criteria above.[51]

2.1.2 (Business) Clusters

The concept of clusters has attracted scholars, policy makers, and multilateral organizations to research the importance of cluster to national and local economies, small firms' performances, and regional economic development. They believe that the formulation of cluster can be beneficial to regional economic development. In their writings, Enright and Ffowcs-Williams found that many countries, local agencies, and multilateral organizations have established their economic development programs based on clusters.[52]

The concept of clusters can be traced from the concept of local economies by Alfred Marshall,[53] Michael Storper,[54] and Masahisa Fujita et al.[55] about dealing with the tight competition of the global economy. Following the local economic process, literature tends to focus on the theme of clusters promoting local development processes. Alfred Marshall found that clusters would be an engine for promoting the local economy referring to his analysis of industrial districts.[56] However, the concept of clusters became known worldwide because of the influential books of Michael Porter. Michael Porter is known as a pioneer of a new theory of economic development as he proposes the concept of clusters in order to increase a nation's competitiveness and boost up regional economic development. His theory has influenced the economic development policies of not only developed but of developing countries as well, namely from the United States of America, Japan, and China, to Finland, Korea, Thailand, Indonesia, and many other countries. In his books, Porter (1990, 1998) has introduced the concept of clusters as the answer to increasing competitiveness

---

51 The importance of defining both SMEs and SMIs is due to the fact that both actors are relevant in this research. Both actors can be found in the two clusters that serve as the case study in this research.
52 Cf. Enright/Ffowcs-Williams 2000, p. 13.
53 See Marshall 1966 (1890).
54 See Storper 1997.
55 See Fujita et al. 2001.
56 See Marshall 1919.

of a nation's product and as a driving force for regional economic growth.[57]

Currently, there are many definitions of a cluster. In a simple definition, a cluster can be put as a concentration of firms producing similar products in one area. Even though there is no single definitions of a cluster, the definition of cluster itself can be traced from a connotation made by Michael Porter in his book "The Competitive Advantage of Nations". Porter (1990) defined a cluster as a group of firms engaged in similar or related activities by links of various kinds.[58] Moreover, he added his definition of clusters as

> "[...] geographic concentrations of interconnected companies, specialized suppliers, service providers, firms in related industries, and associated institutions (for example, universities, standards agencies, and trade associations) in particular fields that compete but also cooperate."[59]

A similar definition came from Möhring (2005), in which she said that "[c]lustering refers to local concentrations of horizontally or vertically linked firms that specialize in related lines of business together with supporting organizations [...]".[60] The term "supporting organization" refers to the private and public sector such as the government, universities, and research centers. Hua Yang et al. (2008) added the definition of cluster as "[...] the phenomenon and mechanism that some local relative enterprises and agencies aggregate to groups in one or more associated industrial value chain to gain competence".[61] Meanwhile, the definition by Meyer-Stamer and Harmes-Liedtke can be put into simple words: "Clusters are [...] a territorial agglomeration of closely related industries".[62]

2.2 Understanding (Business) Clusters

The definition of cluster can be found previously in this chapter. In this section, the writer will explore the conception of clusters such as types of

57 See Porter 1990, Porter 1998.
58 Cf. Porter 1990, p. 131.
59 Porter 1998a, pp. 197-98.
60 Möhring 2005, p. 21.
61 Yang et al. 2008, p. 1.
62 Meyer-Stamer/Harmes-Liedtke 2005, p. 1.

clusters, factors that contribute to a strong cluster, benefits of clustering, and attributes of a cluster.

2.2.1 Types of Clusters

There are many typologies of a cluster. It is not easy to distinguish types of clusters in different countries. Different typologies of clusters will be explained later in this sub-chapter. According to Altenburg and Meyer-Stamer (1999), derived from their research on Latin America's SMEs, clusters are divided into three typologies: the survival clusters of micro and small-scale enterprises, more advanced and differentiated mass producers, and the clusters of transnational corporations (TNCs).[63] The *first* type of clusters, survival clusters of micro and small-scale enterprises, is a group of local firms located in small or even poor areas. This type of cluster mostly produces low-quality goods for local markets. In this type of cluster, the interaction between firms is limited due to a lack of trust among the firms in the cluster, resulting in a minimum degree of cooperation among them. Looking at the case of Latin America's SMEs, the reason why this type has limited interaction and trust among firms is the culture of imitating goods produced by a firm within a cluster, lack of entrepreneurial spirit, which leads to the short average life of SMEs, and the fact that most transactions are done in an informal way. Furthermore, most of the employees in this cluster lack the ability to work with modern management techniques due to a low level of education amongst the employees. The knowledge learned on how to produce particular goods comes from informal relations such as family or friends. The examples of this cluster include the shoe cluster in San Mateo Atenco and San Fransisco del Rincon (Mexico), the metal and repair workshops in Takora (Peru), and the garment industries in Gamarra (Peru) and Netzahualcoyotl (Mexico). The *second* type, a more advanced and differentiated mass production cluster, is a cluster that consists of several firms ranging from medium to large firms. Usually, these firms have good managerial and technological capabilities compared to those of the first type of clusters. This cluster also targets local markets and specializes in particular products such as men's leather footwear in Leon (Mexico) or ladies' leather footwear in Sinos Valley (Brazil). Some of the firms in these clusters also target the interna-

63 Cf. Altenburg/Meter-Stamer 1999, pp. 1695-708.

tional market, such as the home textiles industry in Itajai Valley (Brazil). The *third* type, a cluster of TNCs, is a cluster dominated by big firms in complex technological activities such as electronics and auto industries. They have limited interactions with local firms since most of their production systems use robots or other high-technology equipments. Usually, if they have contact with local firms, it is limited only to simple jobs, for instance packaging materials and printing manuals. Examples of this cluster can be found in the auto industry in Puebla, Ramos Arizpe, and Aguascalientes (Mexico) or in the computer and telecommunications industry in Guadalajara (Mexico).

Ann Markusen (1996) proposed different types of clusters.[64] According to Markusen, there are at least four types of clusters: the Marshallian industrial district (with its Italianate variety), the hub-and-spoke district, the satellite platforms, and the state-anchored district. The Marshallian industrial district is a cluster in which the business structure consists of small and locally owned firms. Since this cluster is dominated by small firms, the degree of economic scale is low. This is also due to the limited interaction and cooperation with firms located outside the cluster. The interesting nature of this cluster is that this cluster is seen as a stable community. Workers in this cluster move from firm to firm, and the owners and their employees live in the same district, which creates a strong local culture within the district. Local financial institutions also actively support the existence of the cluster because of their trust both in information within the district and in the owners of the firms. Compared to the Marshallian district, the Italianate variant has some additional features to it. In the Italianate variant, there is a high degree of cooperation among firms to share risks and innovation in order to stabilize the market. In this variant, the involvement of both business associations and local governments is strong. The business associations provide shared infrastructures such as management, training, marketing, and technical and financial assistance to help firms within the district as well as to provide forums to set up a collective strategy to expand the cluster. The local government also plays an important role by regulating and promoting core industries within the district.

The Hub-and-Spoke district is a type of cluster in which there are a number of big firms (or a single key firm) acting as an anchor or a hub to the regional economy. These big firms can be located inside the cluster or outside the cluster and are surrounded by smaller suppliers and related in-

64 See Markusen 1996, pp. 296-307.

dustries spread out around big firms like the spokes of a wheel. The degree of economic scale is high due to a high degree of cooperation and linkage with external firms. A simple illustration to explain the Hub-and-Spoke district: A key firm buys products from local firms and external suppliers and sells these products to external buyers who may be large buyers or masses of individual buyers. Since there is a high economic scale, local governments participate in regulating and promoting the cluster to both local governments and the central/national government.

The satellite platform is a cluster dominated by large, externally owned and headquartered firms. In this type, a cluster consists only of branch facilities owned by external parent firms. These parent firms and their branch plants have no relations with local suppliers; therefore the important feature of the satellite platform is the absence of any relationships within the region and the cluster, and the high degree of connections and networks between the parent firms and their branch plants.

The last type of cluster, the state-anchored district is a cluster in which a public or nonprofit unit is a key player in the cluster. The public or nonprofit unit can be a university, a research center, a military base or a group of government offices. Hence, the local business structure is dominated by the presence of those units. The economic scale of this cluster then depends on the level of public expenditure of the unit. If the level of public expenditure by, let's say, state-owned or state-dependent facilities is high, the suppliers' sector will grow. However, the existence of the state-anchored district depends on the prospect for the facility at the core of the cluster, and on the extent to which the facility encourages growth within the cluster by generating local suppliers, developing new businesses, or providing labor or other factors of production to the local economy.

The typology of clusters can also be seen from the dimension embedded in a cluster. Christian Ketels (2003) for instance, has defined many dimensions ranging from the production of specific goods and services provided, location preferences, the stage of developments, to the business environment around the cluster.[65] He divided the typology of cluster into three levels. The cluster on the *first* level can be classified by the type of product it produces and sells. Looking at this classification, this shows that different locations play different roles with regard to the cluster. There are clusters in the automotive, media, high technology, and many more industries. The examples include the automotive cluster in Detroit (USA), the

65 Cf. Ketels 2003, pp. 4-5.

telecommunication cluster in Finland, and the shoe cluster in Sino Valley (Brazil). However, many researchers found that the same subject of a cluster can be found in many different locations. The reason is that clusters are distinguished by their specialization, by their focus on specific areas, or by the market segments they target. The example is the footwear cluster which can be found in Northern Italy, Brazil, Romania, China, Vietnam, and Asia.

The *second* level is based on the type of location. The idea is that industries always act in accordance with their interests, mainly economic interests. Thus, at the second level, there are at least three types of clusters. The first is the 'local' industry whose interest is to be close to their customers. This cluster simply produces goods for and serves the local markets. The second is the 'natural resource-dependent' industry whose interest it is to be close to natural resources. This cluster emerges in regions that have abundant natural resources so that this situation helps industries to reduce the cost of production. This type of cluster does not only serve the local market but also expands its business activities to global markets. The third is the 'traded' industry which is free to choose its location based on the attractiveness of a specific location, especially of the business environment. This type of cluster can be found in many regions and countries.

The *third* level of cluster can be classified by the stage of development it has reached. This development depends on two dimensions: the quality of the external business environment where the cluster operates, and the progress the cluster has made in organizing the potential of the business environment through cooperation and internal activities. The former shows that the better the business environment is, the better performance of the cluster will be, while the latter explains that the development of a cluster does not happen automatically; it depends on purposeful action.

Michael Enright of the Harvard Business School divides clusters into three types: working cluster, latent cluster, and potential (wannabe) cluster.[66] A working cluster is a cluster that can explore its potential and produce more than the sum of its portion. A good example of this type of cluster is the Silicon Valley in California (USA), the ceramic tile industry in Sassuolo (Italy), and the flower industry in Holland. According to Enright, in this type of cluster companies are connected to each other and operate collectively to produce more products. This is because a working cluster has the social infrastructures that enables it to share information,

66 Cf. Rosenfeld 1997, pp. 10-12.

ignite new ideas, make networking, and promote new firm start-ups. A latent cluster is a cluster that has the potential and the opportunity to produce but is not exploited and has no synergy among enterprises. An example of this type of cluster are the pharmaceutical industries in North Carolina (USA). They employ around 24,000 workers and have many of the requirements of a working cluster such as the scale, markets, and supports from research centers and universities. However, these industries are heavily dominated by branch plants of multinational companies and create less interaction among firms and workers. The problem with this type of cluster is that it has no vision to face competition, cannot explore the advantage of its competencies, and cannot adapt to the new market situations. Tambunan (2005) stated that most of Indonesian SMEs are categorized as an artisanal cluster due to stagnation, insufficient critical mass, a low degree of interaction among firms, and low access to potential markets and networks.[67] The potential or wannabe cluster is a cluster that has resources and requirements to be a cluster, but some important conditions are missing. Usually, this type of cluster is located in rural areas, for example the wood industries in Oklahoma (USA), the food processing in Ohio (USA), and the microbreweries in Oregon (USA).

In Indonesia, types of clusters can be found in many regions and provinces. This is simply because a cluster is defined as a concentration of enterprises producing similar products in one location.[68] According to Tambunan, looking at the level of development there are at least four types of Indonesian clusters: the artisanal cluster, the active cluster, the dynamic cluster, and the modern/advanced cluster.[69] The *first* type, the artisanal cluster, is characterized by low levels of productivity due to the low quality of human resources and the use of technology as well as the lack of specialization and linkage among SMEs. This type of cluster is similar to what Altenburg and Mayer-Stamer (1999)[70] defined as the survival cluster and to Supratikno's dormant cluster.[71] In Indonesia, about 90 percent of the existing industrial/business clusters are categorized as artisanal or survival clusters.[72] The *second* type, the active cluster, is characterized by an improvement in terms of production system, human resources skills, and

67 Cf. Tambunan (n.d.), p. 18.
68 Cf. ibid., p. 2.
69 Cf. Tambunan 2005, pp. 141-45, Tambunan 2009a, pp. 40-43.
70 Cf. Altenburg/Meter-Stamer 1999, p. 1695.
71 Cf. Marijan 2005, p. 222.
72 Cf. ibid.

marketing networks. The *third* type, the dynamic cluster, is characterized by being a more active cluster in terms of expanding trade networks with international markets, using more advance technology, bigger firm's sizes, and serving more prominent markets. The *last* type, the modern/advanced cluster, is characterized by a high level of inter-firm cooperation that leads to a firm's specialization, and an established business networks among firms, suppliers (such as raw material and components), providers of services, traders, financial institutions, and other supporting agencies. Not only that, this type of cluster also conducts cooperation with the (central and local) government, universities, and research centers. Usually, this cluster is export-oriented with the objective of capturing the domestic market and the international market. An example of this cluster is the Jepara furniture cluster in Central Java.

2.2.2 Factors of a Strong Cluster

A cluster is not only a concentration of similar firms in one region. It must have certain characteristics to be named a strong cluster. Based on a research conducted by Rosenfeld (1997), there are at least 12 (twelve) key factors to support a powerful cluster, namely: research and development capability, knowledge and skills, human resources (labor/worker) development, proximity of suppliers, capital availability, access to specialized services, machine and tools builders, intensity of networking, social infrastructure, entrepreneurial energy, innovation, and shared vision and leadership.[73] The explanations of those factors can be found below:

Research and Development Capability

Producing a product that fits consumer demand and has a high quality of product requires support from the research and development department. This department sometimes is not created by the firms in a cluster but exists because of supporting agencies. As mentioned earlier, the supporting agencies can be training centers created and funded by the government, research centers, or universities. They usually provide training and research to help the cluster coming up with new ideas and innovations.

73 Cf. Rosenfeld 1997, pp. 12-17.

Training is provided to increase both capability and quality of firms in producing their product, while research is conducted to prepare firms in facing the changes of consumer demands and global competition.

Knowledge and Skills

What is meant by knowledge and skills here is human resources' knowledge and skills to produce goods in a cluster. Theoretically, human resources are one of factor of production beside land (assets) and capital. This knowledge and skill is not only given by formal education but also from experiences of the owner. Being in a cluster of course requires high-skilled workers and therefore a cluster is called a large pool of skilled labor. Workers can get knowledge and skills that meet the requirements of a cluster through formal education such as high schools, community colleges, and other educational institutions. However, formal education is sometimes not enough to deal with the changes of consumer tastes and global competition. Experiences of the owner or senior fellow workers can enrich the knowledge and skills of the workers. The case of clusters located in developing countries may explain this phenomenon. Most workers who work in the footwear industrial cluster in Cibaduyut and the decorative ceramic industrial cluster in Plered for instance did not receive the knowledge and skills to produce footwear and ceramic products through formal education but autodidactically from the experiences of the owners or from senior fellow workers.[74] Another example comes from Futorian. The owner of a furniture company in Tupelo (Italy) taught his employees both technical and management skills to run his business. What interesting here is that these employees called themselves graduated from the University of Futorian.[75] There is no doubt that a cluster needs both formal and informal knowledge and skills of its employees to share the knowledge among employees and firms, as well as to increase the quality and quantity of their products.

---

74 A further explanation regarding this statement will be given later in Chapter 5.

75 Cf. Rosenfeld 1997, p. 13.

Human Resource Development

High-skilled workers are vital to the existence and the development of a cluster. For a cluster to produce high technology products, the need to increase its quality of product depends on the capability of its workers. Producing high technology products sometimes relates to the use of computerized and electronic machines. The new developments and inventions of machines put workers into the situation of having to learn more and more of these new equipments. Most SMEs have low-skilled labor to produce their products. Of course, when competing with imported goods, these SMEs must create new innovations and it is impossible to create new innovations without having high-skilled labor and appropriate technology. As a result, technical trainings to increase worker's capability are a must so that workers can match the technical needs of a cluster.

Proximity of Suppliers

Being close to suppliers is an obligation to increase the competitiveness of a cluster. Reduced transaction costs are the key elements of a cluster. Proximity can channel the share of information and technology between firms and suppliers on providing materials. Here, there are at least three reasons for being close to suppliers. *First*, it reduces the cost of business transactions. Being close to suppliers makes a cluster save costs for transporting materials to a firm or a cluster. Also, it reduces the risk of damaging materials due to the shipment process from the suppliers to the firms. *Second*, it reduces the falsity of providing or sending inaccurate materials to a cluster. Sometimes, suppliers send the materials to firms. Of course, it costs not only money to send the wrong materials to the suppliers (in a case of no cover of insurance), but it is also time consuming to have the correct ones coming to the firms. *Third*, it reduces time consumption if the firms have problems with setting up new equipment or with solving problems with using new equipment.

Capital Availability

Capital is another key element in the existence of a cluster. Most clusters consist of SMEs that usually grew from home industries. To expand their business in order to meet the consumer demand, these SMEs need fresh money or capital to do so. The problem sometimes lies on the policy of the lender (banks/financial institutions) to provide them with loans. These SMEs have experienced how difficult it can be to get fresh money (loans) to finance or even to increase their business activities. The government offered some loan mechanisms in order to support SMEs, however, when it comes from the bank administration, it is a different story. Some of these SMEs decided not to further their application for loans because of the complicated administration process of the banks or because of their business being inappropriate to be funded by the bank. Moreover, some of these SMEs have never heard that the government provided these types of loan mechanisms. Hence, most entrepreneurs and SMEs depend on their own money (or that being borrowed from their relatives) to finance their business activities. The support from the financial institutions will promote the creation of a working cluster.

Access to Specialized Services

Specialized services are crucial to a successful cluster. They offer functions for the industry to produce a better quality, and commonly work together closely with the industry. What is meant by specialized industries can be expertise and services provided by the government or research centers to help clusters increase their competitiveness. The case of the Industrial Institute in Ann Arbor (Michigan, USA) to support the auto industry in Detroit (USA) and the Hosiery Technology Centre at Catawba Valley Community College to provide training for technicians can illustrate how important the cooperation between a cluster and providers of specialized services is.

Machine and Tools Builders

Companies that design machine and equipment for firms in a cluster must locate themselves nearby. The goal is not only to provide machines and equipments to the cluster but also to improve the quality of their machines and equipments before selling them to other regions. Those companies can examine whether their product fits the needs of the clusters or if they should improve their product technology so that these machines can produce more goods.

Intensity of Networking

Network here is defined as cooperation among firms in a cluster. This cooperation can be done by producing complementary goods among firms, marketing their products collectively, or sharing orders from consumers in case they fail to fulfill it by themselves. It is a common problem for a cluster when a single firm cannot fulfill orders because of its limited capability and capacity. Thus, to avoid losing orders, this firm asks other similar firms in a cluster to make up for its limitation. Network also means that a cluster has the full support from its supporting industries so that they can reduce the cost of production as well as increase their specialization. Sometimes, the firms in a cluster need a consultation with business associations, research centers, and government institutions to express their needs and goals in order to improve the performance of a cluster as well as the competitiveness of a single firm.

Social Infrastructure

A cluster relies on networks so that it can connect with the market. Rosenfeld (1997) defines social infrastructure as the ability of people to work together in order to achieve the same goal.[76] A simple example of social infrastructure are business associations. Usually, business associations channel firms in a cluster to share ideas or information for the purpose of increasing the firms' competitiveness and a cluster's performance. They typically form a regular group meeting and discussion only to share problems or information of new potential markets. Not only that, business associations sometimes also help firms finding access to financial institutions to receive loans.

Entrepreneurial Energy

The successful element of a firm in a cluster is the entrepreneurial spirit. Entrepreneurial spirit is important because it leads the general direction of a firm. It guides whether a firm spreads only locally, regionally or interna-

76 Cf. Rosenfeld 1997, p. 16.

tionally. It also guides on the management of the existence of a firm. In a bigger picture, it leads to a successful cluster. However, most entrepreneurs have a low level of entrepreneurial spirit. This means that these entrepreneurs do not know how to improve the quality of their products, how to market their products abroad, and how to create innovations to win a tight competition. This is mostly because of the interest in entrepreneurship is declining, especially among young people. These young people think that being an owner of SMEs cannot guarantee their future. These young people tend to work for other people or corporations to avoid the risk of losing money. Thus, the support from external agencies such as business associations, government institutions, and research centers are needed to promote entrepreneurial energy among the young generation as well as to improve the entrepreneurial energy of existing entrepreneurs. Having entrepreneurial energy will direct a cluster into becoming a working and active cluster that promotes both the size of cluster and the regional economic development in the region.

Innovation

In a tight global competition, the need to be innovative is a must in order for firms to stay competitive. Innovation can lead to an increase in production or can help to win (global) competition against similar firms. Innovation is not about producing goods alone, it also refers to strategy in a time of crisis. The owners must deal with how to manage their firm when global demand decreases. They also have to deal with new business regulations issued by the government. Therefore, the spirit of innovation must be in the heart of each firm in order to achieve the common goals and objectives of a cluster.

Shared Vision and Leadership

Shared vision and leadership play an important role in maintaining the existence and the future of a firm and a cluster. Shared vision of a common objective is needed in order to achieve good coordination among firms in a cluster. Shared vision leads to how firms in a cluster work together to fulfill their customers' demand, how they join up on training and skills development, and how they share information, knowledge, and experiences to promote a cluster. This is important so that a cluster can plan the future, formulate strategies, and find potential markets. A strong leadership in a cluster is needed to ensure that this cluster, including firms, research centers, and government institutions, contribute to their full potential to promote the regional economic development.

2.2.3 Benefits of a Cluster

The cluster approach became important for the existence of SMEs lately. Empirical research proved that firms located in a cluster gained more benefits than those located in a different place.[77] Before, SMEs' owners never saw or met other owners producing similar products in their region. As a result, they missed the chance to share information and experiences – related to their products and market opportunities –, and also to cooperate to increase their product's competitiveness to enter potential markets. This is mainly because one SME sees another SME as a competitor instead of a potential partner. Hence, the cluster approach is seen as the best way to reduce that tendency and to bring new ideas on building cooperation among SMEs. Clusters, then, promote cooperation and competition at the same time.[78] Here, competition occurs among firms in a cluster in terms of producing better products and marketing their products. At the same time, cooperation also occurs between firms and related industries and other (local) institutions.

Clusters could promote cooperation among firms. According to Barkley/Henry (2001), cooperation occurs naturally and is common in a cluster because a cluster acts as a pool of integrated activities (of firms), a pool of resources (both human and natural), and a pool of knowledge.[79] In a cluster, firms are working towards a common goal – to increase its competitiveness and to improve social welfare. Marijan (2005) mentions several patterns of cooperation that are undertaken by firms in a cluster.[80] He uses the term of joint action to describe such cooperation. *First,* when firms have the problem of capital, they can form a group (or association) to create a mutual assurance framework in dealing with banks. *Second,*

---

77 See for example Baptista/Swann 1998, Beaudry/Breschi 2003, Europe INNOVA 2008.

78 Cf. Porter 1998b, p. 79.

79 Cf. Barkley/Henry 2001, pp. 5-6.

80 Cf. Marijan 2005, pp. 221-22.

firms in a cluster usually have no adequate production facilities (technology) so that they cannot produce in large quantities. The problem then arises when these firms want to sell their products to the (local or international) markets that require a specific quantity limits. To overcome this, these firms could work together in meeting the target quantity of products requested by the buyers. *Third*, the advantage of being in a cluster is the cooperation related to the chain of production. In this case, there are some companies that produce only up to intermediate goods, and then the process of completion (finishing) is done by another company. Similar advantages are delivered by Tambunan (2005), stating that the advantage of a cluster can be seen in two forms: internal and external networks.[81] The *first*, internal networks, are cooperations among firms within a cluster. This can be done in the form of production, distribution, marketing, or training for the workers. This internal network can be divided into two types: vertical and horizontal cooperation. Vertical cooperation is usually performed by small firms in achieving large orders from buyers or sharing ideas and knowledge to improve the quality of their products. Horizontal cooperation can be done by subcontracting production either to other small firms or to large enterprises. The pattern is similar to the third advantage by Marijan mentioned earlier. The *second*, external networks, are cooperations between firms in a cluster with external actors (outside the cluster) such as local governments, research centers, universities, suppliers, and so on. Burger et al. (2001) added that cooperation among firms in a cluster can be done in form of sharing issues related to the cost of technological change, information on new designs, and information on production techniques.[82] Another example of how business clusters promote cooperation and help SMEs can be found in Sendangsari, Yogyakarta. In Sendangsari, there is a local non-governmental organization called *Kelompok Swadaya Mandiri* (KSM) Sendangsari.[83] The establishment of KSM is to help the small-scale food production and trading producers in the village of Sendangsari, Yogyakarta, in order to face the challenges of the tight competition that has resulted in the decrease of their income. After conducting discussions, these producers decided to form an association called village business association (*Persatuan Wirausaha Desa*) that helps

81 Cf. Tambunan 2005, pp. 139-41.
82 Cf. Burger et al. 2001, p. 290.
83 Cf. Hadiwinata 2003, pp. 153-54.

SMEs and local producers to make a collective purchase of raw materials and to sell their products to outside markets.[84]

Being together in the same location also creates competition not only in order to produce better products (at competitive prices) but also to sell more products and to attract more consumers. Competition is all about a battle among individual enterprises.[85] It includes: competition with other enterprises within and outside a cluster, competition to attract buyers/customers, and competition to secure supply from suppliers. Competition is also about the quality of the business environment in a location, offering unique products and services, maximizing the presence of related and supporting industries, receiving government assistances (grants or loans), searching for potential market information, understanding customer needs, dealing with and maximizing the proximity to (raw material) sources, utilizing high-technology machines, and lowering the production cost in order to maximize profit.[86] Dealing with the business environment, the availability of basic infrastructures (such as roads), the types of buyers, and the government regulations (including a court system) plays an important role for firms in a cluster. Here, firms are asked to anticipate the unavailability of good infrastructures, the sophistication of certain buyers, and a court system that fails to resolve disputes. Firms must find a way, for instance, to understand the needs of sophisticated buyers, whether to imitate another firm's product or to offer unique products (and services). Seeking attention of the buyers is also important and can be done by creating a unique marketing strategy such as displaying their products in order and as neat as possible, promoting their products through websites, or advertising their products through printed advertisements and television. It also happens when dealing with government assistance. Firms must show their feasibility in order to receive government assistances.

Porter (1998) states there are at least three advantages of creating competition within a cluster.[87] *First*, it will increase the productivity of firms (SMEs). *Second*, it will drive innovations of new products. *Third*, it will stimulate the formation of new firms that support current firms and perhaps extend the cluster itself. By having these advantages, a firm will in-

84 Cf. ibid., p. 154.
85 Cf. Huggins/Izushi 2011, pp. 14-15.
86 Cf. Porter 2008, pp. 225-29.
87 Cf. Porter 1998, p. 213.

crease its competitiveness in the midst of global competition. The explanation can be seen as follows.

Cluster and Productivity of SMEs

Being located together with other firms brings advantages for the SMEs' productivity in terms of access to employees, input, information and technology, and motivating product improvements. Clusters can lower the transactional costs for hiring employees. An active cluster can be a signal to attract high-skilled people from other locations to be pooled in one cluster. Labor pooling provides firms with high-skilled and talented employees. Then, firms could avoid the risk of hiring low-skilled individuals as well as reducing the cost for training new employees. These firms have many options of hiring high-skilled and talented people to fulfill their needs. As a result, having this type of employee will benefit firms to produce more and to innovate new products. Stough, Haynes, and Campbell (1998) found that the growth of SMEs in the 'Capital Netplex' in the city of Washington, D.C., in the United States is influenced by the availability of a skilled population with engineering and business technology degrees.[88]

An active cluster also gives benefits in terms of important inputs. The cluster will benefit from being surrounded by many suppliers. Suppliers come and build bases in the cluster areas because there is a guarantee of having buyers for their products. Here, the relations between firms in the cluster and supporting firms (suppliers) can reduce the transaction costs. Reducing the transaction cost means that these firms do not have to spend money on transporting materials from suppliers' facilities – including the problem of late distribution and setting up the inventory for such materials. Moreover, being located in close proximity means these firms can lower their risks of having overpriced materials, or at least these firms can find cheap or competitive prices of the raw materials needed.

As mentioned earlier, proximity can also improve the sharing of information and technology between firms and suppliers on providing materials. Suppliers know far better about what is best for the firms in a cluster. The falsity of producing materials for these firms can be avoided by the suppliers. In terms of technological equipments, suppliers can easily help

88 Cf. Stough et al. 1998, pp. 70-72.

firms to set up equipments and provide maintenance services. Hence, firms can reduce the operational costs for using and maintaining such equipments. Rosenfeld (1997) added that close proximity among enterprises will reduce the costs of business transaction cheaper and easier, resolve businesses' problems faster and more efficiently, and promote new ideas and innovation.[89]

The relations among firms in a cluster tend to improve the firms' products. In a tight competition inside a cluster, firms tend to produce a product that can meet the demands and desires of consumers. Firms will attempt and produce their best in order to outdo their competitors. This is the result of being in a close proximity to each other. Firms can see their competitors' products and they will try to make their own products look good compared to their competitors' products.

Cluster and Innovations

In addition to improving their product, clusters also promote new innovations. Porter (as cited in Huggins/Izushi, 2011) stated that there are three types of innovation: product innovation, marketing innovation, and process innovation.[90] Looking at the second and third type of innovation, it can be interpreted that what is meant by marketing innovation is marketing strategy, while process innovation includes production techniques. As mentioned before, being located close to each other tends to increase the level of competition and the pressure to promote new innovations among firms. In terms of products, each firm tries to produce unique products that no other firms produce or improve the quality of its product. This is the result of having interactions with other firms as competitors as well as their customers. The pride, the feeling of always looking good in the consumer's eyes, and the need to meet customer demands push these firms to produce more and more innovative products. Interactions between firms and experts (or research centers) also contribute to creating new innovations of products. If these conditions simultaneously happen, it is believed that there will be new innovative products coming from a cluster.

89 Cf. Rosenfeld 1997, p. 3.
90 Cf. Huggins/Izushi 2011, p. 12.

Cluster and Formation of New Firms

Clusters always attract the formation of new firms. As indicated before, suppliers will come to an existing cluster because of the guarantee of potential markets. Hence, they do not need to spot market opportunities. As Porter (1998) wrote, there are several reasons for the creation of new firms within the cluster.[91] *First*, a person working in a cluster knows better what is wrong in economic transactions within the cluster. Here, the gap in providing goods and services can be covered by creating new industries by this experienced person. *Second*, it is easy to enter the cluster since it provides many assets and inputs. These assets and inputs can be added together to form a new firm, both a firm that supplies firms with materials or a new firm producing similar products as existing firms. *Third*, it is easy to gain access to financial institutions. New firms have the advantage of having credits since this existing cluster is familiar to financial institutions. Therefore, because of easy access to financial institutions, creating new firms or expanding existing firms will be easier and will enrich the business formation within the cluster.

2.2.4 Attributes of a Cluster

The development of a cluster is related to six attributes that create a competitive advantage for a firm and a nation. The six attributes are: (a) firm strategy, structure, and rivalry, (b) factor conditions, (c) demand conditions, (d) related and supporting industries, (e) the government, and (f) chance. Those attributes can be seen in the following figure.

91 Cf. Porter 1998, p. 84.

Figure 2.1: Porter's Diamond Theory

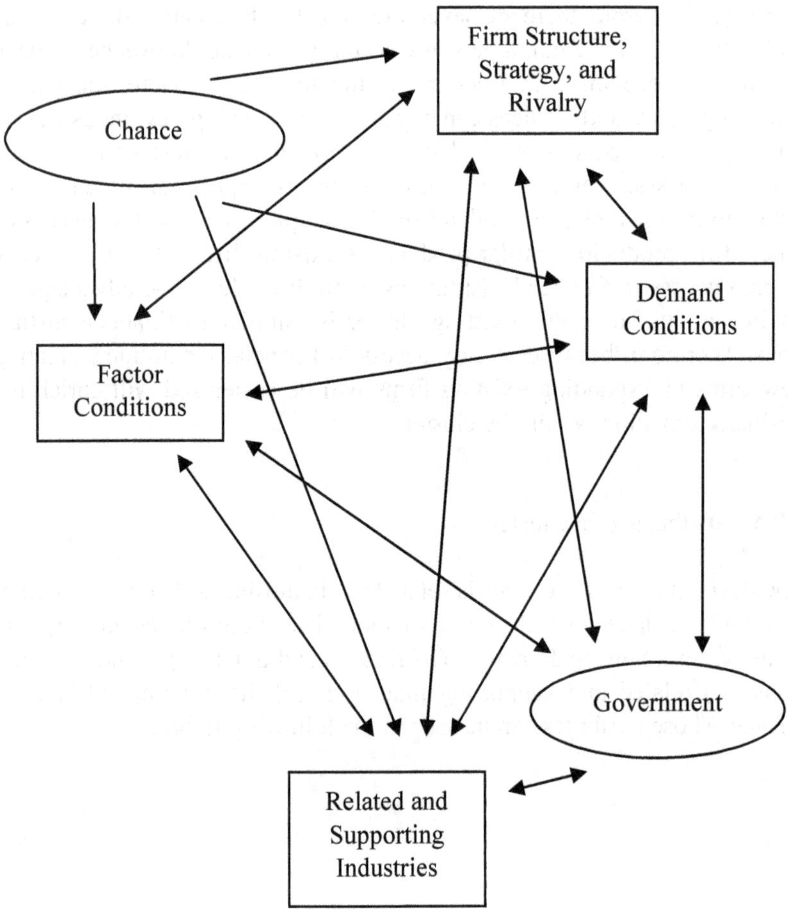

Source: Porter 1990, p. 127

The following will explain each attribute respectively as shown in Figure 2.1.

Firm Strategy, Structure, and Rivalry

According to Porter (2008), this attribute relates to "[...] how companies are created, organized, and managed, as well as the nature of domestic rivalry".[92] Included in this attribute are included: how to design the firm's business strategy (including the corporate structure, production techniques, marketing strategies, relationships with workers and local governments as well as patterns of cooperation with other firms) and how to manage cooperation and competition with other firms in the cluster. In designing a business strategy, a firm must be able to emphasize the focus on its production that will result in high quality products (or at least better quality than other firms), to package its product properly and create marketing techniques that attract buyers, and to make adjustments to a change in the current business trends. The structure of the company should also consider the form and management of this firm, that is whether the company operates based on a familial relationship or is operated by a professional managerial structure. The pattern of cooperation among firms in a cluster can be seen from two patterns. Tambunan (2005) stated that there are two types of cooperation inside a cluster: a horizontal cooperation and a vertical cooperation.[93] A horizontal cooperation is described as cooperation among firms inside a cluster. Here, these firms can work together to optimize large-scale orders for example. A vertical cooperation on the other hand is described as cooperation between firms in a cluster with other firms outside of the cluster. An example of this cooperation is a subcontracting system with other (usually large) firms. Meanwhile, the presence of domestic competition in a cluster is considered very vital. Porter (1990) said that domestic rivalry could force firms to produce better products and provide better service to the buyer.[94] This rivalry is not only focused on goods and services, but also in terms of getting skilled-workers. Porter (2008) said that "[d]omestic rivalry [...] creates pressure on companies to innovate and improve".[95] Here, domestic rivalry pushes firms in a cluster to lower prices (as well as production costs), find new production process (techniques), improve product quality, serve better services to customers,

92 Porter 2008, p. 182.
93 Cf. Tambunan 2005, pp. 140-41.
94 Cf. Porter 1990, p. 107.
95 Porter 2008, p. 197.

and simply create new products.[96] Hence, the domestic rivalry promotes improvements to each firm's performance because other firms' success signals the others to improve.[97]

Factor Conditions

Factor conditions are related to the factors of production such as human resources (skilled labor), natural resources, infrastructure, and capital. Porter (1990) said that factor conditions are similar to the factors of production in the economic term, which are labor, land, and capital.[98] Porter (1990) adds that those factor conditions can be divided into five inputs.[99] The *first* is human resources, which is the availability of workers (in terms of numbers and skills). The *second* is physical resources, which includes the quality, abundance, and accessibility of natural resources such as water and raw materials, climate conditions, and location (to ease business activities and distribute products). The *third* is knowledge resources, which includes the presence of universities and research centers, libraries, and trade associations to support the existence of a cluster (and firms). The *fourth* is capital resources, which is the availability of capital to provide funds for firms and a cluster. The *fifth* is infrastructure, which includes the transportation system and the communication system to support the activity of a cluster. To undertake economic activities, a firm should at least be supported by well-established labors, raw material sources, the availability of capital or funds, and good infrastructure facilities to support production activities including roads, telecommunications networks, and power grids. Not all of these factors should be available within a cluster. For example, the unavailability of raw materials can be managed by buying raw materials from elsewhere. Or the limitation on skilled workers can be overcome by providing trainings for existing workers. The most important is the availability of infrastructure and investment to support economic activities in the cluster.

---

96 Cf. Porter 1990, p. 118.
97 Cf. ibid., pp. 118-19.
98 Cf. Porter 1990, p. 74.
99 Cf. ibid., pp. 74-75.

Demand Conditions

What is meant by demand conditions is the nature of local market and local demand. The importance of the local market (and local demand) for a cluster is that the buyer can give pressure to firms to manufacture their products (at least) in accordance with market's demand especially when there is a sophisticated buyer, which in turn encourages firms to innovate, to improve, and to upgrade their products.[100] According to Porter (1990), a sophisticated and demanding buyer is those who demand high quality products, design, and service from a company.[101] This buyer could put pressure on a firm to continuously make improvements and product innovation. In short, in dealing with competition within a cluster, this demand condition pressures a firm to innovate and produce better than its competitors.

The Presence of Related and Supporting Industries

The presence of related and supporting industries in a cluster is very important. These industries can help companies in reducing production costs, increasing productivity, improving product's quality, and contributing to new innovations. Aside from that, the presence of those industries can speed up the production process of firms in a cluster.[102] Such industries include local governments, research centers, universities, business associations, and suppliers of materials. Proximity between firms and these industries can benefit a cluster in terms of knowledge and information flow and problem solving. Thus, this relation will help firms to innovate and upgrade their products.[103]

Government

The government is the main actor in developing a cluster especially an established cluster and an emerging cluster.[104] In general, there are five roles

---

100 Cf. ibid., p. 86.
101 Cf. Porter 1990, p. 89.
102 Cf. ibid., p. 101.
103 Cf. ibid., p. 103.
104 Cf. Porter 2008, p. 263.

of the government in developing a cluster.[105] *First*, the government should make a macro economy policy and to ensure political stability. *Second*, the government should design programs that are related to the above four attributes (described below). *Third*, the government should provide incentives to encourage productivity. *Fourth*, the government should guarantee to support all existing clusters, not just in one or two clusters only. *Fifth*, the government should create a long-term and sustainable economic policy that involves businesses and society in developing a cluster. According to Porter (1990), the role of the government related to the four attributes mentioned above includes: providing a conducive business climate to attract investors, enforcing the law on competition to ensure fair competition in a cluster, providing good infrastructures to support economic activity (especially in a cluster), establishing universities (research centers) especially for cluster-related technologies, creating skilled workforces through schools or other education institutions, ensuring the economic stability, providing and organizing government offices/departments around clusters, creating related and supporting industries inside a cluster, and so forth.[106] Porter (1990) also adds that the government can act as a buyer of SMEs' products.[107] This can be done by creating regulations to buy local (SMEs') products. Another role of the government is to encourage firms to perform better, to increase productivity, and to innovate more. This can be done by providing not only programs mentioned earlier but also incentives and trainings for the firm.

Chance

Chance is simply an unpredictable event that can give positive and negative impact to the existence of a firm or a cluster.

105 Cf. ibid., pp. 261-62.
106 Cf. Porter 1990, pp. 127-29.
107 Cf. ibid., p. 127.

2.3 The Role of the State in Economic Development

The goal of each nation is to accomplish maximum welfare of society.[108] This can be accomplished by providing public goods such as basic education, defense, maintenance of order, and an engine of economic growth.[109] There is no denying that the government is responsible for all economic and social activities in order to achieve the above goals. In order to accomplish those goals, the government can assign different governmental institutions to create specific policies.

Looking at the purpose of this research, the role of the state is essential in promoting national economic development. The role of government in the development process has been an issue that has attracted the attention of individuals (academicians) and institutions with an interest in economics.[110] The view of classical and neoclassical economic paradigm that favored minimal role of the state in economy has changed recently because of new growth and new trade theories.[111] Not only because of new growth and new trade theories, globalization also plays a role in encouraging state intervention in the economy. El-Mefteh (2005) said that globalization makes the state play an important role in economic development including economic integration, financial capital flows, and productivity growth.[112] Antic (2003) said that: "[...] in modern time, almost all countries that were the most successful in promoting development had very strong role of the state in the economy".[113] Peter Evans (as cited by Antic 2003) stated that a positive role of government could be an influential factor of a rapid industrial growth.[114] This is also supported by Gunnar Myrdal and Ragnar Nurkse (as cited by Brown 1993) that believed the potential of interventionist policies to secure the benefit of more rapid growth.[115]

Reinert (1999) divided the role of the state into three categories: (a) the state as a provider of institutions, (b) the state as a provider of income distribution, and (c) the state as a promoter of economic growth.[116] The *first*

108 Cf. El-Mefteh 2005.
109 Cf. ibid.
110 Cf. Brown 1993.
111 Cf. ibid.
112 Cf. El-Mefteh 2005.
113 Antic 2003, p. 19.
114 Cf. ibid., p. 24.
115 Cf. Brown 1993, p. 2.
116 Reinert 1999, p. 279.

category, what is meant by a provider of institution is that the state creates and assigns a set of institutions as an arm of the government in designing policies and strategies in order to promote economic growth. The *second* category, what is meant by a provider of income distribution can be understood simply as a tool to secure the welfare of individuals. While the *third* category, the state as a promoter of economic growth can be understood as a single actor that has the responsibility to increase national wealth by encouraging economic growth. Looking at these three categories, the first and third categories can be used to explain the role of state in economic development. *First*, using the first category, the state has a duty to establish effective and efficient institutions that can design strategies and policies in order to achieve the targeted goal. Hall and Jones (as cited by Tabellini 2004) found out that countries with better institutional quality have higher levels of labor productivity.[117] The level of economic development of a country lies in the quality of its institutions.[118] Public institutions must be able to design transparent and predictable policies and implement them clearly and effectively.[119] *Second*, using the third category, the state must promote economic growth by having a development strategy. Haggard (1990) defined a development strategy as "[…] packages of policies aimed at steering economic activity into a particular mixture of ownership and sectors".[120] According to Porter (2008b), the basic roles of a government in economic development are: (a) to achieve macroeconomic and political stability, (b) to improve general microeconomic capacity of the economy, (c) to establish the overall microeconomic rules and incentives, (d) to facilitate and upgrade (business) cluster development, and (e) to implement a positive, distinctive, long-term economic action program to upgrade both the general business environment and the array of local clusters.[121] In order to achieve the goal of promoting economic growth, a state must act as a catalyst and challenger to encourage companies to increase their levels of competitive performance[122] if a state focuses on developing its industry or as an enabler of growth and progress.[123] Thus, the policy of economic development of a country should be able to provide a clear direction and

117 Cf. Tabellini 2004, p. 2.
118 Cf. ibid., p. 6.
119 Cf. Wilson/Drysdale 2000, p. 4.
120 Haggard 1990, p. 23.
121 Cf. Porter 2008, pp. 261-62.
122 Cf. ibid., p. 200.
123 Cf. El-Mefteh 2005.

guidance so that the implementation of this policy will be effective and efficient.

An economic policy of a country should be able to answer the challenges of today's globalization. This policy must also able to give a clear picture of the development of the economic sector. Is the focus on the development of industrial sector or on the agricultural sector? Is it better to develop the import substition industrialization (ISI) or the export-oriented industrialization (EOI)? A country should be able to recognize its nature of economic growth.[124] This can be used as a starting point to develop a specific economic sector. Once a country has decided to develop a specific sector, they can focus on developing policies and strategies to create a comparative advantage in their economic sector. This includes: a clear policy and strategy as mentioned before, the need to create skilled labor, the need to provide infrastructure to support economic (industrial) sector, and the implementation of technology to support the production of specific product.[125] Skilled labors are considered important because they could introduce new methods on production and generate technological progress to create innovation.

In short, the role of government in developing its economy should be done by: designing a clear policy and creating strategies on how to achieve the goals, assigning specific governmental institutions to implement those policy and strategies, preparing other supporting actors to be involved in the development process (such as industries, labor, infrastructure, and technology), and evaluating its policy and strategies.

2.4 Policies on Cluster Development in Indonesia

The policy of industrial cluster development in Indonesia started when the New Order government (under President Soeharto) launched a five-year development plan which emphasized on the development of industry-based economic structure. Soetrisno (2009) called this program a takeoff industrial strategy.[126] The most obvious example of development plan is the establishment of the industry-based economy is the establishment of *PT Industri Pesawat Terbang Nurtanio* (IPTN) in 1976. The establishment

124 Cf. Reinert 1999, p. 281.
125 Cf. ibid., pp. 281-82.
126 Cf. Soetrisno 2009.

of this aerospace industry is a good example on how serious the government established PT IPTN by providing good facilities such as infrastructure facilities, human resources, laws and regulations, and other supporting sectors to support the existence of PT IPTN.[127] Looking at the change of the focus of orientation (which used to be based on the agricultural sector), there are some programs that are run by the government of Indonesia with regard to develop industrial (business) clusters in Indonesia. There are two types of programs that are given to develop clusters in Indonesia, namely technical assistance and financial assistance.

For the technical assistance, the early stages of the industrial cluster development in Indonesia began in the 1970s and was marked by the establishment of the small industrial development program (*Program Pembinaan dan Pengembangan Industri Kecil*, BIPIK).[128] This program was aimed to provide training and education to SMEs in order to improve the quality of human resources and the quality of their products. According to Wee (2006), this program was a prototype of cluster formation in Indonesia and was one of the most important programs in developing clusters.[129] Tambunan (2005) mentioned that the BIPIK focused on specific clusters that are considered to have the potential to be developed by providing: the training facilities, equipment/machinery for selected SMEs which participated in the program, loan assistance for purchasing new equipment/machinery, and technical service units (*unit pelayanan teknis*, UPT) in selected clusters.[130] Marijan (2005) further states that the idea of the establishment of UPTs is to help SMEs improve their production quality by introducing the use of (appropriate) technology and knowledge sharing.[131]

127 Previously, the preparation of the establishment of the aircraft industry is marked by the formation of: the Body for Preparation of Aviation Industry (*Lembaga Persiapan Industri Penerbangan*, LAPIP) on December 16, 1961, the Nurtanio Aviation Industrial Institution (*Lembaga Industri Penerbangan Nurtanio*, LIPNUR) in 1966, and PT IPTN as the national aircraft industry as well as industry engaged in the information technology sector, automotive, maritime, and simulation technology, industrial turbine, and engineering services. In 1985, PT IPTN changed its name to *PT Industri Pesawat terbang Nusantara* (IPTN). In 2000, the name was changed to *PT Dirgantara Indonesia* (Indonesian Aerospace). For further details please see: http://www.indonesian-aerospace.com/aboutus.php?m=aboutus&t=aboutus8, accessed January 26, 2014.

128 See Wee 2006, Tambunan 2005, Hill 2001.

129 Cf. Wee 2006, pp. 31-32.

130 Cf. Tambunan 2005, p. 147.

131 Cf. Marijan 2005, p. 218.

Unfortunately, based on the World Bank report (as cited in Wee, 2006) the BIPIK has failed because of the lack of coordination among government agencies responsible for SMEs' development programs, poor design of the development of SMEs (cluster) programs, and the lack of monitoring and evaluation process of existing programs.[132] Other programs carried out to develop the industrial sector (in order to prepare the industrial cluster formation) are small-scale industry areas (*Lingkungan Industri Kecil*, LIK) and small industry estates (*Pemukiman/Perkampungan Industri Kecil*, PIK) programs.[133] What is meant by a small-scale industry area is a particular area within or outside the industrial zone which has infrastructure networks for a number of production units, has common service facilities (CSF), and has the facilities to provide services and trainings. It is expected that small industries inside the LIK can expand themselves and encourage the development of other small industries outside the LIK. While small industrial estate is a particular area that has infrastructure networks and production units which integrate with the houses of businessmen. The purpose of the LIK and PIK is to create an atmosphere of mutual support in promoting industrial growth.

Along with the failure of the BIPIK, the government launched a new program called the Foster Parent Program (*Program Bapak Angkat*) that involves large enterprises and state-owned enterprises.[134] The program is conducted by involving large companies and state-owned enterprises to become business partners of SMEs with the aim of increasing: the capability of SMEs' production, the use of technology, marketing techniques, and access to capital. This program continues to run until today by the name of the Partnership and Community Development Program.[135]

While there are several financial assistance programs provided by the government to the SMEs/SMIs namely: the small investment credit (*Kredit Investasi Kecil*, KIK) and the working capital credit (*Kredit Modal Kerja Permanen*, KMKP) during the period of 1973-1990.[136] The purpose of this program was to provide low-interest loans to small industries to expand their businesses. Unfortunately this program did not go well, charac-

132 Cf. Wee 2006, p. 33.

133 See Pentingnya Pengembangan LIK, PIK, dan SUIK. http://www.bumn.go.id/kim/publikasi/siaran-pers/the-importance-of-lik-pik-suik-development, accessed January 3, 2014.

134 Cf. Wee 2006, p. 33, Soetrisno 2009, Hill 2001, p. 251.

135 See Minister of State-Owned Enterprises Decree No. 236/MBU/2003.

136 Cf. Wee 2006, p. 30.

terized by a high rate of default of the creditors.[137] In 1990, the government introduced a new loan scheme called the Small Enterprise Credit (*Kredit Usaha Kecil,* KUK). Under this scheme, all banks (which were assigned distributing the loans) had to allocate 20 percent of the total loan's funds available for small enterprises. Unfortunately this program did not work well due to a lot of misuse of credit because banks had to achieve the target of distributing 20 percent of their credit portfolio to small businesses. In order to give financial assistance to SMEs, in 2007 (to date), the government issued a new credit scheme called 'people-based small business loans (*Kredit Usaha Rakyat*, KUR).[138] Basically, KUR are intended for those productive and qualified SME that are not yet bankable.

Soetrisno (2009) added that the policy of developing business clusters in Indonesia is also marked by the formation of the Ministry of Cooperatives and SMEs in 1999.[139] To develop the SMEs to be involved actively in the cluster, the ministry established the Agency for Developing Cooperatives Resources and Small and Medium Entrepreneurs (*Badan Pengembangan Sumber Daya Koperasi dan Pengusaha Kecil dan Menengah,* BPS-KPKM). This agency has three functions in order to develop SMEs, which are: (i) business development, in order to expand SMEs' business and market penetration, (ii) investment facilitation, in order to give financial assistance including credit restructuring, and (iii) human resource development, including the provision of trainings as well as research and development.[140]

Not only that, during the administration of President Susilo Bambang Yudhoyono, the government issued two important decisions in the development of industrial clusters in Indonesia. They are: Regulation of the President of the Republic of Indonesia No. 28/2008 on the National Industrial Policy and the Roadmap of National Industrial Cluster Development by the Ministry of Industry. The purpose of these two decisions is to build a strong industrial sector and to improve the competitiveness of the industry through the cluster approach. Descriptions of the national industrial policy and the road map of national industrial clusters will be discussed in another chapter.

---

137 Cf. Marijan 2005, p. 220, Wee 2006, p. 31.

138 For further details see Buku Tanya Jawab Seputar Kredit Usaha Rakyat (KUR), http://www.komite-kur.com.

139 Cf. Soetrisno 2009.

140 Cf. ibid.

3. The Role of the Central Government in Developing Industrial Clusters: Institutions, Policies, and Strategies

This chapter describes the role of the (central) government in developing and empowering SMEs, either through legislation or through programs and policies that guide ministries, government agencies, and local governments in creating their policies and plans. This chapter will begin with the direction of government policies in developing and empowering SMEs, followed by an explanation of policies, programs, and strategic plans of the two ministries in charge of developing and empowering SMEs/SMIs, which are the Ministry of Cooperatives and SMEs and the Ministry of Industry.

3.1 The Importance of SMEs in Indonesia

As a developing economy, the Indonesian economy is characterized by both formal and informal micro, small and medium-sized enterprises (SMEs) that account for almost 99 percent of the total number of economic units. Indonesia, according to the Ministry of Cooperatives and Small Medium Enterprises (SMEs), has more than 52.7 million SMEs who employed more than 96 million workforces in 2009 (Table 3.1).[141] There are about 52.7 million micro and small economic units (accounting for 99 percent of the total number of enterprises), around 546,000 medium-sized enterprises (0.08 percent of the total number of enterprises), and more than 41,000 large enterprises (0.01 percent of the total number of enterprises) in the overall economy consisting of many sectors such as agriculture, mining, manufacture, electricity, gas and clean air supply, construction, trade, hotels and restaurants, transport and communication, finance, rent and service, and services (Table 3.2). In 2010, micro and small economic units accounted for 94.5 percent of total employment, and medium-sized enterprises accounted for 2.71 percent. These SMEs are spread into many categories such as agriculture, industries, and services.

141 Cf. Ministry of Cooperatives and SMEs 2010.

Table 3.1: Number of SMEs, Large Enterprises (LEs), and Workforces in Indonesia, 2006-2009

Indicators	Year							
	2006		2007		2008		2009	
	Total	%	Total	%	Total	%	Total	%
Enterprises	49,026,380		50,150,263		51,414,262		52,769,280	
Micro	48,512,438	98.95	49,608,953	98.92	50,847,771	98.90	52,176,795	98.88
Small	472,602	0.96	498,565	0.99	522,124	1.02	546,675	1.04
Medium	36,763	0.07	38,282	0.08	39,717	0.08	41,133	0.08
Total SMEs	49,021,803	99.9	50,145,800	99.9	51,409,612	99.9	52,764,603	99.9
Large	4,557	0.01	4,463	0.01	4,650	0.01	4,677	0.01

Indicators	Year							
	2006		2007		2008		2009	
	Total	%	Total	%	Total	%	Total	%
Workforce	90,350,778		93,027,341		96,780,484		98,886,003	
Micro	82,071,144	90.84	84,452,002	90.78	87,810,366	90.73	90,012,694	91.03
Small	3,139,711	3.48	3,278,793	3.52	3,519,843	3.64	3,521,073	3.56
Medium	2,698,743	2.99	2,761,135	2.97	2,694,069	2.78	2,677,565	2.71
Total SMEs	87,909,598	97.3	90,491,930	97.2	94,024,278	97.1	96,211,332	97.3
Large	2,441,181	2.70	2,535,411	2.73	2,756,205	2.85	2,674,671	2.70

Source: Modified data from the Ministry of Cooperatives and SMEs 2010

Table 3.2: Proportion of SMEs by Sector, 2008

Sector	Proportion (%)
Agriculture*	51.51
Mining and Quarrying	0.51
Manufacture	6.32
Electricity, Gas, and Water Supply	0.02
Construction	0.34
Trade, Hotels, and Restaurants	28.85
Transportation and Communication	6.25
Finance, Rent, and Services	1.95
Services	4.25

*including agriculture, farms, forestry, and fisheries

Source: Ministry of Cooperatives and SMEs (n.d.)

The data in Table 3.2 shows that the distribution of SMEs by sectors, largely dominated in the agriculture sector, accounted for 51.51 percent. This was followed by trade, hotels & restaurants at 28.85 percent and 6.32 percent for the manufacturing sector. The manufacturing sector here is very diverse ranging from furniture, textiles, garments, footwear, ceramics, food and beverages.

Looking at Tables 3.1 and 3.2 above, the government seems to be obliged to empower Indonesian SMEs by creating policies that favor the SMEs as a backbone of Indonesian economy. It is not surprising that SMEs should get priority for a number of reasons. *First*, SMEs play a vital role in the structure of Indonesian economy. Data in Table 1 earlier shows a comparison of the number of small and medium businesses and large enterprises in the industrial structure in Indonesia from 2006-2009. From that table, it can be seen that SMEs has grown from year to year. In the period of 2006-2009, there was a growth of SMEs from 49,021,803 units in 2006 to 52,764,603 units in 2009 or growing at rate of 7.63 percent compared to a growth of large enterprises from 4,557 units in 2006 to 4,677 units in 2009 or growing at rate of 2.63 percent. The data also shows three important elements which are embedded within SMEs: (a) that the economic structure of Indonesia is still dominated by SMEs; (b) looking at the growth rate that reached 7.63 percent, we can simply interpret that each year new SMEs and new entrepreneurs are born (even though there is no data showing how many enterprise upgraded its size i.e. micro enterprise becomes small enterprise, small enterprise becomes medium enterprise and medium enterprise becomes large enterprise); and (c) SMEs are very important as a provider of employment in Indonesia.

Second, SMEs also can be seen as a provider of employment in Indonesia. Looking back at Table 1, it cannot be denied that Indonesian SMEs are the biggest source of employment. About 97 percent of the total country's workforce is linked to SMEs. This data shows the ability of SMEs to absorb loads of workers that undoubtedly contribute to poverty reduction in Indonesia, and, moreover, not to forget the contribution of SMEs in rural areas. As expressed by Tambunan, the majority of SMEs are located in rural areas so that SMEs can also be called to play an important role in the development of rural areas such as creating employment and generating income.[142] The positive impact of the presence of SMEs in rural areas is the reduction of development gap between cities and rural areas. Sulistyastuti (2004) added that the dominance of SMEs in providing employment opportunities should be appreciated because of the limitations of large enterprises in providing job opportunities due to the number of large enterprises and their requirements such as formal education and others.[143]

Third, the role of SMEs in the national economy can also be seen from their contribution to the Gross Domestic Product (GDP). Tables 3.3 and 3.4 show the contribution and proportion of the GDP contribution of SMEs and LEs to the Indonesian economy.

142 Cf. Tambunan 2009b, p. 1.
143 Cf. Sulistyastuti 2004, p. 144.

Table 3.3: Structure of GDP by size of enterprises (in percent), 2006

Sector	SMEs	LEs
Agriculture	95.7	4.3
Mining and Quarrying	11.4	88.6
Manufacture	23.7	76.3
Electricity, Gas, and Water Supply	8.1	91.9
Construction	66.0	34.0
Trade, Hotels, and Restaurants	96.4	3.6
Transportation and Communication	53.3	46.7
Finance, Rent, and Services	63.6	36.4
Services	48.2	51.8
Total GDP	53.3	46.7

Source: Data is modified from Tambunan (2009a)

Table 3.4: Contribution and Proportion of SMEs and LEs to the Gross Domestic Product in 2007-2008

	Current Prices (based on 2000 prices)				**Constant Prices (based on 2000 prices)**			
	Contribution (in trillion IDR)		Proportion (in percent)		Contribution (in trillion IDR)		Proportion (in percent)	
Enterprise	2007	2008	2007	2008	2007	2008	2007	2008
SMEs	2,105	2,609	56.23	55.56	1,099	1,165	58.40	58.33
LEs	1,639	2,087	43.77	44.44	783	832	41.60	41.67

Source: Data is modified from the Ministry of Cooperatives and SMEs (n.d.)

Looking at the data above, Indonesian SMEs have contributed about more than half of the total GDP between the years 2006-2008. However, when looking at the details, it is the role of large enterprises that have contributed the most to the GDP from 2007-2008 with about 0.01 percent of the total number of business units in Indonesia, large enterprises were able to account for 44.44 percent of total GDP in 2008 comparing to the number of SMEs at 99.99 percent but contributed only 55.56 percent total GDP in 2008 for example. Also, looking at the amount of total GDP's contribution, it is clearly seen that the LEs contribute more than the SMEs. However, apart from the figures above, a high appreciation should be given to Indonesian SMEs for a large contribution to the country's economy.

Fourth, the importance of Indonesian SMEs can also be seen from their contribution on the total export values. Table 3.5 shows the contribution of Indonesian SMEs from their export activities.

Table 3.5: Export of Indonesian SMEs, 2006-2008 (in million USD)

Non-oil and Gas Exports			
Year	SMEs	LEs	Total
2006	12,195.0	65,623.2	77,818.2
2007	14,301.3	75,000.0	89,301.3
2008	18,375.9	91,509.1	109,885.0

Source: Data from Tambunan (2011)

Based on data discussed above, Indonesian SMEs are able to demonstrate their contribution with all limitations (an explanation of the limitations of SMEs will be discussed below). We should underline the increase in the value of exports contributed by Indonesian SMEs even though their contribution is considered small, about 15 percent in 2006 and 16 percent in 2007-2008. There is no denying that the increasing amount of export value indicates the existence of Indonesian SMEs in the midst of the global competition and also in support of government programs.

In addition to the above arguments, Sulistyastuti said that there are at least four strategic positions of SMEs in Indonesia.[144] The *first* one is the issue of capital. SMEs do not require large capital as required by LEs so that the formation of this business unit is not as hard as large firms. The *second* aspect is workforces. Labor needed by the SMEs do not require a formal education. The majority of the workforces required by the SMEs are based on experiences (learning by doing) related to historical factors. For example, as is often found in craft industries, carving and *batik*. The *third* aspect is location. Most of Indonesian SMEs are located in rural areas and do not require large infrastructures like big companies located in urban areas. The *fourth* aspect is survival. Many studies have shown that Indonesian SMEs survived when Indonesia was hit by the crisis in 1997-1998.

144 Cf. Sulistyastuti 2004, p. 145.

The World Bank also added the importance of SMEs in the Indonesian economy as an engine of growth.[145] There are three main arguments behind this view. *First*, SMEs increase competition and entrepreneurship among SMEs and therefore contribute to new innovation and higher number of productivity growth. *Second*, SMEs are generally more productive than large enterprises. Unfortunately, low access to financial services and 'unfriendly' economic conditions hamper the development of SMEs. *Third*, the number of workforces absorbed by SMEs is higher than large enterprises since SMEs are more labor-intensive compared to large enterprises which are capital-intensive. We should acknowledge that with the level of high employment, SMEs have guaranteed the stability of employment, the reduction of unemployment rate, and by becoming the vehicle of creating new entrepreneurs.

SMEs are business activities that can enhance employment and job creation as well as provide economy services to wider community. Not only that, SMEs can contribute in equity and improvement of people's income, driven the economic growth, and can also act as an instrument in the creation of national stability. That is why SMEs are considered as one of the main national economics' pillar that must have the opportunity, support, protection, and wider improvements as a prove of the government's favor to the people's economy's business groups, without necessarily ignoring the role of large enterprises and state-owned enterprises (*Badan Usaha Milik Negara*, BUMN). Unfortunately, even though SMEs have proven their role in the national economy, facts show that SMEs still face many inhibitions and constraints, either internally or externally, in production, marketing, human resources, design and technology, capital, and business climate. Therefore, it is important for the SMEs to be empowered through: (a) the improvement of business climate that can support the development of SMEs and (b) the development and management of SMEs.

The direction and the development policy of SMEs and SMIs have been stated in many regulations, either in the law, government regulation, the presidential decree, the regulation of the President of the Republic of Indonesia, and the presidential instruction. The followings are few of the SMEs development and empowerment's policies in Indonesia:

145 Cf. Tambunan 2007, p. 98.

1. Law No. 20/2008 on Small and Medium-sized Enterprises (SMEs).[146] This law regulates several issues that are related to the development and empowerment of SMEs. In this law, the empowerment of SMEs is defined as an effort that is done by the (central) government, local governments, businesses, and communities as they work together in increasing the economic environment and the development of SMEs so that they can grow into an independent and a strong business.[147] The increase of economic environment is done by establishing laws and policies that in favor of SMEs, covering the aspects of funding, infrastructure, business information, partnership, business licensing, business oppurtunities, trade promotion and institutional support. The goal in SMEs empowerment is to create a balanced, developed, and equitable structure of the national economy, to foster and develop SMEs in becoming strong and independent businesses, and to increase the role of SMEs in promoting regional development, job creation, income generation, economic growth, and poverty reduction.[148] While in this law, the development of SMEs is defined as an effort made by the (central) government, local governments, businesses, and communities to develop SMEs through mentoring assistance and strengthening assistance to develop and enhance the capability and competitiveness of SMEs.[149] What is meant by strengthening assistance is a financial aid given to SMEs via banks, cooperatives, and other non-bank institutions that aims to develop and strengthen the capital of SMEs. These forms include the facilitation of SMEs' business development in the field of production and processing, marketing, human resources, as well as design and technology.
2. Regulation of the President of the Republic of Indonesia No. 5/2010 on the National Medium-term Development Plan 2010-2014.[150] The National Medium-term Development Plan 2010-2014 is used as a guide for ministries or government agencies in preparing strategic plans, which are subsequently taken into con-

146 See Law No. 20/2008.
147 Cf. Article 1 Paragraph 8 of Law No. 20/2008.
148 Cf. Artice 5 of Law No. 20/2008.
149 Cf. Article 1 Paragraph 10 of Law No. 20/2008.
150 See Regulation of the President of the Republic of Indonesia No. 5/2010.

sideration for local governments in preparing and adjusting their local development plans to achieve national development goals. The National Medium-term Development Plan 2010-2014 is the continuation of the National Medium-term Development Plan 2004-2009 which sets three development strategies that pro-growth, pro-jobs and pro-poor. In designing the strategy of economic development, the government has mapped out ten challenges of development in the period 2010-2014.[151] Those ten challenges are: an insufficient achievement of economic growth during the period 2004-2008 which was set at the rate of 6 percent to achieve a prosperous Indonesian society, the acceleration of economic growth by involving all of the population of Indonesia, the persistence of regional disparities, the existing gap between business owners (perpetrators) especially with regard to SMEs, economic growth that threaten environmental sustainability, the quality of infrastructure that not support the economic sector (yet), low level of productivity especially related to the quality of human resources and technology, poor quality of the bureaucracy that impede economic growth, consolidation of democracies especially related to regional autonomy, and weak of law enforcement. In answer to the above challenges, the government issued the National Medium-term Development 2010-2014 that aim to reform Indonesia in all sectors, to improve the quality of human resources, and to increase economic competitiveness.[152] There are five development agenda in the National Medium-term Development 2010-2014, namely: the economic development and people's welfare improvement, the improvement of governance, upholding the pillars of democracy, the law enforcement and anti-corruption, and the promotion of an inclusive and equitable development. From those agendas, the government issued eleven priority programs which are also used as a basis for making strategic plans of ministries and government agencies, namely: bureaucratic reform and governance, education, health, poverty alleviation, food security, infrastructure, investment and business

151 Cf. Kementerian Perencanaan Pembangunan Nasional/Badan Perencanaan Pembangunan Nasional 2010a, pp. 18-21.

152 Cf. Kementerian Perencanaan Pembangunan Nasional/Badan Perencenaan Pembangunan Nasional 2010a, p. 25.

climate, energy, environment and disaster especially in frontier, outer, and post-conflict areas as well as culture, creativity, and technological innovation. There are at least four priority programs that later became the main focus of development programs and empowerment of SMEs which are priorities on bureaucratic reform and good governance, poverty alleviation, infrastructure, and business and investment climate.

3. Presidential Instruction No. 1/2010 on Accelerating the Implementation of National Development Priorities 2010.[153] This instruction refers to the priority programs/plans in the National Medium-term Development 2010-2014. If the plan is associated with the development and empowerment of SMEs, there is several priority programs that became the foundation strategic plan government ministries and agencies associated with the presence of SMEs. *First*, the priority of bureaucratic and governance reform that is focused on structuring the concept of regional autonomy, especially with regard to the harmonization and synchronization of legislation at national and local levels. *Second*, the priority of poverty reduction that is focused on the development and expansion of employment opportunities, the improvement of supporting credit guarantee, and the expansion of the KUR to SMEs. *Third*, the priority on infrastructure that is focused on improving domestic connectivity to support the distribution of goods and services between regions. *Fourth*, priority of the investment climate and business that is focused on simplifying the procedure of business license/permit and business investment, and improving labor regulations such as wage system, labor protection, social security.
4. Regulation of the President of the Republic of Indonesia No. 28/2008 on the National Industrial Policy.[154] In this regulation, the purpose of the national industrial policy is to improve the competitiveness of the industry. In supporting this objective, the ministry in charge and responsible in the field of industry prepares and establishes road map of the priority industrial cluster development including the industrial manufacturing base, agro-based industry, transportation industry, electronics and telematics industry, supporting industries of creative industries and the crea-

153 Cf. Presidential Instruction No. 1/2010.
154 Cf. Regulation of the President of the Republic of Indonesia No. 28/2008.

tive industries on particular SMIs.[155] In addition to those priority industries, the Ministry of Industry also prepares and establishes a road map of provincial industrial development and guide road map of industrial districts and municipality's development.[156] Until now it has mapped the development of industry in the eleven provinces covering: the province of DI Yogyakarta (Leather Processing Industry and Wood Processing Industry), the province of Central Sulawesi (Cocoa Processing Industry, Manufacturing Seaweed Industry, and Fish Processing Industry), the province of Papua (Cocoa Processing Industry, Manufacturing Coffee Industry, and Sweet Potato Processing Industry), the province of West Sumatra (Cocoa Processing Industry, Fish Processing Industry, and Snack Industry), the province of South Sumatra (Rubber Processing Industry), the province of Lampung (Cassava and Corn Processing Industry), The province of East Kalimantan (Cocoa Processing Industry and Rubber Processing Industry), the province of South Sulawesi (Cocoa Processing Industry and Manufacturing Seaweed Industry), the province of Gorontalo (Maize Manufacturing and Marine Product Processing Industry), the province of East Nusa Tenggara (Corn Processing Industry and Manufacturing Seaweed Industry), and the province of West Nusa Tenggara (Beef Processed Food Industry, Corn Processing Industry, Manufacturing Seaweed Industry, Fish Processing Industry, and Industrial Craft).[157] Moreover, since 2006 the Directorate General of Small and Medium Enterprises of the Ministry of Industry has studied the counties and cities industry's core competencies which include: the regency of Katingan, the area of West Nusa Tenggara (Rattan Industry, Rubber Industry, Palm Oil Industry, Food Processing Industry, and Peat Commodities Industry),[158] the regency of Konawe, the area of Southeast Sulawesi (Skipjack Manufacturing Industry, Cocoa Processing Industry, Rattan Industry, Oil Industry, and Manufacturing Bricks Indus-

155 Cf. Article 2 of Regulation of the President of the Republic of Indonesia No. 28/2008.

156 Cf. Article 6 of Regulation of the President of the Republic of Indonesia No. 28/2008.

157 Cf. Kementerian Perindustrian (n.d.a).

158 Cf. Departemen Perindustrian dan PT INDULEXCO (n.d.).

try),[159] the regency of West Lampung, the area of Lampung (Desiccated Manufacturing Coconut and Coconut Coir Processing Industry),[160] the city of Palu, Central Sulawesi (Rattan Industries), and the regency of East Sumba, East Nusa Tenggara (Seaweed Processing Industry).[161]

In developing and empowering SMEs in Indonesia, there are two government agencies that directly intersect with the program in developing and empowering SMEs. They are: the Ministry of Cooperatives and SMEs and the Ministry of Industry. Although there are several other government agencies that also intersect with SMEs' sector such as the Ministry of Commerce, the Ministry of Manpower and Transmigration, and the National Planning Agency (*Badan Perencanaan Nasional*, Bappenas), however this study will only focus on the two ministries mentioned earlier. The following will illustrate profiles, strategies, and policies of the two ministries in developing and empowering SMEs as mandated in the National Medium-term Development Plan (Indonesia) 2010-2014.

3.2 The Ministry of Cooperatives and SMEs

Empowering SMEs is an integral part of national development, which is aimed at establishing a just and prosperous society. In the 1945 Constitution, it is explicitly emphasized the implementation of principle of brotherhood (Article 33 Paragraph 1) and the implementation of the national economy activity based on economic democracy (Article 33 Paragraph 4).[162] Like other countries, the Indonesian government has the responsibility for promoting economic growth at national and local levels to increase people's welfare. In order to achieve this goal, the president of Republic of Indonesia, President Susilo Bambang Yudhoyono (SBY) said his concern is to overcome unemployment and poverty. His concern is then formulated into a triple track strategy: pro-growth, pro-jobs and pro-poor.[163]

---

159 Cf. ibid.
160 Cf. ibid.
161 Cf. ibid.
162 Cf. Kementerian Koperasi dan UKM 2010, p. 1.
163 Cf. Triple Track Strategy: Upaya Mengurangi Pengangguran dan Kemiskinan, http://www.presidenri.go.id/index.php/topik/2006/12/21/44.html, accessed January 5, 2014.

The *first* track is to increase economic growth by prioritizing the export sector and investments. The *second* track is to promote the real sector to create jobs. The *last* track is to revitalize agriculture, forestry, marine and rural economy to reduce poverty.

Looking at the development and empowerment programs of SMEs in Indonesia, such programs will be directly related to the life and welfare for the vast majority of Indonesia (pro-poor). In addition, the potential and the strategic role of SMEs have proved as a pillar of strength and growth of the national economy (pro-growth). While SMEs are dominant, their presence as a national economic actor is also a vital subject in the context of development, particularly in the expansion of job opportunities for new entrepreneurs and employment as well as to reduce unemployment rate (pro job). Consistently with the above strategy, the Ministry of Cooperatives and SMEs design vision, mission, goals, strategies, and policies as guidelines for policy making by all stakeholders in developing and empowering SMEs in Indonesia.

3.2.1 Vision and Mission

Referring to Presidential Regulation No. 47/2009 on the Establishment and Organization of Ministry, the role of the Ministry of Cooperatives and SMEs is to handle government affairs in order to sharpen, coordinate, and synchronize all government's programs in empowering SMEs.[164] In addition, referring to the (Indonesia) National Medium-term Development Plan 2010-2014[165] and the purpose of empowering SMEs as stated in Law No. 20/2008 on Micro, Small and Medium-sized Enterprises,[166] the Ministry of Cooperatives and SMEs establish its vision which is: To be a Credible Ministry to Achieve Tough and Independent Cooperatives and SMEs as Soko Guru of the National Economy. In order to achieve this vision, the Ministry of Cooperatives and SMEs designs its mission statement which are: (1) to contribute to the national development through the formulation of national policies, the coordination of plans, the execution, and the con-

---

164 Cf. Articles 3c and 47 of Regulation of the President of the Republic of Indonesia No. 47/2009.

165 Cf. Kementerian Perencanaan Pembangunan Nasional/Badan Perencanaan Pembangunan Nasional 2010b, pp. 64-65.

166 Cf. Article 1 Paragraph 8 of Law No. 20/2008.

trol of policies in empowering SMEs and (2) to enhance synergies and active role of the public and the business community in order to increase productivity, competitiveness, and independence of SMEs in a systematic, sustained, and integrated way.[167] There are three big parts in achieving those vision and missions:[168]

a. Growing and developing the entrepreneurial spirit of SMEs,
b. Improving the competitiveness of SMEs, and
c. Developing financial access and financial guarantee for SMEs.

To achieve those vision and missions, the Ministry of Cooperatives and SMEs has launched the purposes of developing and empowering SMEs as mandated by Law No. 20/2008 on Micro, Small and Medium-sized Enterprises which is to build a national economy based on a just economic democracy as follows:[169]

1. Increasing the number and role of SMEs in the national economy,
2. Increasing the empowerment of SMEs by developing policies and programs based on research and improving the quality and skills of SMEs' human resources,
3. Increasing the competitiveness of SMEs' products by improving the ability of SMEs in developing creative, innovative, high quality, and competitive products,
4. Increasing the marketing of SMEs' products by improving institutional organization, marketing network, and market share of SMEs,
5. Increasing the access to financing and guarantee for SMEs by providing and expanding access scheme to financing in accordance with the needs of SMEs,
6. Developing the entrepreneurial spirit of SMEs by creating new and innovative entrepreneurs, raising awareness of entrepreneurship as a culture, and developing entrepreneurial spirit among the community, and

---

167 Cf. Kementerian Koperasi dan UKM (n.d.).
168 Cf. Kementerian Koperasi dan UKM 2010, p. 10.
169 Cf. ibid., pp. 10-11.

7. Improving the business climate that favors SMEs by improving the quality of public service that is transparent, accountable and credible as well as creating regulations that favor SMEs.

3.2.2 Strategic Objectives

There are a number of strategic objectives to be achieved by the Ministry of Cooperatives and SMEs towards the development and empowerment of SMEs in Indonesia.[170] Those objectives are:

a. Increasing the number and role of SMEs in the national economy which is characterized by an increase in productivity of SMEs by 5 percent per year, an increase in the contribution of SMEs to the GDP by 6 percent per year, an increase in the average number of SMEs' employment by 5 percent per year, an increase in the average of the total investment's value of SMEs by 10 percent per year, and an increase in the value of SMEs' export by 15 percent per year,
b. Increasing the empowerment of SMEs which is characterized by: an increase in the number of human resources of SMEs who join training (conducted by the ministry), the implementation of entrepreneurial training for prospective entrepreneurs, an increase in the number of places of business skills practice in rural educational institutions, an increase in the number of SMEs that apply information technology and appropriate technology in their activity, and an increase in the number of SMEs' business partnership,
c. Increasing the competitiveness of SMEs which is characterized by: an increase in the use of SME's product within the country, a stable of 65 percent market share of SMEs in the retail business, and an increase in the value of non-oil exports of SMEs or at least at the rate of 20 percent per year,
d. Increasing the marketing of SMEs' products which is characterized by: an increase number of trading house across the province, an increase in the quality of facility and infrastructure of production and marketing, more promotion for SMEs' products, an increase in the number and quality of modern retail shop owned by

170 Cf. Kementerian Koperasi dan UKM 2010, pp. 12-14.

SMEs, stronger marketing of SMEs' products in business centers including in the less developed areas, remote areas, and borders, and the realization of SMESCO as an icon for creative industry and empowerment of national SMEs,

e. Providing access to financial and guarantee for SMEs which is characterized by: the availability of financing scheme that is easy, affordable, and prompt for SME's credit guarantee, an increase in the number and quality of financial (micro finance) institutions, and a stronger capital for SMEs in business centers including in the less developed areas, remote areas, and borders,
f. Improving the business climate that favors SMEs which is characterized by: the implementation of the good governance concept that is effective, efficient, and responsible, the implementation of regulations and policies in favor of the empowerment of SMEs, the harmonization of programs and activities in empowering SMEs through cross-sectoral coordination at the level of central (government) , provincial, district, and city, and the availability of prospective studies and policies in empowering SMEs, and
g. Developing the entrepreneurial spirit which is characterized by: the creation of 5,000 new entrepreneurs among scholars and the availability of modules to raise awareness of entrepreneurship.

3.2.3 Organizational Structure

In implementing its vision and missions as well as designing national policies to develop and empower SMEs, the Ministry of Cooperatives and SMEs assisted by seven (7) deputies which consist of:

1. Deputy for Cooperatives and SMEs' Institutional, this deputy is responsible for preparing policy's formulation and coordinating the implementation of such policy which is mainly related to: policies on Cooperatives and SMEs in accordance with current regulations, a coordination on the supervision of such policy with other working unit in the Ministry of Cooperatives and SMEs and other relevant government agencies, and an arrangement of the implementation of agreement that is related to SMEs,
2. Deputy for Production, this deputy is responsible for setting policy formulation and coordinating policy implementation in the area of production especially related to the plan and development

program in the production of SMEs. All SMEs' sector engaged in the agriculture and horticulture crops, the forestry and horticulture, the fisheries and animal husbandry, the handicraft industry and mining, and the electricity and miscellaneous business are under the responsibility of this deputy,

3. Deputy for Finance, this deputy is responsible for preparing policy formulation and coordinating policy implementation in the field of SMEs' financing especially concerning on the implementation of agreements and the establishment of qualification requirements for SMEs that will get financial aid,
4. Deputy for Marketing and Business Network, this deputy is responsible for setting policy formulation and coordinating policy implementation in the areas of marketing and business networks especially concerning on marketing of SME's products in domestic market, export and import activities of SMEs, facility and infrastructure of marketing SMEs' products, the establishment of business networks and partnerships for SMEs, and the publication of business information regarding to SME products,
5. Deputy for Human Resource Development, this deputy is responsible for setting policy formulation and coordinating policy implementation in the field of human resource development especially concerning on the implementation of the technical functions of SMEs' empowerment in the field of human resource development, the preparation of education and training's standards for the development training modules for SMEs, and the creation of new entrepreneurial development system,
6. Deputy for Business' Development and Restructuring, this deputy is responsible for preparing policy formulation and coordinating policy implementation especially related to an increase in the productivity and quality of SMEs' products, the empowerment of business development institutions for SMEs, and the facilitation of investment ot develop SMEs, and
7. Deputy for SMEs' Resource Assessment, this deputy is responsible for preparing policy formulation and coordinating policy implementation especially related to researches on SMEs, researches on the resources of SMEs, and the development and regeneration of SMEs.

Looking at the organizational structure of the Ministry of Cooperatives and SMEs, these deputies are supported by several assistant deputies. The following is the organizational chart of the Ministry of Cooperatives and SMEs:

Figure 3.1: The Organizational Chart of the Ministry of Cooperatives

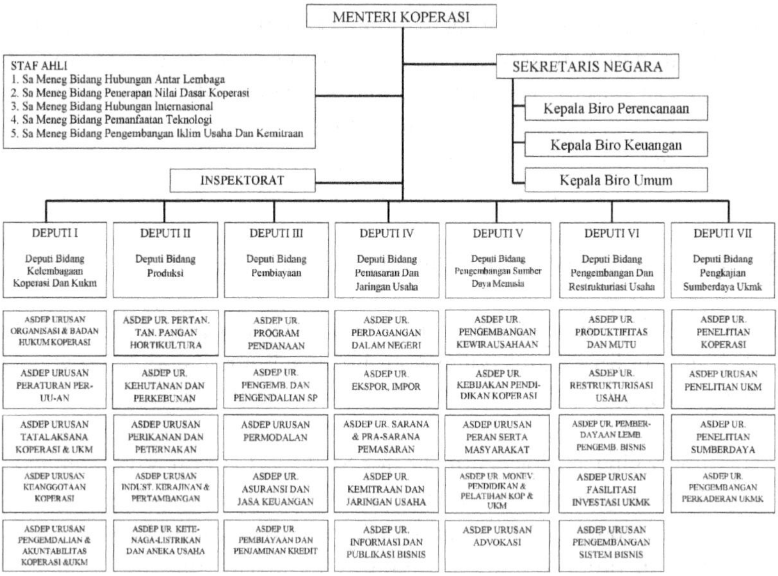

Source: modified from Kementerian Koperasi dan UKM, http://www.depkop.go.id/images/struorg 100.png, accessed January 7, 2014

In carrying out the mandate to develop and empower SMEs in Indonesia, the Ministry of Cooperatives and SMEs formulate national policies and strategies to develop and empower SMEs in Indonesia. These policies and strategies are based on the First Agenda of the 2010-2014 National Development Vision and Mission which is the Economic Development and the Improvement of Public Welfare.[171] This agenda emphasizes on increasing revenue, decreasing unemployment, and improving people's quality of life including poverty alleviation and employment creation. In line with the

171 Cf. Kementerian Perencanaan Pembangunan Nasional/Badan Perencenaan Pembangunan Nasional 2010a, pp. 38-67.

earlier agenda, the direction of this policy direction is aimed at improving access to finance for SMEs, in particular in providing KUR for SMEs. It is expected that an increase in the access to financing of SMEs will reduce poverty rate and improve the livelihoods of the poor. The strategy of empowering SMEs is directed towards the development of innovation and technology competencies so that SMEs can play a greater role in supporting the sustainable growth of the national economy. To support this, there should be an action to improve a more conducive business environment for the sake of improvement of the competitiveness of SMEs, to increase business access to productive resources for SMEs, and to increase the capacity, competence and productivity efforts of SMEs.

3.2.4 Policies to Develop and Empower SMEs

Referring to the above strategy, the Ministry of Cooperatives and SMEs put its focus on four major policies in the development and empowerment of SMEs. They are:[172]

1. Improving business climate for SMEs. This policy is intended to achieve a more coordinated and participative SME's empowerment program that is supported by an increase in the role of private institutions and communities, to provide regulations and (national and local) policies that support the empowerment of SMEs, and to lower fee that inhibit the development of SMEs. An important aspect in the improvement of the business climate is the development of regulations and policies that facilitate and favor the growth of SMEs nationwide. Included in this is the arrangement of regulation concerning the development of SMEs and the synchronization of such regulation at the national and regional levels such as local regulations (provincial decree), regency and district regulation. Not only that, improving the business climate can also be done through the development of financial sector policies such as the establishment of microfinance institutions and cooperatives for savings and credit, by increasing capacity and quality of personnel especially in the local region, by supporting the development of adaptive assessment activities in order to im-

172 Cf. Kementerian Koperasi dan UKM 2010, pp. 24-29.

prove the value added of SMEs' product, the establishment of international cooperation for SMEs, the development of the model in the application of technology and research in line with the needs of SMEs, as well as the development and improvement of the quantity of information for SMEs including the development of information systems and networks. Before, there has been a legal basis for the improvement of business climate for SMEs as set out in Presidential Instruction No. 3/2006 on the Policy Package for Improving the Investment Climate that are mainly related to the empowerment of SMEs.[173] In this Presidential Instruction, there are 3 (three) programs that focus on the improvement of business climate for SMEs, namely: improving regulations related to licensing for SMEs, developing consulting services for SMIs, and strengthening partnerships with large enterprises with SMEs.

2. Increasing access to productive resources. This policy is intended to increase SMEs' access to financial resources that meet with the need of SMEs. Here, the strategy of increasing financial access for SMEs is done by strengthening capital for SMEs in various forms of credit schemes, particularly the People Based Small-Business Loans and other schemes in accordance with the conditions and the needs of SMEs, including financing for the issuance of land certificates. To provide more extensive coverage, in addition to direct support and funding to SMEs, this development of productive resources is also aimed at the microfinance institutions and cooperatives for saving and credit. In this case, it is necessary to lower interest rates on loans and other various facilities for SMEs. Moreover, what is meant by productive resources is also associated with an increase in the access to technology and the access to markets and marketing for SMEs. The President through Presidential Instruction No. 3/2006 had instructed the improvement of the access of SMEs to financial resources and other productive resources.[174] Those instructions are: the formulation of national policies and strategies for developing microfinance[175]

173 Cf. Chapter V of the Appendix of Presidential Instruction No. 3/2006.

174 Cf. Chapter V of the Appendix of Presidential Instruction No. 3/2006.

175 Previously there was a joint decision between the Minister of Finance, the Minister of Home Affairs, the Minister of Cooperatives and SMEs as well as the Governor of Bank Indonesia to develop microfinance institutions by assisting the legal status of microfinance institutions that do not have a legal status. Detail of

(this proposal has submitted since 2010 and was approved by the House of Representatives in December 2012),[176] the development of investment credit scheme for SMEs (before, there has been a mechanism to finance SMEs as stipulated in Regulation of the Minister of Cooperatives and SMEs No. 14/2006 on the Technical Guidelines and Financing Credit Guarantee Fund for Cooperatives and SMEs),[177] the availability of fiscal incentives for SMEs that utilize innovative technology (the government through the Ministry of Home Affairs has set up incentives for SMEs in the region),[178] the handover of land certification for SMEs to increase access to bank credits, and the development of SMEs' industrial region.

3. Developing SMEs' product and marketing for SMEs. This policy is intended to develop a competitive, high-quality, innovative and creative SMEs' product not only in domestic market but also in the international market. An important aspect is the increase in the production of value-added products of SMEs by applying technology accompanied by developments in science that can generate new innovations of SMEs' product. Another important is the aspect of marketing network to strengthen a business network which is aimed to dominate the domestic market and increase the export's value and markets. Actually, the government has regulated the development of and marketing SMEs' product as stipulated in Government Regulation No. 32/1998 on Building and Developing Small Business and in Presidential Instruction No. 10/1999 on Empowering Medium Business.[179] Unfortunately, until today there are still no optimal results from the two decisions.
4. Improving the competitiveness of human resources of SMEs. This policy is intended to increase the capacity and productivity of

---

this joint decision can be found in the Joint Decree of the Minister of Finance, Minister of Interior, Minister of Cooperatives and SMEs as well as the Governor of Bank Indonesia on Strategic Development of Microfinance Institutions.

176 Cf. Harian Kontan 2012.

177 Cf. Articles 4 and 6 of Decree of Minister of Cooperatives and SMEs No. 14/2006.

178 Cf. Articles 9, 11, 13, 14, 16, 19, and 36 of Regulation of the Minister of Home Affairs No. 64/2012.

179 Cf. Article 7 of Government Regulation No. 32/1998, the second part of Presidential Instruction No. 10/1999.

SMEs by improving the quality and quantity of entrepreneurship. There are two legal basis to support the improvement of the competitiveness of human resources SMEs which are, the Memorandum of Understanding between the Minister of Cooperatives and SMEs with the Minister of National Education on Enhancing the Role of University in Empowering Cooperatives, Micro, Small and Medium-sized Enterprises and Regulation of Minister of Cooperatives and SMEs No. 2/2008 on Empowering Business Development Services-Providers (BDS-P) for the Development of Cooperatives, Micro, Small, and Medium-sized Enterprises. The goal of the BDS-P program is to promote an entrepreneurship's culture in the university level, to create experts/professional assistants for SMEs, and to provide mentoring and business development services to SMEs. In addition, the efforts to increase the competitiveness of human resources of SMEs can be done by: (a) the development of new entrepreneurial growth system by formulating and developing policies to promote and cultivate the entrepreneurial spirit and by forming and developing education and training institutions to undertake education, training, and counseling related to motivation and business creativity, technical and basic skills, as well as the creation of new entrepreneurs, (b) the development of expertise and technical skills of SMEs by encouraging the application of modern management for SMEs, and (c) the development of SMEs' training institution to revitalize and to grow the training institutions and incubators through collaboration and partnerships with universities as well as private, national, and foreign enterprises.

3.3 The Ministry of Industry

The President of the Republic of Indonesia has proclaimed the development and construction of the national industrial sector by issuing Regulation of the President of the Republic of Indonesia No. 28/2008 on the National Industrial Policy. It cannot be denied that Indonesia's industrial sector is one of the national economy's backbones so that it is necessary to have a comprehensive national industrial policy in order to improve the competitiveness of national industry. If explored further, SMIs become one of the industrial sector to get serious attention from the government. In the book of Ministry of Industry's Strategic Plans 2010-2014, it is said that SMIs have been a major driver of the national economy in the period of 2005-2009 with a contribution to the GDP of the industrial sector amounted to 24.95 percent, the employment in the manufacturing sector with a total of 2,552,507 workers during the period 2005-2009 (or an average of 519,137 workers per year), and the total income of the investment in the industrial sector worths IDR 52.88 trillion.[180]

3.3.1 Vision and Mission

In carrying out the mandate to make fundamental improvements to achieve the industrial vision of strengthening the competitiveness of the industrial manufacturing base as well as the establishment of a sustainable future mainstay industry, the Ministry of Industry outlines the vision, mission and objectives of its the policy and program for the year 2010-2014. The vision of the Ministry of Industry is: Strengthening Competitiveness of the Industrial Manufacturing Base and the Establishment of a Sustainable Future Mainstay Industry.[181] To achieve this vision, the Ministry of Industry launched its primary mission, which is to[182]

a. promote an increase in the value added of the industry,
b. encourage an increase of the market share at home and abroad,
c. encourage the improvement of supporting industries,
d. facilitate mastery of industrial technology,
e. facilitate strengthening of the industrial structure,
f. encourage the spread of industrial development outside Java Island, and
g. encourage an increase in the contribution of SMIs to the value of the gross domestic product.

180 Cf. Kementerian Perindustrian 2010, p. 8.
181 Cf. ibid., p. 41.
182 Cf. ibid., p. 84.

3.3.2 Strategies to Promote the Industrial Sector

Looking at the direction of industrial sector development in Indonesia, there are three time stages in setting the national industrial policy for the purpose of making a strong and resilient Indonesian industrial sector:[183]

1. The *first* phase, 2010-2014, is to make fundamental improvements to achieve the vision of strengthening and sustaining the competitiveness of the manufacturing industry base as well as the establishment of a mainstay future pillar industry,
2. The *second* phase, 2015-1019, is the period to make Indonesia as the a new industrialized country, and
3. The *third* phase, 2020-2025, is the period to make Indonesia as one of the powerful world's industrialized country.

Looking at the direction of the development of national industry, there are still problems faced by the industrial sector, either inhibit the growth of industry in general or specifically faced by certain industries. The problem is divided into two major parts, namely the internal problems and external problems.[184] The internal problems include: the structure of the industry that is still not strong, the basic industry who acts as a supplier of raw materials and auxiliary materials that is still limited both in number and quality so the dependence on import's sector is still high, the production capacity is still not optimal, the limited number of high-tech industries, the low performance of industrial sector due to the global crisis, the disruption of the domestic market share (mainly due to smuggling actions), lack of quality and design mastery, lack of funding for research and development of local industrial products, raw materials and component support in the domestic market has not standardized resulting in difficulty in the manufacturing process, and the roles of SMIs are not maximized. While external factors faced by the industrial sector are: lack of infrastructure (roads, electricity, ports, railways, and gas supply), government bureaucracy that is not pro-business, the high illegal flow of imported goods, labor issues (regional minimum wages, severance pay, health insurance, etc.), the problem of legal certainty, the high rate of credit interest, and lack of partisanship and public awareness to use of domestic products.

183 Cf. Kementerian Perindustrian 2010, p. 45.
184 Cf. ibid., pp. 14-15.

To achieve targets and provide solutions to the existing problems, well-structured and measurable efforts are needed. They must be translated into a strategic plan that accommodates the desires of stakeholders in the form of strategic outcomes which consist of: *First*, an increase in the value added of the industry; *second*, an increase of the market share at home and abroad; *third*, the development of a strong supporting industries; *fourth*, an increase of the ability of innovation and technology industry that is energy efficient and environmentally friendly; *fifth*, a strong and complete of industrial structure; *sixth*, the increasing spread of industrial development, and the seventh, the increasing importance of SMIs to the value of Gross Domestic Product.

3.3.3 Organizational Structure

In performing its duties, the Ministry of Industry has the following organizational structure:

Figure 3.2: The Organizational Chart of the Ministry of Industry

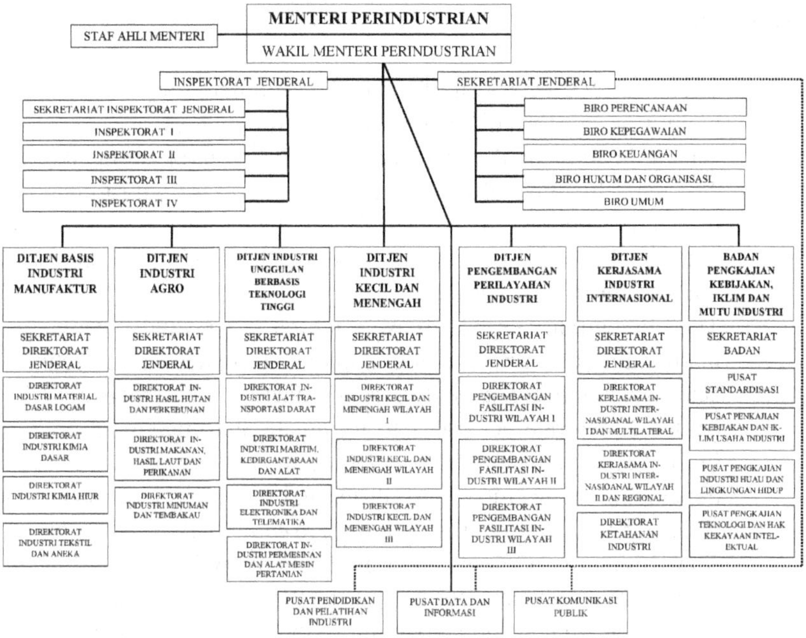

Source: modified from Kementerian Perindustrian, http://www.kemenperin.go.id/struktur/kemenperin, accessed January 7, 2014

In accordance with Regulation of the President of the Republic of Indonesia No. 24/2010, the main task of Ministry of Industry is to assist the President in conducting business (issues) in the industrial sector with the principal function of which are: (a) the formulation, the determination and the implementation of policies in the industrial sectors and (b) providing technical guidance and supervision over the policies of the Ministry of Industry in the region.[185]

185 Cf. Kementerian Perindustrian 2010, p. 36.

The Ministry of Industry oversees seven directorate generals who have duties and functions as set out in Regulation of the Minister of Industry No. 105/2010 on the Organization and Administration of the Ministry of Industry as follows:

1. The Directorate General of Industrial Manufacturing Base has the main task to formulate and implement policies and technical standardization in the field of industrial manufacturing base.[186] The main function of this directorate general is to formulate and implement policies in industrial manufacturing base sectors including the making of road map for developing an industrial manufacturing base cluster.[187]
2. The Directorate General of Agricultural (Agro) Industry has the main duty to formulate and implement policies and technical standardization in the field of agro industry.[188] The main function of this directorate general is to formulate and implement policies in the field of agro industry including the making of road map for developing an agro industry cluster and providing technical guidance and evaluation in the field of agro-industry.[189]
3. The Directorate General of High Technology-based Leading Industry has a fundamental duty to formulate and implement policies and technical standardization in the field of high technology-based leading industry.[190] The main function of this directorate general is to formulate and implement policies in the high technology-based industry including the making of road map for developing a high technology-based industry cluster.[191]
4. The Directorate General of Small and Medium-sized Industries has a fundamental duty to formulate and implement policies and technical standardization in the field of SMIs.[192] This directorate

186 Cf. Article 108 of Regulation of the Minister of Industry No. 105/2010.
187 Cf. Articles 109a and 109b of Regulation of the Minister of Industry No. 105/2010.
188 Cf. Article 211 of Regulation of the Minister of Industry No. 105/2010.
189 Cf. Articles 212a, 212b, and 212c of Regulation of the Minister of Industry No. 105/2010.
190 Cf. Article 294 of Regulation of the Minister of Industry No. 105/2010.
191 Cf. Articles 295a and 295b of Regulation of the Minister of Industry No. 105/2010.
192 Cf. Article 397 of Regulation of the Minister of Industry No. 105/2010.

general has a principal function to formulate and implement policies in the SMI sectors including the making of road map for developing a small and medium-sized industrial cluster.[193]

5. The Directorate General of Industrial Area Development has a fundamental duty to formulate and implement policies and technical standardization in the field of industrial area development.[194] The main function of this directorate general is to formulate and implement policies in the field of industrial area development including the making of road map for developing potential/leading regional (in provincial level as well as district/municipal levels) industrial clusters and providing technical guidance and evaluation in the field of regional area development.[195]
6. The Directorate General for International Industrial Cooperation has the main duty to formulate and implement policies and technical standardization in the field of international industrial cooperation.[196] This directorate general has principal functions to formulate and implement policies in the field of international industrial cooperation including promotion of (local) industry and treatment for industrial barriers.[197]
7. The Agency of Assessment of Policy, the Climate, and Industry Quality has duties and functions to carry out research, assessment, and the development of medium and long-term macro industrial policy, to formulate policies regarding the development of the priority industrial cluster, and the priority industrial cluster development policy as well as the development of the business climate and industrial quality.[198] This directorate general has principal functions to formulate and implement policies, plans, research programs in the field of medium and long-term macro industrial policy including the development of the priority industrial cluster as well as to monitor, to evaluate, and to make reports of research

193 Cf. Articles 398a and 398b of Regulation of the Minister of Industry No. 105/2010.
194 Cf. Article 480 of Regulation of the Minister of Industry No. 105/2010.
195 Cf. Articles 481a, 481b, and 481d of Regulation of the Minister of Industry No. 105/2010.
196 Cf. Article 551 of Regulation of the Minister of Industry No. 105/2010.
197 Cf. Articles 552a, 552b, and 552d of Regulation of the Minister of Industry No. 105/2010.
198 Cf. Article 661 of Regulation of the Minister of Industry No. 105/2010.

and studies in the field of industrial development and industrial clusters.[199]

3.3.4 Strategic Objectives

In supporting the implementation of its vision and mission, the Ministry of Industry sets seven strategic objectives for the period of 2010-2014 consisting of:[200]

1. Strategic Objective I: A high value added of the industry that is characterized by: a high rate of growth of industry that creates value added and a contribution of the manufacturing industry to the national gross domestic product.
2. Strategic Objective II: A high market share at home and abroad which is characterized by: an increase of the export market share of national industrial products and an increase of the market share of national industrial products to the demand in the domestic market.
3. Strategic Objective III: A strong development of supporting industries which is characterized by: an increase in the level of productivity and capability of industrial human resources as well as an increase of the national industrial climate index.
4. Strategic Objective IV: A high ability of innovation and technology industry that is characterized by: a growing number of research and development of industrial technology and an increase rate to use of innovative applied research and development by industrial sectors.
5. Strategic Objective V: A stronger, complete, and deeper industrial structure which is characterized by: the growth of basic upstream industries (such as metal and chemical industries), the growth of the automotive part, electronics, and machinery industries as well as other the growth of other industry.
6. Strategic Objective VI: The spread of industrial development which is characterized by: the increasing contribution of manufac-

199 Cf. Articles 662a, 662b, and 662c of Regulation of the Minister of Industry No. 105/2010.

200 Cf. Kementerian Perindustrian 2010, pp. 84-86.

turing industries outside Java Island to the GDP as well as the increasing amount of new investment in supporting industries and industrial components' industries that absorb many workforces.

7. Strategic Objective VII: The increasing importance of SMIs to the value of the GDP that is characterized by: the growth of small industries above the average of national economic growth, the growth of the middle industries twice over small industry, and the increasing number of SMIs' output being 'outsource' by large industries.

To implement the above strategic objectives, the Ministry of Industry uses two approaches, namely the *top-down* approach and the *bottom-up* approach.[201] The *top-down* approach is done by determining the priority industrial clusters that are considered to be able to compete in the domestic and international markets. While the *bottom-up* approach is done by encouraging regional self-reliance based on the local potentials in order to build and develop an independent economy of the province, city, and district. This *bottom-up* approach is done to acquire inputs from the regional areas for later being accommodated into government programs.

In the *top-down* approach, the government (the Ministry of Industry) has mapped out 35 priority industrial clusters to be developed which are divided into six groups of industrial clusters, namely: (a) a cluster for the group of the industrial manufacturing base, which is composed of the steel industry, cement industry, petrochemical industry, ceramic industry, machinery industry (such as electrical machinery and electrical equipment), the labor-intensive manufacturing industry (such as textiles and textile products as well as footwear); (b) a cluster for the group of agro industry which consists of 12 branches of industry: oil palm, rubber, cocoa, coconut processing, coffee processing, sugar, tobacco, fruit processing, furniture, fish processing, paper and milk processing; (c) a cluster for the group of transportation equipment industries which focuses on improving the productivity and quality of the motor vehicle industry, shipbuilding, aerospace, and railway; (d) a cluster for the group of the electronic and telematics industries, which are devoted to the development of electronics, telecommunications, and computer industries; (e) a cluster for the group of the supporting creative industry and certain creative industries such as the fashion industry, software and multimedia industry as well as the art and

201 Cf. Kementerian Perindustrian 2010, pp. 42-44.

craft industries; and (f) a cluster for the group of certain SMIs that are focused on the development of precious stones and jewelry industrial clusters, salt industrial clusters, pottery and decorative ceramics industrial clusters, the *atsiri* (aromatic) oil industry, and snacks industrial clusters.

While the *bottom-up* approach is done by developing the potential of local industries in areas considered to support national development and regional economic development. The focus of this approach is the development of the industrial sector based on regional industrial core competency.[202] The establishment of regional core competency is done by adopting the concept of One Village One Product (OVOP), which has been developed in Oita, Japan, and the concept of SAKASAKTI (*Satu Kabupaten/Kota, Satu Kompetensi Inti*, 'one regency/city, one core competence') which must have a criteria of: having a high value added, having regional uniqueness, having strong linkages with local resources, and having the opportunity to penetrate the international market.

In implementing the vision, mission, and strategic objectives above, the Ministry of Industry developed a national industrial policy that is consistent with Regulation of the President of the Republic of Indonesia No. 28/2008 on the National Industrial Policy and the Medium-term National Development Plan 2010-2014. Referring to the Medium-term National Development Plan 2010-2014, the 2014 vision to be achieved by the government of Indonesia is to realize a prosperous, democratic, and equitable of Indonesia. To achieve this vision, the government established the following missions:

1. Continuing development toward a prosperous Indonesia,
2. Strengthening the pillars of democracy, and
3. Strengthening the equity (justice) dimension in all areas.

The big agenda which being implemented to support the vision and mission above are:

a. Promoting economic development and improving people's welfare,

---

202 What is meant by regional industrial core competency is a set of regional industrial advantage or uniqueness of resources (including natural resources) for the purpose of regional economic development which has a unique local characteristics and the availability of adequate human resources.

b. Improving governance's bureaucracy,
c. Strengthening the pillars of democracy,
d. Enforcing law enforcement and anti-corruption, and
e. Encouraging inclusive and equitable development.

In connection with the strategic objectives that have been previously described, there are ten program activities of the Ministry of Industry, which are focused on the empowerment and development of manufacturing industries as well as SMIs. Those ten programs are: the revitalization and growth of potential manufacturing base industry, the revitalization and growth of potential agro industry, the revitalization and growth of potential high technology-based leading industry, the revitalization and growth of developing potential SMIs, the development of potential industrial area, the international industrial cooperation, the quality assessment and industrial policy, the monitoring and improving the accountability of the Ministry of Industry state apparatus, the management and technical support of Ministry of Industry, and the improvement of the Ministry of industry officials' facility and infrastructure.[203] Related to the focus of this study, the author will focus only on the two programs as follows:[204]

I. The Program of Revitalization and Growth of Potential for the Manufacturing Base Industry. The program aims to restore the industry's performance that was affected by the global financial crisis, particularly the industrial sector undertaking export activities to Europe and the United States. This program not only seeks to provide solutions to the problems faced by the industry, but also to produce formulation and policy of developing an industrial manufacturing base clusters. Based on the Road Map of the Development of Industrial Manufacturing Base Cluster, there are eight industrial clusters to be developed in the period of 2010-2014, namely: the steel industrial cluster, the cement industrial cluster, the petrochemical industrial cluster, the ceramic industrial cluster, the electrical machinery and equipment industrial cluster, the general equipment industrial cluster, the textiles and textile products industrial cluster, as well as the footwear industrial clus-

203 Cf. Kementerian Perindustrian 2010, pp. 88-118.
204 Cf. ibid., pp. 88-92 and 97-99.

ter.[205] There are two major indicators for the successful of this program: (a) the achievement of the target by the end of 2012 which is the recovery (100 percent) of industry sectors affected by the crisis to the condition before crisis and (b) the achievement of the target by the end of 2014 which is the production capacity's utilization (by 80 percent) in the industrial sector. Moreover, the activities carried out in the period of 2010-2014 are focused on the revitalization and growth of the textile and various industry by restructuring the industrial machinery for textile, footwear, and leather tanning, developing the footwear industrial cluster, improving the business climate in the textile and miscellaneous industries, developing human resources in the industry's sectors, and increasing the design of textile products. An example of a policy issued by the Ministry of Industry in supporting those activities that have been designed is the issuance of Regulation of the Minister of Industry No. 98/2011 on the Program to Restructure of SMIs' Machinery/Equipment (then replaced by the new regulation which is Regulation of the Minister of Industry No. 13/2013 on the Program to Restructure of SMIs' Machinery/Equipment).[206] The purpose of this program is to replace and/or to add a more efficient and productive machinery or equipment so that these SMIs are able to produce a high-quality and competitive product.[207]

II. The Program of Revitalization and Growth of SMIs. The program aims to formulate policies for the development of SMIs, to increase the value added of the products of SMIs, to increase the number of SMIs, to utilize resources including regional natural resources, to develop the concept of OVOP, to spread the industry's development to various area as part of the equitable distribution of the national industrial growth, to promote regional cooperation, and to develop small and medium-sized industrial clusters. There are two key indicators to evaluate the effectiveness of this program, namely: (a) the industrial ratio in Java and outside Java reaches a position of 60:40 in 2014 and (b) the contribution of

205 Cf. Departemen Perindustrian 2009a, p. iii.

206 Cf. Regulation of the Minister of Industry No. 98/2011 and Regulation of the Minister of Industry No. 13/2013.

207 Cf. Article 4 Paragraph 2 of Regulation of the Minister of Industry No. 98/2011.

gross domestic income of the SMIs reaches 34 percent in 2014. The activities carried out in the period 2010-2014 are focused on:

a. The spread and development of SMIs in the region I (Sumatra and Kalimantan), region II (Java and Bali), and region III (Sulawesi, Nusa Tenggara, Maluku, and Papua) which its action plans is the development of small and medium-sized industrial clusters, the development of creative industries, the development of concept of OVOP, and the development of entrepreneurial spirit. The development in region I is focused on the development of small and medium-sized industry clusters of craft and art products, of snacks, of *atsiri* oil, and of fashion. For region II is focused on the development of small and medium-sized industrial clusters of craft and art products, of precious stones and jewelry, of decorative pottery and ceramics, of salt, of snacks, of *atsiri* oil, and of fashion. While the development of region III is focused on the development of small and medium-sized industrial clusters of art and craft products, of snack, of *atsiri* oil, of fashion, of salt, and of pottery and decorative ceramics.

b. The formulation and evaluation of SMIs revitalization and growth's programs that emphasize on improving coordination and the improvement of cross-sector (among government agencies) activities.

c. The development of the Indonesian footwear industries with the main focus to improve the quality of the footwear products and human resources through the development of product design and promotion of shoe product, the development of cooperation with the business world, the improvement of capability and ability of human resources by formulating training modules, the improvement of Indonesia's footwear product quality by improving shoe production's technology.

4. The Role of the Local Government in Developing Industrial Clusters: Offices, Policies, and Strategies

4.1 Introduction

The development of industrial clusters in the region of West Java is done with some considerations, namely: (a) to understand customer needs and market opportunities, (b) to improve business relationships among business people (both core industry and supporting industry), (c) to strengthen the competitiveness of the product, (d) to improve the quality of the product, (e) to reduce internal costs, and (f) to have access to government agencies and financial institutions.[208] Not only that, the development of industrial clusters is also a practical implementation of regional autonomy as stipulated in Law No. 32/2004 on Regional Autonomy as well as a tool for driving local economic growth and creating employment. The role of the local governments is vital to the development of the industrial clusters within their regions. In this case the local government must provide adequate infrastructure facilities for the development of clusters and create a friendly business climate to attract foreign investment.

4.2 The Profile of the Province of West Java

Since 2008, the province of West Java has 17 registered districts, nine cities with 625 districts and 5,877 villages. The organizational structure of the government of the West Java Province itself consists of one regional secretariat with 12 bureaus/offices and the parliament secretariat, 20 regional offices, 17 sub-regional offices, 17 technical institutions, three other institutions, three regional government-run hospitals, 121 technical services units, and one sub-technical services unit. In running its daily operations, the government of the West Java Province has issued the policies stated in the Medium-term Development Plan of the West Java Province 2008-2013. This medium-term development plan is a guide for regional

---

208 Interview with D. from the Office of Industry and Trade of the Province of West Java on January 28, 2013 in Bandung.

offices and organizations in preparing the regional offices/organizations' strategic plan and a guide for the local government (district/municipality) in drafting/adjusting the development plan of their respective regions in order to achieve the development targets of the West Java Province.

4.2.1 Vision and Mission

The policy direction and development focus of West Java, especially in relation to economic issues and SMEs/SMIs for the years of 2008-2013 are aimed at reducing the poverty rate, improving the quality of life, expanding employment opportunities, developing strategic and basic infrastructure, and improving the competitiveness of the industrial sector.[209] Considering the potential, conditions, problems, challenges, and opportunities in West Java, the government of the West Java Province has made it its government's vision to achieve an independent, dynamic, and prosperous community of West Java. The meaning of this vision is as follows.[210] An independent community is defined as a condition in which people are able to meet their needs by relying on their own abilities and strengths. A dynamic society is defined as the attitude and condition of the people who are actively able to respond to opportunities and challenges of globalization and contribute in the development process. While prosperous society is defined as a condition of the people who get a sense of security and prosperity in life.

In order to achieve that vision, the Government of the West Java Province made the five following missions.[211] The *first* mission is to create productive and competitive human resources in which West Javans are characterized by being religious, having a noble character, being healthy and intelligent, having moral and a champion spirit, and being ready to compete figures. The *second* mission is to enhance the regional economic development based on local potential which is indicated by a competitive economic structure of West Java and by exploiting its comparative advantage. The *third* mission is to improve the availability and the quality of the infrastructure in the region which is marked by an infrastructure that is ready to support high economic growth. The *fourth* mission is to increase

209 Cf. Government of the West Java Province (n.d.).
210 See Appendix II of West Java Provincial Regulation No. 25/2010.
211 Cf. ibid., p. V-3.

the carrying capacity and the capacity of an environment for promoting and ensuring sustainable development in the region. Lastly, the *fifth* mission is to improve the effectiveness of local governance and the quality of democracy, which is characterized by the reliable administration to support regional development.

4.2.2 Policies to Develop and Empower SMEs/SMIs

Referring to the second mission mentioned above as well as to the empowerment and development of SMEs/SMIs in West Java, the Government of the West Java Province issued West Java Provincial Regulation No. 10/2010 on the Empowerment and Development of Cooperatives, Micro, Small and Medium-sized Enterprises as the basis for regional economic development.[212] Looking at Article 1 of the law, the office which is responsible for empowering and developing the SME sector is the Office of Cooperatives and Micro, Small and Medium-sized Enterprises of the Province of West Java. Moreover, looking at Article 3 Paragraph 1, the purpose of the empowerment and the development of SMEs is to realize and to enhance the regional economy and the welfare of the society through the increasing role of SMEs in a sustainable manner. The goals of empowering and developing SMEs (in accordance with Article 3 Paragraph 2) are to (1) develop SMEs to become strong and independent businesses, (2) develop and enhance the capabilities and competitiveness of SMEs, (3) provide protection and business support for SMEs, and (4) enhance the creation of new businesses and foster entrepreneurship. To carry out the purposes of the empowerment and development of SMEs, the focus of this provincial regulation is divided into two parts. The first part is focused on the growth of a friendly business climate, and the second part is focused on the development of SMEs.

In order to grow a friendly business climate to empower and develop SMEs, the Government of the West Java Province focuses on several aspects such as funding, facilities and infrastructure, business information, partnership, business licensing, business opportunities, trade promotion, business protection, and institutional support.[213] The focus on funding is done by expanding funding sources and facilitating local SMEs in access-

212 Cf. West Java Provincial Regulation No. 10/2010.

213 Cf. Chapter VIII of West Java Provincial Regulation No. 10/2010.

ing bank credit and non-bank financial institutions, increasing funding and expanding its network so it can be accessed by SMEs in the region, providing support in obtaining funding, and helping businesses in the region to obtain financing and other financial services or products that use either conventional systems or the sharia system.[214] Moreover, the Government of the West Java Province facilitates financing and guarantees for SMEs which includes bank credits, venture capital, funds from the state-owned enterprises (SOEs) and the regional-owned enterprises, and grants.[215] Related to the funds from the SOEs, the Ministry of State-owned Enterprises has arranged for such assistance in Regulation of the Minister of State-owned Enterprises No. 236/2006 on the Partnership Program with the Small Business and the Community Development Program which funds for partnerships of 1-3 percent are sourced from profit after tax allowance and funds for community development program of a maximum of 1 percent are sourced from profit after tax allowance.[216]

The focus on facilities and infrastructure is done by providing a basic infrastructure that can encourage and develop the growth of SMEs such as the opening of showrooms and providing certain tariff remission for SMEs.[217] The focus on business information is done by forming and facilitating the use of data and business information network of SMEs in the region that are integrated with business data and network in the national and international levels, organizing and disseminating information about the market, financial sources, commodity, underwriting, design and technology as well as the quality of SMEs' product in the region, and ensuring transparency and equal access for SMEs in the region.[218]

The focus on the partnership is done by forming a partnership among SMEs in the region and realizing partnership with large enterprises as stipulated in Government Regulation No. 44/1997 on Partnership. The regulation itself is made to encourage business partnerships between/among SMEs in the region, to encourage partnerships between SMEs and large enterprises in the region, to develop partnerships to improve the bargaining position of SMEs in the region, to form the market

---

214 Cf. Article 11 of West Java Provincial Regulation No. 10/2010.
215 Cf. Article 25 of West Java Provincial Regulation No. 10/2010.
216 Cf. Article 8 of Regulation of the Minister of State-owned Enterprises No. 236/2003.
217 Cf. Article 12 of West Java Provincial Regulation No. 10/2010.
218 Cf. Article 13 of West Java Provincial Regulation No. 10/2010.

structure that ensures fair, and to prevent the market share and concentration by individuals or groups that harm SMEs in the region.[219]

Looking at the regulation, what is meant by a partnership is cooperation between businesses and small to medium businesses or large businesses along with mentoring by medium-sized businesses and large enterprises on the principle of mutual need, mutually reinforcing and mutually beneficial to each other.[220] Furthermore, partnerships can be done in the form of: the core-plasma, sub-contracting, general trading, franchising, and agency.[221] The core-plasma relationship is the relationship between small enterprises which acts as a plasma and medium and large enterprises as a core. Here, both medium and large enterprises will help with developing small enterprises by providing production facilities, technical guidance, and the marketing of their production system in order to increase efficiency and productivity of small enterprises.[222] The sub-contracting program is the relationship where SME provide and produce components required by large enterprise as part of their production system.[223] The benefit of this relationship is as follows: *first*, the contract guarantees a clear and continuous relationship between SME and large enterprise. *Second*, there will be a process of technology transfer from the large enterprise to SME. In general trading activities, a partnership between large enterprise and medium-sized enterprise with small enterprise is done in the form of marketing cooperation, provision of business premises, or receiving supplies from small enterprise as business partner to meet the needs of large enterprise and medium-sized enterprise.[224] The franchising program is conducted where large and medium-sized enterprises that intend to expand their business by giving the franchise should give the opportunity and prioritize small enterprise to act as a franchisee.[225]

The focus on business licensing is done by simplifying licensing procedures with a one-stop service system. The Indonesian Chamber of Commerce and Industry (KADIN) found out that the process of issuing business trading license and company registration by local authorities is too

219 Cf. Article 14 of West Java Provincial Regulation No. 10/2010.
220 Cf. Article 1 of Government Regulation No. 44/1997.
221 Cf. Article 37 Paragraph 2 of West Java Provincial Regulation No. 10/2010.
222 Cf. Article 3 of Government Regulation No. 44/1997.
223 Cf. Article 4 of Government Regulation No. 44/1997.
224 Cf. Article 5 Paragraph 1 of Government Regulation No. 44/1997.
225 Cf. Article 7 Paragraph 1 of Government Regulation No. 44/1997.

long (it is up to 16-21 working days through 3-5 different offices).[226] This system is already set in Regulation of the Minister of Home Affairs No. 24/2006 on The Guidelines on One Stop System to waive the cost of licensing for micro businesses and provide waiver for small business licensing fee as set out also in Regulation of the Minister of Home Affairs No. 24/2006 on the Guidelines for One Stop System.[227] While the types of businesses that have a licensing fee exemptions and waivers include: agriculture, mining and quarrying, manufacturing, electricity, gas and water, construction, trade, hotels and restaurants, transport and communications, finance, leasing, and services company, and other services.[228]

The focus on the business opportunity is done by the following ways.[229] *First*, provincial government is required to determine the designation of a place of business which includes the provision of: location in the market, shopping area, location of industrial centers, location of smallholder agriculture, artisanal mining location, reasonable location for street vendors, and other locations. *Second*, large businesses are required to provide at least 10 percent of their business premises to be dedicated and built only for SMEs. *Third*, local governments, district/city governments, and businesses are required to provide protection and development of traditional markets. *Fourth*, provincial government is required to develop areas and types of business activities, with a special process, labor-intensive, and has a cultural heritage that is specific and hereditary. *Fifth*, provincial government is required to establish lines of business devoted to SMEs and lines of business open to large businesses with a condition that they must cooperate with SMEs. *Sixth*, provincial government is required to protect SME businesses that are strategic. *Seventh*, provincial government is required to prioritize the use of the products produced by SMEs through direct procurement. *Eighth*, provincial government is required to prioritize SMEs in the region in the provision of goods or services, in chartering the

---

226 For further explanation see Indonesian Chamber of Commerce and Industry (KADIN), 2010. Key Challenges Faced By Entrepreneur: Indonesia. Paper presented at the Workshop on Reducing Start-Up and Establishment Time of Business, Hiroshima, March 1-2, 2010. Can be accessed at http://mddb.apec.org/Documents/2010/EC/WKSP1/10_ec_wksp1_006.pdf.

227 Cf. Article 4 Paragraphs 1 and 2 (a and b) and Article 4 Paragraph 2f of Regulation of the Minister of Home Affairs No. 24/2006, Article 15 of the West Java Province Regional Regulation No. 10/2010.

228 Cf. Article 15 Paragraph 2 of West Java Provincial Regulation No. 10/2010.

229 Cf. Article 16 Paragraph 1 of West Java Provincial Regulation No. 10/2010.

work undertaken by the local government and district/city governments, and in providing legal advice and advocacy assistance.

The focus on the promotion of trade is done by increasing the promotion of SMEs in the region for regional, national, and international markets, expanding sources of funding for the promotion of SMEs in the region, and facilitating the ownership of intellectual property rights (IPR) for the improvement of product quality and design of SMEs areas in their business activities (local and international business).[230] The focus on business protection is done by providing protection to empower and develop SMEs by including elements of society and paying attention to the element of fair competition.[231] While the focus on the institutional support is done by developing and improving the function of business incubators, business development services institutions, financial consultants bank partners, Credit Guarantee Agency (see for example the Credit Guarantee Agency of West Java which will start operating in 2013), and other similar professional bodies as supporting institutions for the development of SMEs in the region.[232]

Looking back at the second focus of West Java Provincial Regulation No. 10/2010 which is the development of SMEs, the Government of the West Java Province which is about the development of SMEs, the Government of the West Java Province emphasized its focus on the production and processing, marketing, human resources, and design and technology.[233] The focus on production and processing is done by increasing the production and processing techniques as well as the management capabilities of SMEs in the region, providing waivers on provision of facilities and infrastructure, production and processing, raw materials, auxiliary materials, and packaging for products of SMEs in the region, encouraging the application of standardization in production and processing, and improving engineering design capabilities for medium-sized businesses.[234] The focus on marketing is done by doing research and marketing studies, disseminating market information, performing management skills and marketing techniques, promoting trading house for SMEs' product, providing promotional support products, network marketing, and distribution, and

230 Cf. Article 17 Paragraph 1 of West Java Provincial Regulation No. 10/2010.
231 Cf. Article 18 of West Java Provincial Regulation No. 10/2010.
232 Cf. Article 19 of West Java Provincial Regulation No. 10/2010.
233 Cf. Chapter XI of West Java Provincial Regulation No. 10/2010.
234 Cf. Article 21 of West Java Provincial Regulation No. 10/2010.

providing professional consultants in the field of marketing.[235] The focus on human resources is done by socializing and cultivating entrepreneurial spirit, improving the technical and managerial skills of entrepreneurs, establishing and developing educational and training institutions to promote the creation of new entrepreneurs.[236] While the focus on design and technology is done by increasing capacity in design and technology as well as quality control, improving collaboration and technology transfer especially with large companies, improving the ability of SMEs in the field of research to design and develop new technologies, providing incentives to SMEs in the region which develop technologies and preserve the environment, and encouraging SMEs to obtain a certificate of IPR.[237]

In support of program development and empowerment of SMEs as defined in the above regulation, one of the Government of the West Java Province's missions includes an orientation to improve the competence of all the existing resources in West Java to create economic activities effectively and efficiently.[238] The ability of the economy to create jobs and reduce poverty continues to be the main focus of the Government of the West Java Province. West Java's regional economic policies are aimed at achieving a sustainable economic growth through the development of core businesses that is based on local potential to reduce welfare disparities between regions. To support its regional economic policy, there are several targets to be achieved. They are: (a) increasing regional economic activities based on local potentials, (b) promoting job opportunities and job creation, (c) increasing the role of institutional and economic capital in the development of local SMEs, and (d) increasing investments that encourage jobs. In achieving this mission, the Government of the West Java Province provides a series of targets to support the achievement of the mission. The *first* target is the increasing regional economic activities based on local potential, in this case the increased activity of SMEs based on local potential. To achieve this goal, the focus is on growing and revitalizing SMEs' *sentras*, encouraging the growth of potential industries (for example agribusiness), encouraging mastery of the technology industry,

235 Cf. Article 22 of West Java Provincial Regulation No. 10/2010.

236 Cf. Article 23 of West Java Provincial Regulation No. 10/2010.

237 Cf. Article 24 of West Java Provincial Regulation No. 10/2010.

238 See the second mission (to achieve West Java's vision) in previous page. The second mission is to enhance regional economic development based on local potential which is indicated by a competitive economic structure of West Java by exploiting its comparative advantage.

and strengthening the industrial structure in order to improve productivity of SMEs. The *second* target is the growing business opportunities and employment opportunities. Strategies used to achieve these two objectives are: encouraging the creation of a conducive business climate, encouraging the creation of business opportunities/markets, increasing expertise/skills/work culture in the community, and creating new entrepreneurs in various business sectors. The *third* target is the growing role of institutions and capital of SMEs in developing a competitive local economy. Strategy needed to achieve this goal is to create a credit guarantee agency to support the development and empowerment of SMEs.

Programs undertaken by the Government of the West Java Province above are also in tune with President of the Republic of Indonesia Regulation No. 5/2010 on the National Medium-term Development Plan 2010-2014 which serves as a guideline for the preparation of materials and improvement of the medium-term regional development plans,[239] Presidential Instruction No. 1/2010 on Accelerating Implementation of National Development Priorities in 2010 which includes poverty reduction programs and the creation of investment climate and business climate,[240] and Presidential Instruction No. 3/2010 on Equitable Development Program which includes programs that are: pro-people, justice for all, and the achievement of the Millennium Development Goals.[241] To support government programs especially those related to poverty alleviation through development and empowerment of SMEs as well as the creation of investment climate and business climate, the following will explain the policies and programs of the Government of the West Java Province through the Office of Cooperatives and SMEs and the Office of Trade and Industry.

4.3 The Responsibility of Regional Offices

In implementing the vision and missions above especially related to the empowerment of SMEs, the Government of the West Java Province in accordance with West Java Provincial Regulation No. 21/2008 on the Or-

239 Cf. Article 2 Paragraph 3b of Regulation of the President of the Republic of Indonesia No. 5/2010.
240 Cf. Presidential Instruction No. 1/2010.
241 Cf. Presidential Instruction No. 3/2010.

ganization and Administration of the Department of the West Java Province, assigned the Office of Cooperatives and SMEs and the Office of Trade and Industry to develop and empower SMEs and SMIs.

Based on Article 17 of West Java Provincial Regulation No. 21/2008, the organizational structure of the Office of Cooperatives and SMEs consists of: cooperatives section, partnerships and SME product development section, financing and technology section, and supervision section.[242] While according to Article 18 of West Java Provincial Regulation No. 21/2008, the members of the Office of Industry and Trade consists of: metal industry, machinery, transportation equipment, miscellaneous textiles, and telematics section, various industrial fields, crafts, and chemical section, agro industrysection, domestic trade section, international trade section, and the promotion and cooperation of industry and trade section.[243] For the purposes of this study, not all areas are covered in this chapter, only the areas related to the development and empowerment of SMEs and SMIs will be discussed. This chapter will also discuss the programs undertaken by both offices related to the coordination, integration, and synchronization of their program with the other offices in West Java and offices outside West Java.[244] The following will discusse the profile of the two offices.

4.3.1 The Office of Cooperatives and SMEs

The Indonesian government's attention to SMEs are very dominant especially after the economic and financial crises in mid-1997 which resulted in the collapse of several major industries, especially industries that relied heavily on imported materials. SMEs development is an alternative option in strengthening the national industrial sector as well as achieving the focus and purpose of the central government in terms of poverty reduction (as described in the previous chapter). Referring to the existing conditions, the role of SMEs in the national economy still needs to be cultivated.[245]

242 Cf. Article 17 Paragraphs c, d, e, and f of West Java Provincial Regulation No. 21/2008.

243 Cf. Article 18 Paragraphs c, d, e, f, g, and h of West Java Provincial Regulation No. 21/2008.

244 Cf. Article 28 Paragraph 1 of West Java Provincial Regulation No. 21/2008.

245 For more discussion on the challenges and conditions faced by Indonesian SMEs, please see Pakpahan, Aknolt K. (2013). Micro, Small, and Medium-Sized Enter-

Organizational Structure

The Office of Cooperatives and SMEs was formed in accordance with West Java Provincial Regulation No. 15/2000 on the Regional Working Units and West Java Provincial Regulation No. 21/2008 on the Organization and Administration of the Province of West Java Regional Offices.[246] In its organizational structure, the Office of Cooperatives and SMEs oversees four sections consisting of: cooperatives, partnership and SMEs' product development, financing and technology, and supervision. Of the four sections mentioned above, there are two sections that specifically deal with the empowerment and development of SMEs: (1) partnership and SMEs' product development and (2) financing and technology. The following will explain a brief profile of both sections.

1. The Partnership and SMEs' Product Development has the main task to conduct assessment on the material for formulating technical policies related to the partnership and SMEs' product development including conducting partnership among SMEs, facilitating and developing SMEs' product as well as marketing and promoting SMEs' product. In carrying out its main task, this section has a function of: (a) conducting assessment on technical policies and guidance for promoting partnership among SMEs and SMEs' product development, (b) conducting technical activities for promoting partnership among SMEs and SMEs' product development, and (c) conducting coordination and cooperation with other related agencies in dealing with activities for promoting partnership and SMEs' product development. In supporting its main tasks and functions, this section is assisted by the three sub-sections, namely:
   a. The sub-section of Partnership, which is the executive body on formulating technical policies on SMEs' partnership, materials for promoting SMEs' partnership, and forms of SMEs' partnership.

---

prises in Indonesia: Towards More Coordinated Policies and More Competitive-based SME. In: Heise, Matthias/Rucktäschel, Kathrin (eds.). Indonesia's Search for Democracy: Political, Economic, and Social Developments. Baden-Baden: Nomos, pp. 299-318.

246 Cf. Dinas Koperasi dan Usaha Mikro, Kecil, dan Menengah Provinsi Jawa Barat (n.d.a).

   b. The sub-section of Facilitation and SMEs' Product Development, which is the executive body on formulating guidelines and technical policies on facilitating and developing SMEs' products as well as formulating and implementing materials on facilitating SMEs' product development.
   c. The sub-section of Promotion and Marketing of SMEs' Product, which is the executive body on formulating guidelines and technical policies on promoting and marketing SMEs' products.
2. The Finance and SMEs' Technology has the main task to conduct assessment on the materials for formulating technical policies related to financial access for cooperatives and SMEs as well as to develop entrepreneurial spirit and SMEs' technology. In carrying out its main task, this section has a function of: (a) conducting assessment on technical policies and guidance related to financial and technological issues for SMEs, (b) conducting activities of the assessment of financing cooperatives and SMEs as well as developing entrepreneurial spirit and technology for SMEs, and (c) conducting coordination and cooperation with other related agencies in dealing with activities for assessing the financial access for cooperatives and SMEs as well as developing entrepreneurial spirit and technology for SMEs. In supporting its main tasks and functions, this section is assisted by the two sub-sections, namely:
   a. The sub-section of Assessment of Financing SMEs, which is the executive body on formulating guidelines and technical policies on financing SMEs.
   b. The sub-section of Development of Entrepreneurial Spirit and Technology for SMEs, which is the executive body on formulating guidelines and technical policies on developing entrepreneurial spirit and technology for SMEs.

Vision and Mission

In conducting its duties and functions of development and empowerment of West Java's SMEs, the Office of Cooperatives and SMEs has a vision to create West Java's cooperatives and SMEs, which has the independence, competitiveness, and high productivity on a national and international level.[247] Moreover, the mission of this office is to create a superior cooperatives and SMEs at the national and international levels.[248]

Problems of Developing and Empowering West Java's SMEs

The Office of Cooperatives and SMEs has mapped out several crucial problems in developing and empowering SMEs in West Java.[249] Some of the problems are:

a. The limitations of SMEs in gaining access to increase the capability of their human resources, access to finance, and access to market information so that these SMEs cannot grow into business units that supports regional economic growth in West Java,
b. The high level of consumer credit compared to investment credit by the SMEs inhibits the SMEs to support the real sector,[250]
c. The pressure in the midst of globalization that led to SMEs' products are being excluded and are not competitive compared to imported products,
d. The business climate that does not fully support the development and empowerment of SMEs,
e. The high rate of poverty and the low quality of people's standard of living that results in the low quality of human resources in the SME sector, and
f. The expansion of employment opportunities through the growth of new entrepreneurs is still low.

247 Cf. Dinas Koperasi dan Usaha Mikro, Kecil, dan Menengah Provinsi Jawa Barat (n.d.b).

248 Cf. ibid.

249 Cf. Dinas Koperasi dan Usaha Mikro, Kecil, dan Menengah Provinsi Jawa Barat (n.d.a).

250 Consumer credit is simply funds provided to fulfill an individual's needs while investment credit is funds to buy goods and services for the company (in this case SMEs).

Activities to Empower SMEs

In overcoming the above problems, in 2009, the Office of Cooperatives and SMEs emphasizes on two programs, namely:[251]

a. The Development of Entrepreneurship and Competitive Advantage which includes activities to: develop rural economy through a cooperative approach, strengthen cooperatives, strengthen the capability of human resources for SMEs, facilitate graduate assistant to give assistance in improving SMEs' performance as well as increase and empower the capacity of SMEs.
b. The Development of Supporting System for SMEs which includes activities to: empower SMEs through the facilitation of financing and the use of appropriate technology, develop market access for SMEs' product, promote SMEs' partnership, and support activity on developing SMEs' products.

In further detail, the details of the programs conducted by this office consist of:

1. Program of Developing Rural Economy through a Cooperative Approach as follows:

No.	Programs/Activities	Target Group(s)
1.	Development of SMEs' business capacity in rural area:	
	Meeting to give guidance on the technical production management and sales management for SMEs	300 SMEs in the village
	Seminar in Developing Cooperatives in Growing Village.	100 managers/members of cooperatives in the village
2.	Development of a Conducive Agribusiness Climate for SMEs:	
	Meeting to give guidance on technical assistance for rice business	150 managers/members of Food-base Cooperatives in 16 regencies

251 Cf. Dinas Koperasi dan Usaha Mikro, Kecil, dan Menengah Provinsi Jawa Barat (n.d.a).

	Meeting for developing stock of raw materials	150 managers/members of Food-base Cooperatives in 16 regencies
3.	Implementation of rural economy growth program in the regency of West Bandung: Meeting in establishing Participation Rural Appraisal (PRA)[252] and *Zielorientierte Projektplanung* (ZOPP)[253]	 100 cooperatives and SMEs in three villages in the regency of West Bandung
4.	Optimization of Rural Economy Growth Management Team: Ten months honorarium for the management team consisting of representatives from the regional organization (city/regency), the West Java Cooperative Council, consultants, and elements of the West Java Office of Cooperatives and SMEs	 45 people of the management team

2. Program of Increasing the Capacity of SMEs' Human Resources as follows:

No.	Programs/Activities	Target Group(s)
1.	Consolidation and evaluation of training: Consolidation to harmonize the curriculum syllabus, target par-ticipants, methods, media, place, and organizing training	 Elements of university, businesses, the Office of Cooperatives and SMEs, Regional Chamber of Commerce, the West Java Cooperative Council, and other stakeholders

252 PRA is an interactive method that emphasizes local (community) participation so that local community can contribute their ideas and thoughts to make the assessment, analyze, and plan a certain program. Cf. Abdullah et al. 2012, p. 15.

253 *Zielorientierte Projektplanung* (Goal-Oriented Project Planning) is a project planning method that emphasizes goal-oriented project plan approach in planning a regional development. Cf. Satriawan/Oktavianti 2012, p. 98.

	Evaluation of training is carried out after the implementation of the overall training	Training's alumni
2.	Training on Management Skills and Entrepreneurial Spirit: Training on business feasibility, the making of business proposals, the making of business plans, accounting for cooperatives, financial managment, marketing management, distribution management, human resource management, import-export, and cooperative taxation	 30 accountants for 900 cooperatives and SMEs in West Java, 60 accountants for coopera-tives and SMEs in the city/regency in West Java, 10 accountants for 102 graduate assistants
3.	Training on Bookkeeping and Basics of Cooperatives	60 accountants for cooperatives and SMEs in the city/regency in West Java
4.	Publishing of Training Modules/ Materials	Cooperatives and SMEs in the region of West Java

3. Program of Facilitating Graduate Assistant to Increase the Performance of SMEs as follows:

No.	Programs/Activities	Target Group(s)
1.	Mentoring consolidation	102 graduate assistants
2.	Placement and mentoring evaluation: Placement of 102 graduate assistant in 26 cities/regencies in West Java. Monthly mentoring evaluation	 102 graduate assistants 102 graduate assistants

4. Program of Increasing the Capacity of SMEs as follows:

No.	Programs/Activities	Target Group(s)
1.	Participatory development for developing cooperatives and SMEs: Formulation of programs to empower SMEs for the year of 2010	 150 SMEs' stakeholders in West Java
2.	Formulation of Control System Program to empower SMEs	Officials from the Office of Cooperatives and SMEs
3.	The improvement of information system for cooperatives and SMEs: Operating the online network system to	 IT teams

	record data on cooperatives and SMEs in West Java Formulation of a monograph on cooperatives and SMEs in West Java	 Officials from the Office of Cooperatives and SMEs
4.	Consolidation to empower and strengthen cooperatives and SMEs	140 people from regional offices, SMEs, and other stakeholders
5.	Coordination to empower and strengthen cooperatives and SMEs in order to create networks with other cooperatives and SMEs outside the region	Officials from the Office of Cooperatives and SMEs
6.	Monitoring, controlling, and evaluating the Program of Supporting Cooperatives and SMEs in West Java (2009)	The Office of Cooperatives and SMEs
7.	The improvement of information on the West Java SMEs through electronic and printed media	10 advertisements on printed media and 16 advertisements on television
8.	The publishing of a book on the role and development of SMEs to the GRDP in 2008	The Office of Cooperatives and SMEs
9.	Evaluation on the impact of supporting SMEs' market access especially those which attended exhibitions at home and abroad	The Office of Cooperatives and SMEs
10.	Evaluation on the development of leading commodity center (*sentra*) in West Java especially those which have earned endorsement facilitation	137 cooperatives of the leading commodity center
11.	Recording SMEs in West Java	3,600 West Java SMEs

5. Program of Empowering SMEs through Financial Facilitation and the Use of Appropriate Technology as follows:

No.	Programs/Activities	Target Group(s)
1.	Consolidation with the financial institutions and other financial institutions to open access to SMEs: Meeting with all stakeholders in order to open financial access to financial institu-	 150 cooperatives and SMEs' stakeholders, the West Java

	tions and other financial institutions	Cooperative Council, Regional Cha-mber of Commerce, P3UKM, banks, universities, and graduate assistants
2.	Meeting with state-owned enterprises and private companies that will conduct the Corporate Social Responsibility (CSR) program and the Partnership and Community Development Program in West Java	150 SMEs in West Java.
3.	Optimization of the Memorandum of Understanding (MoU) between the Governor of West Java and Askrindo Corp. in order to guarantee loans for SMEs in West Java	150 SMEs in West Java
4.	Assistance in SMEs' financial feasibility: Preparing SMEs' business feasibility in West Java by the assistance of graduat assistants	1,300 SMEs in West Java
5.	Intermediate SMEs with financial institutions and other financial resources	1,300 SMEs in West Java
6.	Guidance and consultation on financial aspects using the hedging system: Conducting guidance on alternative financing resources for SMEs in five cities/regencies of five different commodities	375 SMEs in the center of mangos teen in Tasikmalaya in the center of star fruit in Depok, in the center of pineapple in Subang, in the center of sweet potatoes in Kuningan, and in the center of tomatoes in the regency of West Bandung
7.	Guidance and consultation of financing warehouse especially for rice commodity	100 SMEs in rice commodity in Karawang and Indramayu
8.	The Utilization of appropriate technology for SMEs: Providing technical guidance on the application of appropriate technology based	50 SMEs in 26 cities/ regencies in West Java

	on local potentials with the involvement of the Indonesian Institute of Sciences and Research Center of the University of Pasundan	
9.	Growing entrepreneurial spirit and making business plan	250 SMEs in West Java which were selected from about 1,300 SMEs receiving business feasiblity assistance/mentoring

6. Program of Developing the Market Access for SMEs' Product as follows:

No.	Programs/Activities	Target Group(s)
1.	The South African International Trade Exhibition in Johannesburg, South Africa in collaboration with the West Java Investment and Promotion Coordination Board	Five handicraft SMEs
2.	The 6th Cooperative Fair of West Java (annual event in order to celebrate the Cooperative Day)	224 SMEs in West Java
3.	Ramadan Fair (annual event during the Ramadan)	150 SMEs in West Java
4.	Exhibition of women SMEs' product that has export potential in Bandung Gender Exhibition	100 women SMEs and 100 export potential SMEs
5.	Inacraft Exhibition in Jakarta in collboration with the Association of Exporters and Producers of Indonesian Handicrafts	8 SMEs in West Java
6.	The 24th Trade Expo Indonesia in Jakarta	8 SMEs in West Java
7.	Business Meeting: Business meeting that was held at the Cooperative Fair Business meeting that was held at the Gender Exhibition	 200 SMEs in West Java 150 SMEs in West Java
8.	The 2009 Jakarta Fair in collaboration with the West Java Investment and Promotion Coordination Board	8 SMEs in West Java

7. Program of Developing Partneships for SMEs as follows:

No.	Programs/Activities	Target Group(s)
1.	Consolidation for developing business clusters	150 people from the business centers (*sentra*), regional offices, and graduate assistants
2.	The participatory planning on common perception about business clusters, development of business clusters, and formulation of program to develop business clusters	240 people from regional offices and graduate assistants
3.	Providing technical guidance of business development	100 SMEs in West Java
4.	Increasing the capacity building of business clusters' managers	200 SMEs in West Java, regional offices, and graduate assistants
5.	Facilitation of the development of inter-regional SMEs' networks: Conducting meeting between the West Javan SMEs and the Pekanbaru SMEs	 10 SMEs in West Java
6.	Partnership meeting between the West Javan SMEs and local potential buyers	120 SMEs in West Java

8. Program of Supporting of SMEs' Product as follows:

No.	Programs/Activities	Target Group(s)
1.	Socialization and facilitation of the legal aspect of halal products	300 SMEs in West Java
2.	Socialization and facilitation of the legal aspect of IPR	50 SMEs in West Java
3.	Providing technical guidance in design by the Association of Exporters and Producers of Indonesian Handicrafts and technical guidance in product packaging and diversification by the University of Pasundan	200 SMEs in West Java

Activities and Strategic Plans of Empowering the West Javan SMEs in 2010-2013

To follow up programs that have been conducted in 2009, the Office of Cooperatives and SMEs made a strategic plan for the year 2010-2013 with the aim of achieving the vision of the Province of West Java. Its aim is the achievement of an independent, dynamic and prosperous community of West Java, by creating a productive and competitive human resource in West Java, increasing regional economic development based on local potentials, improving the availability and quality of infrastructures, improve capability and capacity of environment for a sustainable regional development, and improving the effectiveness of local governance and the quality of democracy.[254]

To implement this mission, the Office of Cooperatives and SMEs sets objectives as the basis for making the SMEs' Strategic Plan in 2010-2013. The objectives of this office are:[255]

a. To have the personnel (human) resources with competency in providing public services to SMEs,
b. To coordinate policies on the empowerment and development of SMEs with all relevant agencies in West Java (including the city/regency agencies),
c. To expand networks of cooperation among SMEs in West Java.

To support the objectives above, the strategic plan of this office emphasizes on two major development programs which are:

1. Program on developing entrepreneurial spirit and competitive advantage of SMEs includes program to: increase cooperation and partnership of SMEs, promote and maket SMEs' products, strengthen the SMEs, and increase the capacity of SMEs' human resources.
2. Program on developing a support system for SMEs which includes programs to: facilitate development of SMEs' products, facilitate financial access for SMEs, develop entrepreneurial spirit

254 Cf. the Government of the West Java Province (n.d.).
255 Cf. Dinas Koperasi dan Usaha Mikro, Kecil, dan Menengah Provinsi Jawa Barat (n.d.c).

for SMEs' owners, facilitate the use of an appropriate technology for SMEs, record the activity of SMEs as well as monitor, control, and evaluate the empowerment of SMEs' program.

Details of the two programs above are as follows:

1. Program on Increasing Cooperation and Partnership of SMEs as follows:

Programs/ Activities	Year				Target Group(s)
	2010	2011	2012	2013	
Development of SMEs' Networks	x	x	x	x	SMEs in West Java and the Office of Co-operatives and SMEs
Development of SMEs products' trading house abroad	x	x	x		Selected countries
Development of SMEs products' trading house outside the province	x	x	x	x	Selected provinces
Development of bilateral partners with partners (SMEs) outside the province	x	x	x	x	Selected provinces
Business Meeting for selected SMEs	x	x	x	x	SMEs in cities/ regencies in West Java
Optimization of the West Java SMEs Business Center	x	x	x	x	SMEs in West Java

The idea to establish the trading house is actually done to help the marketing of SMEs' products in not only the international market but also the domestic market. Before, the marketing of SMEs' products are carried out independently by the SMEs' owner. The utilization of a partnership with the trading house is expected to develop SMEs and their products as well as to increase the value added and the bargaining position of SMEs in regional economic growth. Trading house according to the Ontario Association of Trading Houses is defined as a commercial brokerage services that have specialized the trading of goods and services provided by long-term other parties.[256] The function of the trading house is to facilitate the process of buying and selling of goods between producers and consumers both in domestically and abroad. Until now, the Government of Indonesia has two trading houses in Jeddah, Saudi Arabia (for the Arab countries and Africa's markets) and in Bulgaria (for Eastern European markets).[257]

The SMEs' business center (*Sentra Bisnis UKM, Senbik*) is a supply chain system of SMEs' products from producers to consumers that is organized effectively and efficiently to increase the value added of the SMEs' products.[258] Several reasons for the formation of a *Senbik* are: *First*, the province of West Java does not have the central marketing of SMEs' products; *second*, many SMEs' products are sold independently and find it difficult to meet the demand in the domestic market or international market in large numbers; *third*, there is difficulty of SMEs in developing business networks because of the limited market information; and *fourth*, the realization of the tough and independent of the economic development of West Java. Looking at these reasons, the creation of a *Senbik* is aimed to accelerate economic transactions at the regional level so as to achieve an equitable economic development in the entire region of West Java, which in turn can improve the welfare of society. The function of a *Senbik* itself is: a means to collect superior (leading) products of West Java's SMEs, a means to market superior (leading) products of West Java's

256 Cf. Ontario Association of Trading Houses (n.d.).

257 For further details see The Need to Develop SMEs Global Market Network, Purpose: Information, Submitted by: Indonesia, paper presented at the 26th SMEWG Meeting, Kaohsiung, Chinese Taipei, March 30-April 4, 2008. http://www.oath.on.ca/publications/PDF_En/EN_TradingHousesPractical.pdf, accessed January 6, 2014.

258 Cf. Dinas Koperasi dan Usaha Mikro, Kecil, dan Menengah Provinsi Jawa Barat (n.d.d.).

SMEs, a center of business activities of SMEs in West Java, and a means of SME's business information center in West Java.

2. Program on Promoting and Marketing SMEs' Products as follows:

Programs/Activities	**Year**				**Target Group(s)**
	2010	2011	2012	2013	
Facilitation to attend exhibitions at domestic exhibitions	x	x	x	x	SMEs in West Java
Facilitation to attend exhibitions abroad	x	x	x	x	SMEs in West Java
The involvement of SMEs in the Cooperatives Fair	x	x	x	x	SMEs in West Java
The involvement of SMEs in the Ramadan Fair	x	x	x	x	SMEs in West Java
Facilitation of Exhibitions for Superior (Leading) SMEs' Products	x	x	x	x	SMEs in West Java
Facilitation of Exhibitions for Halal Products	x	x	x	x	SMEs in West Java
Facilitation of Exhibitions for SMEs' Products that have export potentials	x	x	x	x	SMEs in West Java
Facilitation of Exhibitions for Women SMEs' Products	x	x	x	x	SMEs in West Java
The opening of the West Java SMEs Outlets	x	x	x	x	SMEs in West Java

Promotional activities that are carried out by the Office of Cooperatives and SMEs are aimed not only to introduce the West Java SMEs' products to the local market and the international market but also to increase productivity, to increase exports, and to increase the value added of such products at the same time. Some examples of the exhibition organized and held regularly annually by the West Java Investment and Promotion Coordination Board in cooperation with the Office of Cooperatives and SMEs and the Office of Industry and Trade of the Province of West Java are: Cooperative Fair in July to celebrate the cooperative day, Ramadan Fair that is held during the month of Ramadan and to celebrate Idul Fitri, Halal Fair which is held in September, Women SMEs' Products Exhibition in March, the Braga Festival in December, and the Exhibition for Domestic Product also in December.[259] While other regular exhibitions at the national scale include: the Jakarta Fair, the Jakarta International Handicraft Trade Fair (INACRAFT) in February, the Trade Expo Indonesia in October, and SMEs' products exhibition held in SMESCO Building in Jakarta by Indonesian SMESCO Company (a private sector organization which was created by a decree of the State Ministry of Cooperative and SMEs). In SMESCO Building itself, it can be found stands and displays of various products produced by SMEs in West Java including Cibaduyut's footwear and Plered's decorative ceramics. There are also several international exhibitions that are attended by the West Java SMEs and is facilitated by the West Java Investment and Promotion Coordination Board in cooperation with the Office of Cooperatives and SMEs such as: the International Frankfurter Messe Germany every year attended by the SMEs in the decorative ceramic cluster in Plered and the China ASEAN Expo in October.

Facilitation of marketing of the West Java SMEs' products is also helped with the opening of SMEs' online outlet.[260] The Office of Cooperatives and SMEs has officially launched the SMEs' online outlet at the exhibition of the Women SMEs' Products. The purpose of this website is as a means of promotion of SMEs' products in order to introduce its products in both regional and international levels. It is hope that this SMEs' online outlet can expand market share and information to the community and consumers. Through this online outlet, shopping can be done anytime and anywhere around the world through the internet.

259 Other programs and routine activities can be found at the website of the West Java Investment and Promotion Coordination Board, http://westjavainvest.com/in/index.php?option=com_content&task=view&id=274&Itemid=96.

260 Cf. Dinas Koperasi dan Usaha Mikro, Kecil, dan Menengah Provinsi Jawa Barat (n.d.e.).

3. Program on Developing and Strengthening the Capacity of SMEs as follows:

Programs/Activities	Year				Target Group(s)
	2010	2011	2012	2013	
SMEs' mentoring program by graduate assistants	x	x	x	x	SMEs in West Java
Creating of new entrepreneurs and strengthening the entrepreneurial spirit	x	x	x	x	SMEs in West Java
The publishing of a book on the role and development of SMEs in the West Java Gross Regional Domestic Product (GRDP)	x	x	x	x	SMEs in West Java
The publishing of a book on Guidelines on Local Regulations to Develop SMEs	x	x	x	x	SMEs in West Java
The publishing of database on the growth of the total export's value and quantity of the West Java SMEs	x	x	x	x	SMEs in West Java
The establishment of 'One Village One Product' in potential business center (*sentra*) in West Java	x	x	x	x	SMEs in West Java
Business mentoring through business incubator programs for SMEs in rural areas	x	x	x	x	SMEs in rural areas in West Java

Improving market information system for SMEs in rural areas	x	x	x	x	SMEs in rural areas in West Java
Growing entrepreneurial spirit of SMEs in rural areas	x	x	x	x	SMEs in rural areas in West Java
Development of rural SMEs in the economic region of West Java	x	x	x	x	SMEs in rural areas in West Java

The development and strengthening of SMEs' programs are conducted by providing graduate assistant to inform the SME's business owners on the process of obtaining financing from the banking sector, the process of increasing the production capacity of SMEs, and the expansion of marketing network for SMEs' products. In addition, this mentoring program is also a continuation of the program of Increasing the Role of Universities in Developing BDS-P and the Empowerment of SMEs as instructed by the resident in Presidential Instruction No. 6/2007 on the Acceleration of Real Sector and Development of Micro, Small and Medium-sized Enterprises that effectively began in June 2007.[261]

While the OVOP program is done to follow up Presidential Instruction No. 6/2007 which focuses on the development of SMEs through the OVOP approach.[262] The OVOP program itself is a program to develop local potentials to produce a world class product that has a unique characteristic of the area and has advantage of local resources.[263] The main objective of the OVOP program is to increase the number of small industries' products that have high a value added and have international competitiveness.[264] This program is aimed on certain product that has market potential for both domestic and international markets which has been done for generations by local communities so that these communities are culturally in-

261 Cf. Chapter II A.2 of Presidential Instruction No. 6/2007.
262 Cf. ibid.
263 Cf. Article 1 of Regulation of the Minister of Industry No. 78/2007.
264 Cf. Article 3 Paragraph 2 of Regulation of the Minister of Industry No. 78/2007.

tegrated with the resulting products. One example of the OVOP program in West Java is the decorative ceramic cluster in Plered.

4. Program on Increasing the Capacity of SMEs' Human Resources as follows:

Programs/Activities	**Year**				**Target Group(s)**
	2010	2011	2012	2013	
Training on Management Skills and Entrepreneurial Spirit	x	x	x	x	SMEs in West Java
Substantive technicals training for SMEs	x	x	x	x	SMEs in West Java
The publishing of training modul and syllabus for SMEs' training	x	x	x	x	The Office of Cooperatives and SMEs

Activities carried out by the Office of Cooperatives and SMEs are aimed to improve managerial capacities of SMEs in West Java. Usually the training provided are not only carried out by the Office of Cooperatives and SMEs initiatives, but also because of the demand of SMEs' perpetrators in West Java. One example of the activities initiated by this office is the Managerial and Entrepreneurship Training for Cooperatives and SMEs which is regularly held every year in the auditorium of the Office of Cooperatives and SMEs.

5. Program on Facilitating the Development of SMEs' Products as follows:

Programs/Activities	**Year**				**Target Group(s)**
	2010	2011	2012	2013	
Facilitation of Establishing Business Clinic for SMEs in the cities/regencies in West Java	x	x	x	x	SMEs in West Java

Facilitation of the legal aspect of SMEs' Products (halal products and IPR)	x	x	x	x	SMEs in West Java
Development of OVOP in potential business centers in the cities/regencies in West Java area	x	x	x	x	SMEs in West Java
Facilitation on the Development of Product Design, Brand, Packaging, and Diversification of SMEs' Products	x	x	x	x	SMEs in West Java

The function the business clinic is to provide services to SMEs including coaching, mentoring, and empowering small and medium businesses. One example of the business clinic in West Java is the Promotion Agency and Business Linkages (*Badan Promosi dan Pengelola Keterkaitan Usaha,* BPPKU) under the coordination of the Bandung Chamber of Commerce and Industry.[265] The purpose of this clinic is to: (a) improve the quality of potential SMEs in the city of Bandung, (b) strengthen the entrepreneurial spirit and enhance the managerial capabilities of SMEs in the city of Bandung, (c) build communities and networks of SMEs in order to strengthen SMEs, (d) increase job creation and the amount of total sales of SMEs, (e) improve the quality of small business management with the parameter of each SME at least having the business plan and business reporting system.

6. Program on Facilitating Financing for SMEs as follows:

Programs/Activities	**Year**				**Target Group(s)**
	2010	2011	2012	2013	
Assistance in SMEs' business feasibility	x	x	x	x	SMEs in West Java

265 Cf. Kadin Bandung (n.d.).

Intermediate SMEs with financial institutions and other financial resources	x	x	x	x	SMEs in West Java
Consolidation with the financial institutions and other financial institutions to open access to SMEs by the Association of Development and Assistance Center for Small and Medium Enterprises	x	x	x	x	SMEs in West Java
Advocacy on SMEs' credit guarantee	x	x	x	x	SMEs in West Java
Guidance and consultation of financial aspect using the hedging system	x	x	x	x	SMEs in West Java
Optimization of SMEs' Financing through the CSR and the Partnership and Community Development Program	x	x	x	x	SMEs in West Java

The facilitation of SMEs' financing is focused on finding a solution of capital issues faced by SMEs in West Java. One example of assistances is the establishment of the Association of Development and of the Assistance Center for Small and Medium Enterprises (*Pusat Pengembangan Pendamping Usaha Kecil Menengah,* P3UKM) in Bandung whose job is to provide advice and assistance to access financing both in financial institutions or non-bank institutions. Not only that, the facilitation of SMEs' financing is also done by optimizing the CSR program and the partnership and community development (PCD) program by private companies and regional (West Java) state-owned enterprises in West Java. Unfortunately due to the nature of CSR that is voluntary, not many CSR programs are conducted to give assistance on financial issues to the West Java SMEs. Therefore, to support the CSR and PCD programs in West Java, the Government of the West Java Province issued West Java Provincial Regulation No. 21/2011 on (Capital) Investment which requires investors in West

Java to implement social responsibility programs to SMEs and also Regulation of the City of Bandung No. 13/2012 on the Obligation of Implementating Social Responsibility Program.[266] One example of the implementation of the regulations above is the Program of Creating and Growing New Entrepreneur by PT Bank Pembangunan Daerah Jabar Banten.[267]

7. Program on Developing the Entrepreneurial Spirit as follows:

Programs/ Activities	Year				Target Group(s)
	2010	2011	2012	2013	
Creating new entrepeneurship	x	x	x	x	SMEs in West Java
Providing business incubator for SMEs in rural area	x	x	x	x	SMEs in rural area in West Java
Implementing the entrepreneur's program based on local potentials	x	x	x	x	SMEs in West Java
Entrepreneurial practices of SMEs	x	x	x	x	SMEs in West Java

Programs to create new entrepreneurs are constantly conducted to increase the number of SMEs in West Java as well as to reduce the number of unemployment rate. Each year, the Office of Cooperatives and SMEs conducts entrepreneurship training that is aimed at graduates who are unemployed. It is expected by joining such training these graduates can start their own businesses and create jobs for other job seekers. One example of such trainings is the SMEs' Assistance Program Through Business Incubator which is the collaboration of the Office of Cooperatives and SMEs with the Institute of Research and Community Service of Bogor Agricul-

266 Cf. Article 25b of West Java Provincial Regulation No. 21/2011, Article 9 of Regulation of the City of Bandung No. 13/2012.

267 Cf. AntaraJawaBarat.com 2012. Other CSR programs that are conducted by PT Bank Pembangunan Daerah Jabar Banten can be accessed at http://www.bankbjb.co.id/csr/index_en.html, accessed January 15, 2014.

tural Institute.[268] This program is aimed at college graduates who are interested in doing business in the field of agribusiness, agroindustries, and green products.

8. Program on Facilitating the Appropriate Technology for SMEs as follows:

Programs/Activities	Year				Target Group(s)
	2010	2011	2012	2013	
Assistance for the implementation of appropriate technology for SMEs	x	x	x	x	SMEs in West Java
Assistance for facilities of appropriate technology for SMEs	x	x	x	x	SMEs in West Java
Dissemination of appropriate technologies for SMEs	x	x	x	x	SMEs in West Java
Application of appropriate technologies based on local potentials	x	x	x	x	SMEs in West Java
Increasing the application of appropriate technology for SMEs through CSR and PCD programs	x	x	x	x	SMEs in West Java

The facilitation of appropriate technologies for SMEs is based on Regulation of the Minister of Home Affairs No. 20/2010 on Community Empowerment through the Appropriate Technology Management. The aim of this program is to boost the economy and to develop entrepreneurial spirit.[269]

268 For further details see Inkubator Agribisnis dan Agroindustri – Institut Pertanian Bogor. http://inkubatoripb.com/index.php?nama=Home, accessed January 6, 2014.

269 Cf. Article 3 Paragraphs 1a and 1b of Regulation of the Minister of Home Affairs No. 20/2010.

It is with hope that through the use of appropriate technology and supported by reliable human resources, the quality of SMEs' products could be improved so that it can compete with foreign products and increase total sales and value-added products. The Province of West Java has formed a team to coordinate the establishment of appropriate technology's center at provincial and district level in West Java to support the small and medium businesses in utilizing appropriate technology.[270] At the district and village level, there are the appropriate technology service center (*Pos Pelayanan Teknologi Tepat Guna, Posyantek*) and the appropriate technology outlet (*Warung Teknologi Tepat Guna, Wartek*) to provide information, technical services, and orientation about the importance of using appropriate technology to unemployed people, teenage dropout, and poor families in the entire region of West Java.

9. Program on Recording SMEs' Database as follows:

Programs/Activities	**Year**				**Target Group(s)**
	2010	2011	2012	2013	
Identification of potential SMEs in West Java	x	x	x	x	SMEs in West Java
Identification of SMEs which have export potentials	x	x	x	x	SMEs in West Java
The publishing of monographs on the evaluation of SMEs' performance	x	x	x	x	SMEs in West Java
Establishment and facilitation of SMEs' online database system in West Java	x	x	x	x	SMEs in West Java
Assistance for utilizing the online networks for the West Java SMEs	x	x	x	x	SMEs in West Java

270 Cf. http://www.inilah.com/read/detail/1608902/pemprov-jabar-genjot-teknologi-tepatgu-na, accessed June 15, 2011.

Advertising the West Java SMEs through electronic and printed media	x	x	x	x	SMEs in West Java

The activity of recording SMEs' data is aimed to provide information to the public and consumers about SMEs' products. One of the initiatives undertaken by the Office of Cooperatives and SMEs is to create an online website (*Gerai KUMKM*)[271] and a business center (*Senbik*) as mentioned earlier. Not only that the leading products of the West Java SMEs are also promoted through the website that is managed by the Ministry of Cooperatives and SMEs. The example of such websites is: the SMECDA, the SME's Center, and the Indonesian Products.[272] Unfortunately, the profile of these websites are not intersting; in fact, one of the three websites is not accessible anymore.

10. Program on Monitoring, Controlling, and Evaluating the Empowerment of SMEs as follows:

Programs/Activities	**Year**				**Target Group(s)**
	2010	2011	2012	2013	
Monitoring and evaluating the performance of graduate assistant for SMEs	x	x	x	x	SMEs in West Java
Monitoring and evaluating the program on Empowerment of SMEs	x	x	x	x	SMEs in West Java

The program of monitoring, control, and evaluating the empowerment of SMEs is conducted every year by the Office of Cooperatives and SMEs in order to see the effectiveness of programs conducted in previous years. Unfortunately, there is no detailed information on how the monitoring and

271 The Office of Cooperatives and SMEs has launched a specific website to promote SMEs' products in West Java. Previously, the address of this website could be found at www.geraikumkm.com, unfortunately this website is no longer available.

272 For further details see www.smecda.com, www.indonesian-products.biz, and formerly www.sentrakukm.com, which unfortunately is no longer available.

controlling program is conducted and what kind of evaluation is made as a follow-up of the assessment of previous programs.

4.3.2 The Office of Industry and Trade

The Office of Industry and Trade was formed in accordance with West Java Provincial Regulation No. 21/2008 on the Organization and Administration of the Province of West Java Regional Office.[273] The main task of this office is to conduct local government affairs in the field of industry and trade based on the principles of (local) autonomy. The establishment of this office is expected to develop the industrial sector in West Java especially the import-substitution industries and the export-oriented industries by developing and empowering existing industrial clusters. In order to realize this goal, the Office of Industry and Trade creates its vision and mission as follows. The vision of the Office of Industry and Trade is: The Realization of Leading Industry in West Java and Optimization of Domestic and International Markets In 2013.[274] While the missions that are carried out by this office are: (a) to increase the growth of leading local industry, (b) to improve the smoothness of the distribution, to secure the domestic market and provide consumer protection, (c) to increase the foreign trade activities, and (d) to manage internal organization (and human) resources in order to support its main tasks.[275]

Organizational Structure

In its organizational structure, the Department of Trade and Industry oversees six sections consisting of: (a) Metal, Machinery, Equipment, Miscellaneous Textile, and Telematics industries, (b) Assorted, Crafts, and Chemical industries, (c) Agroindustry, (d) Sub-section of Domestic Trade, (e) Sub-section of International Trade, and (f) Promotion and Cooperation for Industry and Trade. In addition, the Office of Industry and Trade also oversees six technical service units namely: the Industrial Development Center, the Bandung Metrology Center, the Bogor Metrology Center, the

273 Cf. Article 18 of West Java Provincial Regulation No. 21/2008.
274 Cf. Dinas Perindustrian dan Perdagangan Provinsi Jawa Barat 2009, p. IV-3.
275 Cf. ibid., p. IV-4.

Karawang Metrology Center, the Tasikmalaya Metrology Center, and the Cirebon Metrology Center. Looking at these six sections and six technical service units, there are at least six units that are directly related to the development of SMEs/SMIs. They are: (1) the Section of Metal, Machinery, Equipment, Miscellaneous Textile, and Telematics industries, (2) the Section of Assorted, Crafts, and Chemical industries, (3) the Section of Domestic Trade, (4) the Section of International Trade, (5) the Section of Promotion and Cooperation for Industry and Trade, and (6) the Industrial Development Center. The following will explain a brief profile of those sections.

1. The Section of Metal, Machinery, Equipment, Miscellaneous Textile, and Telematics industries, which has the fundamental duty to conduct assessment on the material for formulating technical policies related to the facilitation of metals, machinery, textiles and textile products, transportation, telecommunications, and electronics industries.[276] In carrying out its main task, this section has a function of conducting technical assessment of industrial development policy of metals, machinery, textiles and textile products, transportation, telecommunications, and electronics including monitoring and evaluation program.[277] The main tasks of this section are: (a) to conduct assessment of materials on policy and technical considerations including the protection of industrial enterprises, the program planning to develop industry, the mastery of technology, the improvement of the quality of human resources, capital, the dissemination of industrial information, and the supervision of industry performance and (b) the facilitation and coordination to develop the metals, machinery, textiles and textile products, transportation, telecommunications, and electronics industries.[278] In supporting its main tasks and functions, this section is assisted by the three sub-sections, namely:[279]

276 Cf. Article 8 Paragraph 1 of Regulation of the Governor of West Java No. 69/2009.

277 Cf. Article 8 Paragraph 2 of Regulation of the Governor of West Java No. 69/2009.

278 Cf. Article 8 Paragraph 3 of Regulation of the Governor of West Java No. 69/2009.

279 Cf. Articles 9, 10, and 11 of Regulation of the Governor of West Java No. 69/2009.

a. The sub-section of metal and machinery has the main task of formulating technical policy for the development of metal and machinery industries.
b. The sub-section of industrial transportation, telecommunications, and electronics formulates technical policy for the development of transportation, telecommunications, and electronics industries.
c. The sub-section of textiles and textile products' main task is to formulate technical policy for the development of textiles and textile products industries.

2. The Section of Assorted, Crafts, and Chemical industries, which has the fundamental duty to conduct assessment on the material for formulating technical policies related to the development of assorted, crafts, and chemical industries.[280] In carrying out its main task, this section has a function of conducting technical assessment of industrial development policy of assorted, crafts, and chemical industries including monitoring and evaluation program.[281] The main tasks of this section are: (a) to conduct assessment of materials on policy and technical considerations including the protection of industrial enterprises, the program planning to develop industry, the mastery of technology, the improvement of the quality of human resources, capital, the dissemination of industrial information, and the supervision of industry performance and (b) the facilitation and coordination to develop the assorted, crafts, and chemical industries.[282] In supporting its main tasks and functions, this section is assisted by the three subsections, namely:[283]
   a. The sub-section of the assorted industry has the main task of formulating technical policy for the development of assorted industry.

280 Cf. Article 12 Paragraph 1 of Regulation of the Governor of West Java No. 69/2009.
281 Cf. Article 12 Paragraph 2 of Regulation of the Governor of West Java No. 69/2009.
282 Cf. Article 12 Paragraph 3 of Regulation of the Governor of West Java No. 69/2009.
283 Cf. Articles 13, 14, and 15 of Regulation of the Governor of West Java No. 69/2009.

   b. The sub-section of the craft industry formulates technical policy for the development of craft industry.
   c. The sub-section of the chemical industry's main task is to formulate technical policy for the development of chemical's industry.
3. The Section of Domestic Trade, which has the fundamental duty to conduct assessment on the material for formulating technical policies related to the development of domestic trade, legal metrology, future trading, warehouse receipt financing alternatives, and auction market.[284] In supporting its duty, this section is assisted by the three sub-sections, namely:[285]
   a. The sub-section of market development has the main task of formulating technical policy for facilitating future trading, auction market, marketing and distribution.
   b. The sub-section of business and trade facilities formulates technical policy for facilitating business development and trade facilities.
   c. The sub-section of consumer protection and supervision's main task is to formulate technical policy for coordinating and facilitating trade supervision and consumer protection.
4. The Section of International Trade, which has the fundamental duty to conduct assessment on the material for formulating technical policies related to the development of international trade.[286] In supporting its duty, this section is assisted by the three sub-sections, namely:[287]
   a. The sub-section of industrial export and mining has the main task of formulating technical policy for coordinating and facilitating industrial export and mining activity.
   b. The sub-section of import formulates technical policy for coordinating and facilitating import activity.

---

284 Cf. Article 20 Paragraph 1 of Regulation of the Governor of West Java No. 69/2009.

285 Cf. Articles 21, 22, and 23 of Regulation of the Governor of West Java No. 69/2009.

286 Cf. Article 24 Paragraph 1 of Regulation of the Governor of West Java No. 69/2009.

287 Cf. Articles 25, 26, and 27 of Regulation of the Governor of West Java No. 69/2009.

   c. The sub-section of export of agricultural, plantation and forestry products' main task is to formulate technical policy for coordinating and facilitating export of agricultural, plantation and forestry's products especially in the provincial scale.

5. The Section of Promotion and Cooperation for Industry and Trade, which has the fundamental duty to conduct assessment on the material for formulating technical policies related to industrial cooperation, marketing and promotion of industrial products, international trade cooperation, and export development.[288] The main tasks of this section includes the facilitation of promoting partnerships between SMIs and large industry, the facilitation of promoting international cooperation, cross-sectoral (and regional) cooperation, and the dissemination on international trade agreements and bilateral cooperation.[289] In supporting its duty, this section is assisted by the three sub-sections, namely:[290]
   a. The sub-section of export promotion has the main task of formulating technical policy for facilitating and developing export promotion.
   b. The sub-section of trade cooperation formulates technical policy for facilitating trade cooperation.
   c. The sub-section of industrial cooperation's main task is to formulate technical policy for facilitating and coordinating industrial cooperation.
6. The Industrial Development Center, which is a representative of the local government agency (in this case the Office of Industry and Trade) in conducting daily technical tasks in the field.[291] In supporting its duty, this center is assisted by several sub-sections, two of them are: the Office for the Development of the Small and Medium-sized Shoe Industry in the city of Bandung and the Office for the Development of the Small and Medium-sized Ceramic Industry in the regency of Purwakarta.

---

288 Cf. Article 28 Paragraph 1 of Regulation of the Governor of West Java No. 69/2009.

289 Cf. Article 28 Paragraph 3 of Regulation of the Governor of West Java No. 69/2009.

290 Cf. Articles 29, 30, and 31 of Regulation of the Governor of West Java No. 69/2009.

291 See Regulation of the Governor of West Java No. 113/2009.

Issues in Developing Industry in the Province of West Java

In achieving the vision and mission that has been mentioned earlier, there are several issues that could affect the industrial activity in West Java.[292] *First*, the business climate remains unfavorable in West Java. Some aspects that do not support the creation of a conducive business climate includes: a high interest rate which results in a low interest of the public in borrowing funds, the inventory management and distribution costs are still high which affects product prices, the rampant labor demonstrations, the increasing price of oil and electricity tariff which resulted in the increase of production costs, and the unsatisfactory implementation of local autonomy, especially regarding coordination between the central government, local governments, and regency/city governments. *Second*, the business relationship (partnership) among industries is still low. *Third*, mastery of science and technology in industry development is still low which results in the lack of product development and innovation. *Fourth*, a high dependence on imported raw materials for several industrial sectors which can cause instability in output especially if there is price fluctuations and supply issues overseas. *Fifth*, the organizational effectiveness rate is still low due to the low quality of human resources and lack of organizational discipline. *Sixth*, the environmental issues and the impact of international trade agreements that led to few industrial products that can enter the international market (because it does not meet international standards).

The Importance of SMIs for West Java's Economy

Seeing the potential of the industrial sector in West Java, it is not surprising that the Government of the West Java Province pays great attention on this sector. The following table shows data on the number of business units, workforces, and investment in industrial sector in West Java from 2008-2011. Data on industrial sector is divided into SMIs and large industries.

292 Cf. Dinas Perindustrian dan Perdagangan Provinsi Jawa Barat 2009, pp. III-1-III-8.

Table 4.1: Number of Business Units, Workforces, and Investment in the Industrial Sector in West Java, 2008-2011

	2008	2009	2010	2011
Small and Medium-sized				
Business Units	197,134	198,478	199,537	199, 723
Workforces	2,206,532	2,280,375	2,291,053	2,294,825
Investment (in million IDR)	4,673,985.54	6,040,433.30	6,274,804.67	10,206,094.00
Large				
Business Units	3,309	3,475	3,523	3,592
Workforces	1,830,817	1,914,235	1,925,618	1,925,260
Investment (in million IDR)	3,016,397.00	119,882,497.00	123,845,893.64	202,323,541.94

Source: Data is modified from Dinas Perindustrian dan Perdagangan Provinsi Jawa Barat (n.d.)

Between 2008-2011, there were: a growth of number of SMIs from 197,134 units in 2008 to 199,723 units in 2011 or growing at rate of 1.31 percent, a growth of number of workforces from 2,206,532 in 2008 to 2,294,825 in 2011 or growing at rate of 4 percent, and a growth in the total value of investment from IDR 4,673,985.54 million in 2008 to IDR 10,206,094 million in 2011 or growing at rate of 118.35 percent. Looking at the growth rate of number of SMIs that reached 1.31 percent, we can simply interpret that each year new SMIs and new entrepreneurs are born (even though the growing rate of large industries is bigger, which is 8.5 percent). The same interpretation also occurs in the number of workforce that reached 4 percent; this means each year these SMIs absorb new workers (creates job opportunities). The increase in business units, workforces and total investment (that reached 118 percent from 2008 to 2011) should be the basis of the policies and programs of local governments to develop and empower SMIs in West Java. However, when looking at the details above, it is the role of large industries that have contributed the most of total investment especially in 2011 (that growing at rate of 6.607 percent).

The following table shows the comparison of the number of SMIs' entrepreneurs in West Java from 2008 to 2011.

Table 4.2: Number of Entrepreneurs of Small, Medium, and Large Industries in West Java, 2008-2011

Item	2008	2009	2010	2011
Small	72,112	19,257	19,893	32,227
Medium	12,233	3,902	4,038	4,335
Total (small+medium)	84,345	23,159	23,931	36,562
Large	4,015	1,752	1,794	1,879

Source: Data is modified from Dinas Perindustrian dan Perdagangan Provinsi Jawa Barat (n.d.)

Looking at Table 4.2 above, the average ratio between the SMIs with large industries during the period of 2008-2011 was 94.1 percent to 5.8 percent (that the SMIs are accounted for 94.14 percent of total enterprises while large industries are accounted for 5.86 percent). Indeed, there was a sharp decline in the number of business units in small, medium, and large industries in 2009, but it cannot be avoided especially related to the economic (financial) crisis in Southeast Asia that affected the existence of industries in the region. However, looking at the above data, in the period of 2009-2011 there was a growth in number of SMIs especially in 2011 or growing at average rate of 67.35 percent. This data shows that the economic (industrial) structure of West Java is still dominated by SMEs.

Looking at the potential of SMI sector in West Java, it is not surprising that the Office of Industry and Trade must pay special attention to this sector. It is also aligned with the direction and focus of the policy of regional economic development in West Java, which focuses on poverty reduction, expanding employment opportunities, and improving the competitiveness of industrial sector.

Programs of the Office of Industry and Trade

Looking at the potential of SMIs in West Java and the need to overcome issues mentioned earlier, the Office of Industry and Trade designed its programs which are focused on:[293]

1. Program on Developing Small and Medium-sized Industries. The purposes of this program are to: increase the number of SMIs, improve the employment of SMIs, and improve service to small and medium businesses. There are several main programs that are aimed at developing SMIs in West Java, namely: increasing the capacity building of SMIs (such as organic fertilizer and food processing), developing product design and diversification of SMIs' products (such as electonics and telematics), product development of tile, pottery, and decorative ceramic through the development of creative industries community, increasing the competence of human resources (especially in footwear and lether products industries), facilitating of the legal aspect of creative industries, developing the packing house industry, facilitating the implementation of national product standards (*Standar Nasional Indonesia*, SNI) and of ISO certification, and improving market access for industrial products.
2. Program on Strengthening the Structure and Increasing the Capability of Industrial Technology. The aims of this program are to: increase the synergy to promote industrial development, improve the mastery of industrial technology, and increase employment by industrial sector. There are several programs that are designed namely: strengthening of priority industrial clusters (such as footwear, furniture, metal goods/machinery, fruit, essential oils as well as pulp and paper), facilitating cooperation and partnership among creative industries, improving the technology capacity for industries (such as agroindustry, rattan, wood, and bamboo), developing the fashion-based creative industry, developing the processed food creative industry, developing the automotive-based manufacturing industry, developing handicraft industry, developing information technology-based creative industry, and the development of tobacco industry.

293 Cf. Dinas Perindustrian dan Perdagangan Provinsi Jawa Barat 2009, pp. V-1-V-4.

3. Program on Developing the Domestic Trading System. The objectives of this program are to: improve public distribution of essential goods and other strategic goods and increase the use of domestic products. Programs that are designed to achieve those objectives are: revitalizing of traditional markets, facilitating future trading, and increasing the use of domestic products.
4. Program of Consumer Protection and Protection of Domestic Trade. The aims of this program are to: increase control of goods in circulation and increase the protection of consumers and producers. There are two main programs that are aimed at protecting consumer and domestic trade, namely: increasing supervision of goods in circulation and improving metrology services.
5. Program on Improving and Developing Export. The aim of this program is to increase the volume and value of the West Java SMIs' exports. There are four main programs that are aimed at improving and developing export, namely: increasing export competitiveness of West Java products, increasing (foreign) market access, strengthening institutional functions to support foreign trade, and monitoring the performance of foreign trade (to see market potential).
6. Program on Development Communication, Information, and the Utilization of Information Technology with the aim to improve services of and information on industry and trade to the public.

Some examples of the programs undertaken by the Office of Trade and Industry for developing the footwear industry in West Java, especially with regard to the above six programs are:

No.	Programs	Date
1.	Facilitation on Training for Footwear Production Techniques (for two classes)	March-April 2012
2.	Facilitation on Training for Entrepreneurial Spirit of Footwear's SMIs	September-November 2012
3.	Assistance to attend domestic exhibitions	January-December 2012
4.	Training on Techniques and Design of Leather Product	May 2012
5.	Training on Footwear Production Techniques	June 2012

6.	Socialization on Restructuring of Leather and Leather Products' Machinery	March 2012

Source: Data is modified from the West Java Office of Industry and Trade

Looking at the above programs, there are many programs that are designed to develop the footwear industry in West Java. Program on footwear production techniques is aimed at 80 SMIs that are registered on the Office of Industry and Trade. The aim of this program is to improve the quality of products produced by the footwear industry in Cibaduyut and Ciomas to dominate the domestic shoe market as well as to produce products that can compete with imported (similar) products especially products coming from China and Vietnam.[294]

The assistance to attend domestic exhibitions is given in 2012, namely: Expo on Leather Shoes and Fashion 2012 in Jakarta, the Indonesian Creative Products Exhibition in South Sulawesi, the Trade Expo Indonesia in Jakarta, Expo on Domestic Products in Balikpapan – East Kalimantan, the West Java Expo 2012, and the Bandung Air Show 2012. Unfortunately, there is no report on the effectiveness of these programs. Moreover, there is no published research on the effectiveness of these industries to improve the quality and quantity of their products (especially the footwear industry and decorative ceramic industry) after receiving training and facilitation by the local government and relevant agencies.

294 Interview with Mr. D. from the Office for Developing the Small and Medium-sized Shoe Industry in Cibaduyut in Bandung.

5. The Implementation of Business Clusters in the Cibaduyut Footwear Industrial Cluster and the Plered Decorative Ceramic Industrial Cluster

To answer the research questions that have been mentioned in the earlier section of this study, the author used two industrial cluster locations. The selection of these two sites is done with the following considerations: *first*, the location of the two clusters is not far from the city of Bandung so that the interview process and observations at the site are easier in order to complete the research process. *Second*, the location of these two industrial clusters has been formed since the 1900s in a form of *sentra* before being formalized into industrial clusters in 2009. *Third*, the government and the Ministry of Industry had chosen these two sites to be developed into a dynamic cluster by issuing Regulation of the President of the Republic of Indonesia No. 28/2008 on the National Industrial Policy which used as the basis of the issuance of Regulation of the Minister of Industry of the Republic of Indonesia No. 110/M-IND/PER/10/2009 on the Roadmap of the Development of the Footwear Industrial Cluster and Regulation of Minister of Industry of the Republic of Indonesia No. 135/M-IND/PER/10/2009 on the Roadmap of the Development of Pottery and Decorative Ceramic Industrial Cluster.

This chapter will discuss the role of the central government through the Regulation of the Minister of Industry that regulates the formation of the industrial clusters of shoe and ornamental pottery and ceramics as well as profiles of the two industrial clusters location, i.e. the Cibaduyut Footwear Industrial Cluster, Bandung, and the Plered Decorative Ceramic Industrial Cluster, Purwakarta, and also problems that arise in the two industrial clusters.

5.1 The Role of the Central Government

In order to support the target for Indonesia's economic growth, which was announced by the *Kabinet Indonesia Bersatu II* (the Cabinet of United Indonesia II) 2010-2014, the industrial sector is expected to be the main driver to achieve the target of the economic growth by an average of 7 percent per year.[295] The government through Presidential Regulation No. 28/2008 has issued the National Industrial Policy to support achieving the objective mentioned earlier by improving the industrial competitiveness so that the Indonesia's national industry has a strong industrial structure. This chapter will not discuss the entire road map of the priority industrial cluster development, but will only focus on two guide maps on the cluster development, which are the development of footwear industrial cluster and the development of pottery and decorative ceramics industrial cluster, which are in accordance with the primary focus of this research.

5.1.1 The Development of the Footwear Industrial Cluster

The development of the footwear industrial cluster is administered because this manufacturing industry is one of the industries that deserve attention from the government. The footwear industries that are included in the general guide map consist of the shoe industry for daily use, sport shoe industry, shoes for engineering or industrial purposes, and other footwear industry. The main reason of the development of the industries is based on the value of shoe exports, which is significantly high. Data and figures from the Ministry of Industry show that there was an increase in the value of total exports of Indonesian leather products, leather goods, and shoes/footwear in the last three years, as follows: in 2009 the number was USD 1,888,082,911, in 2010 the number increased to USD 2,665,634,728, and in 2011 which reached USD 3,450,898,952.[296] Looking at the increased export values especially in the last three years, the government focused on the development of the footwear industry by forming a footwear industrial cluster. The guideline (roadmap) of this industrial cluster is based on Regulation of the Minister of Industry of the Republic of Indonesia No. 110/M-IND/PER/10/2009.[297] This guideline is compiled as: (a) an operational guideline for all government agencies to support, complementary and synergistic, the successful of the implementation of the industrial development programs in accordance with each agency's duty, (b) a

295 Cf. Departemen Perindustrian, 2009a, p. iii.
296 Cf. Kementerian Perindustrian (n.d.b).
297 See Departemen Perindustrian 2009a, pp. 189-221.

guideline for actors and stakeholders in the footwear cluster industry, including employers and other institutions to actively involve in the industrial cluster, and (c) a guideline for making cross-sectoral coordination as well as between related government institutions whether at the national level or local (provincial and districts) level.[298] Looking through the three intentions above, it can be concluded that the guideline is intended to provide guidance to the central and local government institutions as well as the industrial actors in synergizing programs to encourage the creation of a stronger national footwear industry sector.

Looking deeply at the guideline of the development of the footwear industrial cluster, there are at least three groups of footwear industry involved which are divided into:

1. The upstream industry, which consists of leather tanning industry, artificial leather industry, crumb rubber industry, yarn spinning industry, and aromatic chemicals industry.
2. The inbetween industry, which is comprised of rubber/plastic soles industry, accessories industry made of metal, weaving cloth industry (canvas, ply fabric, and cloth tape), embroidery industry (labels), adhesive/glue industry, shoe laces and knitting industry.
3. The downstream industry, which consists of the footwear industry for daily use, sport shoe industry, technical shoe industry (for industrial purposes), and other footwear industry.

These three industries are the main target of the industrial cluster development so hopefully these three industries can work together to achieve the goals and objectives of the development of national footwear industrial cluster.

In the guideline of the footwear industrial cluster, the goals and objectives of this industrial cluster are divided into two time periods, medium-term goals (from 2010-2014) and long-term goals (from 2010-2015). Both have their own qualitative and quantitative goals and objectives.

---

298 Cf. ibid., p. 194.

The medium-term goals and objectives are as follows:[299]

1. The medium-term qualitative targets consist of:
    a. The development of the national shoe brand to meet the needs of domestic demands and to be gradually directed to be able to compete in the international market,
    b. The increasing numbers of export destinations especially for shoes that have a high value added and competitive advantage (uniqueness) such as party shoes,
    c. The increasing use of domestic demand in local shoe products,
    d. The decreasing number of imported shoe products and a lesser activity of illegal and unfair import practices,
    e. The creation of a supportive (friendly) business environment,
    f. The increasing numbers of supporting industries and the lessening dependence over imported raw materials, and
    g. The increasing competitiveness of local footwear product in the international market.
2. The quantitative targets consist of
    a. The increasing number of an annual average export value by 10 percent so that in the year of 2014 the export value of the footwear will reach USD 3.2 billion,
    b. A significant addition to the number of total workforces in the national footwear industry that reaches an annual average 4 percent per year, and
    c. An additional of new investment and an enhancement of the old investment by USD 500 million per year.

Meanwhile, the long-term goals and objectives are:

1. The following qualitative targets:
    a. The national brand has dominated the domestic and international market,
    b. An increase in the number of employment for footwear industry sector,
    c. The increasing role of footwear industry in the national economic growth,

299 Cf. Departemen Perindustrian 2009a, pp. 201-02.

   d. The strong development of footwear industrial cluster as a supporting partner of the growth of SMEs in order to increase the role of SMEs as well as to create business and employment opportunities,
   e. A solid structure of footwear industrial structure and the growth of other supporting industries,
   f. The increasing role of the research and development institutions in technology, designs, and human resources sectors, and
   g. The increasing role of the footwear industry cluster in the development of the footwear industry outside Java Island.
2. The following quantitative targets:
   a. Indonesia is seen as a world-class footwear exporter with a 7 percent market share value,
   b. An additional number of workforces in the footwear industry by 10,000 workers per year, and
   c. An additional of new investment and an enhancement of old investment by USD 500 million per year.

Looking at the goals or targets above, we can come into conclusion that in the mid-term range, the target achievements are the development of the national shoe brands to fulfill domestic market (demand) and to campaign the use of local product while in the long-term range is more focused on the improvement of the quality of local shoe product through research and development as well as to strengthen the industrial cluster for competing in the international market. To achieve those goals and targets, it is necessary to design some strategies and policies in the development of footwear cluster industry.[300] These strategies and policies are based on the vision of the footwear industry, which is to make Indonesia as a world-class footwear exporter and to improve its product competitiveness by strengthening the production (supply-push) and creating market (demand-pull). These strategies and policies are focused upon the strengthening of industrial institutions (micro) and to create a better business environment (macro). The following table describes the general strategies of the development of the national footwear industry.

300 Cf. Departemen Perindustrian 2009a, pp. 203-12.

Table 5.1: General Strategy of Footwear Industry Development

	Micro	Macro
Supply-Push	a. Developing of the supporting industry (tanning leather, synthetic leather, rubber, and accessories), b. Improving of human resource ability and productivity, c. Improving product quality, d. Increasing the role of research and development agencies, e. Improving technological aspect in the footwear industry.	a. Giving incentive especially to the new investment of the footwear supporting industry, b. Creating a supportive bussiness environment (through local [government] regulations), c. Strengthening the footwear industry structure and building a relation with the small medium enterprises/industries, d. Strengthening infrastructure facility to support the development of industrial cluster, e. Giving easy access / facility for loans / capital with a competitive interest.
Demand-Pull	a. Developing national shoe's brands, b. Improving design and product quality, c. Promoting product diversity, d. Increasing promotion and advertisement in the local and international market, Improving the export value by improving the ability to control networks in the export market, e. Increasing the use of local footwear domestically.	a. Developing the domestic market by improving the quality and the use of local (national) product, b. Improving the surveillance of the illegal (import) activity, c. Facilitating the billateral and multilateral economic cooperations in order to enhance export market, d. Facilitating the participation of local industries in international exhibitions.

Source: Departemen Perindustrian 2009a, p. 204

There are several main focuses in implementing the above strategies. *First*, in developing the national footwear industry, it also has to develop relevant supporting industries for such as: (a) a core industry like casual leather shoes, formal leather shoes, leather sandals, and sport shoes made from synthetic leather, (b) a supporting industry like leather tanning, processed rubber industry (for shoe soles), component industries and yarn industries, and (c) a related industries, like packaging industries, machinery industries, lasting and molding, labels industries, and shoelaces industries.

Second, the strategy to promote the development of technology is directed to reorganize equipment and machinery including its supporting industry, to improve designs, and to strengthen research and development institutions.[301] Examples of technology sector that being developed are: the development of eco-friendly leather tanning technology; the prevention and extermination of pests and diseases as well as foot and mouth disease virus (FMD) that involves the Institute of Research and Community Empowerment of the Bogor Agricultural University, the Yogyakarta Leather Technology Academy (*Akademi Teknologi Kulit*, ATK), the Yogyakarta Center for Leather, Rubber, and Plastics (*Balai Besar Kulit, Karet, dan Plastik Yogyakarta*, BBKKP), and Gadjah Mada University (Yogyakarta); the rubber processing technology development which is processed raw rubber material into sport shoes and formal shoes soles that involves the North Sumatera Rubber Research Institute, the BBKKP, the ATK, and the Bogor Plantation Research Institute (*Balai Penelitian Perkebunan*, BPP); the development of molding machinery to make footwear that involves Institut Teknologi Sepuluh November (ITS) Surabaya and the BBKKP; and the development of synthetic leather making technology that involves Petrokimia Gresik Corp. and the Agency for the Assessment and Application of Technology (*Badan Pengkajian dan Penerapan Teknologi*, BPPT).

Third is the strategy to improve the workforce's abilities and productivity. This improvement is essential to be delivered because the type of this cluster is a labor-intensive industry. The third focus is based on the research conducted by Aspiranti, Nurfahmiyati, and Sundaya (2008) who found that one of the main problem faced by the Cibaduyut shoe industry is in the production management aspect as a result of the lower level of education in their workforce.[302] Therefore, the aspect of human resource has to be constantly improved especially in fields that are related with technology and design production, the skills of using sewing machine,

301 Cf. Departemen Perindustrian 2009a, pp. 205-06.
302 Cf. Aspiranti et al. 2008, p. 1.

shoelast making process, sewing method, and the creation of patterns and standard sizing.

Fourth, related to the development of marketing products, there are several to be done as follows.[303] In developing the domestic market, there are some strategies to be offered which are: introducing national brands to local people, encouraging the domestic market/people to use local products through cooperation with government institutions and business actors, setting up tax sales reduction so that the products' cost can be competitive with imported brand, and giving protection to the domestic products through a non-tariff policy. Meanwhile, in developing networking in the international market can be done by: building communications with importer countries especially those with international brand holders, improving the product quality and establishing international standard in the product to strengthen exports activities, opening the non-conventional market (e-commerce) through Indonesian product's promotion, and improving communications with the designated export countries.

The locations of the cluster development according to the Regulation of the Ministry of Industry are as follows:[304]

a. A core industry, is divided into: (1) sport shoes, that will be developed in Tangerang and Serang (Banten), Bekasi and Bandung (Jawa Barat), Surabaya, Mojokerto, Sidoarjo, Pasuruan (East Java), also Medan and Deli Serdang (North Sumatera), (2) casual and formal shoes, that will be developed in Bandung and Bogor (West Java), Sidoarjo, Magetan, Mojokerto (East Java), Medan (North Sumatera), and Yogyakarta, and also (3) sandals which are being developed in Tangerang (Banten), Bogor and Bandung (West Java) as well as Sidoarjo and Mojokerto (East Java).
b. A supporting and related industry, is divided into: (1) leather tanning industry, that will be developed in Surabaya, Malang, Pasuruan (East Java), Bogor, Bandung, Garut (West Java), Tangerang and Serang (Banten), Magelang and Semarang (Central Java), Yogyakarta, Jakarta, Padang Panjang (West Sumatera) as well as Medan and Deli Serdang (North Sumatera), (2) rubber soles and accessories industry which are developed in North Sumatera and West Java, (3) synthetic leather industry, that will be

303 Cf. Departemen Perindustrian 2009a, p. 207.
304 Cf. ibid., pp. 216-17.

developed in the area of Banten and Central Java, and (4) accessories industry from textile and metal that will be developed in the area of Banten, West Java and East Java.

The above goals and strategies will be implemented by involving government and non-governmental institutions. Those institutions are: the Ministry of Industry, the Ministry of Cooperatives and SMEs, the Ministry of Education and Culture, the Ministry of Manpower and Transmigration, the Ministry of Finance, the Ministry of Trade, the Ministry of Agriculture, the Ministry of Public Work, the Ministry of Transportation, the Ministry of Foreign Affairs, Bank Indonesia (Indonesian Central Bank), the National Standardization Agency of Indonesia (*Badan Standardisasi Nasional*, BSN), the Indonesia Investment Coordinating Board (*Badan Koordinasi Penanaman Modal*, BKPM), the Indonesian Institute of Sciences (*Lembaga Ilmu Pengetahuan Indonesia*, LIPI), local governments (including related offices/agencies), and universities as well as research centers. The following table describes the involvement of those institutions in working together to run the programs of the development of the national footwear industrial cluster.

Table 5.2: Medium-term Plan of the Footwear Cluster Industry Development, 2010-2014

No.	Programs/Action Plans	Stakeholder(s)
1.	Improving investments for supporting industry by giving facilities and easy of doing business	Ministry of Industry, Ministry of Finance, BKPM, local/regional governments
2.	Improving the role of research and development institutions to develop the main and substitution materials, supporting materials, and accessories	Ministry of Industry, LIPI, local/regional governments, research and development institutions, universities
3.	Simplifing the procedure for importing the raw leather materials	Ministry of Industry, Ministry of Trade, Ministry of Finance
4.	Improving the quality of raw skin in the abattoir	Ministry of Industry, Ministry of Agriculture, local/regional governments
5.	Developing the domestic farm animals	Ministry of Agriculture, local/regional governments

6.	Improving the quality and product's diversity of the leather imitation industry	Ministry of Industry, research and development institutions, universities
7.	Strengthening the leather tanning industries' UPT by supporting the availability of the raw leather materials to increase services for small industries in order to support the availability of raw materials	Ministry of Industry, Ministry of Finance, local/regional governments
8.	Improving the human resource skills in designs and production technique through workshops and internships	Ministry of Industry, Ministry of Cooperatives and SMEs, Ministry of Education and Culture, Ministry of Manpower and Transmigration, universities
9.	Improving the footwear quality through the application of product standard and quality management	Ministry of Industry, Ministry of Manpower and Transmigration, BSN, universities
10.	Improving the use of technology through revitalizing/restructuring machinary and industrial equipment	Ministry of Industry, Ministry of Cooperatives and SMEs, Ministry of Finance, universities
11.	Improving coordination with stakeholders which related to employment policies, minimum wages, and employment terminations.	Ministry of Industry, Ministry of Manpower and Transmigration, local/regional governments
12.	Improving coordination for infrastructure improvements for industry	Ministry of Industry, local/regional governments
13.	Facilitating working groups and cluster's facilitators to work upon strategic alliance	Ministry of Finance, Bank Indonesia
14.	Improving coordination of buying raw materials through fiscal incentive and the removal of value added tax	Ministry of Industry, Ministry of Trade, Ministry of Finance, Bank Indonesia
15.	Deregulating permits/regulations and reviewing local regulations that are not pro-investment to promote investment expansion or to have new investment	Ministry of Industry, Ministry of Finance, BKPM, local/regional governments
16.	Improving and promoting national shoe brands to the domestic and international market	Ministry of Industry, Ministry of Trade, Ministry of Foreign Affairs

17.	Improving the road condition so that the transportation of goods from the industrial locations to the market place can be done smoothly	Ministry of Public Work, Ministry of Transportation, local/regional governments
18.	Building and developing ports at the particular business locations	Ministry of Public Work, Jasa Marga, PT Pelindo
19.	Promoting cooperations with local market (malls and department stores) and building a specialized footwear market place	Ministry of Industry, Ministry of Trade, local/regional governments
20.	Improving the potential international markets through international cooperations	Ministry of Industry, Ministry of Trade, Ministry of Foreign Affairs
21.	Improving promotion and advertisement in the local and international markets through exhibition	Ministry of Industry, Ministry of Trade, Ministry of Foreign Affairs

Source: Departemen Perindustrian 2009a, pp. 213-15

Looking at Regulation of the Minister of Industry of the Republic of Indonesia No. 110/M-IND/PER/10/2009 on the Roadmap of the Development of the Footwear Industrial Cluster, the expected type of business cluster in Cibaduyut is the Markusen's Marshallian industrial district (with the Italianate variant)[305] or Tambunan's dynamic cluster.[306] According to Markusen's types of clusters, the Marshallian Italianate variant is characterized by: (a) a high degree of cooperation among firms to share risks and innovation in order to stabilize market, (b) a strong involvement of both business associations and local governments, (c) the involvement of business associations to provide training, marketing information, technical and financial assistance to help firms within the district as well as provide forums to set up collective strategy to expand the cluster, and (d) the role of local governments to regulate and promote core industries within the district. While a dynamic cluster is characterized by more active cluster in terms of expand trade networks with international markets, use more advance technology, bigger firm's size, and served more prominent markets.

305 Cf. Markusen 1996, p. 298.
306 Cf. Tambunan 2009a, p. 41.

5.1.2 The Development of the Pottery and Decorative Ceramic Industry Cluster

The development of pottery and decorative ceramic industry is developed based on the National Industrial Policy, which regulates the development of particular small and medium cluster industries.[307] The pottery and decorative ceramic industry that are mentioned in the road map of national cluster development consist of clay/ceramic industries, industries of building materials made of clay/ceramics, and other clays/ceramic industries. The development of this industrial cluster is regulated in Regulation of the Minister of Industry of the Republic of Indonesia No. 135/M-IND/PER/10/2009.[308] This guideline is compiled as: (a) an operational guideline for all government agencies to support, complementary and synergistic, the successful of the implementation of the industrial development programs in accordance with each agency's duty, (b) a guideline for actors and stakeholders in the footwear cluster industry, including employers and other institutions to actively involve in the industrial cluster, and (c) a guideline for making cross-sectoral coordination as well as between related government institutions whether at the national level or local (provincial and districts) level.[309] Referring to those three objectives, it can be concluded that the guideline is used to provide guidance to the central and local government institutions as well as the industrial actors in synergizing programs to encourage the creation of a stronger national footwear industry sector, so that they could combine their planned programs to improve the pottery and ceramic industry as a local economic driving force (in terms of number of unit, number of worker, and increasing the total production value).

The understanding of pottery industry is the industry that made from raw clay into pottery production process.[310] While a decorative ceramic industry is the industry that turns raw clay, feldspar, silica sand, and kaolin into a decorative ceramics production process.[311] According to Regulation of the Minister of Industry of the Republic of Indonesia No. 135/M-

307 Cf. Chapter 2 of Presidential Decree No. 28/2008.
308 See Departemen Perindustrian 2009b, pp. 63-94.
309 Cf. ibid., p. 68.
310 Cf. ibid., p. 73.
311 Cf. ibid.

IND/PER/10/2009, the pottery and decorative ceramic industry is grouped into:

1. The upstream industry, which includes the pottery and decorative ceramic material industries, such as clay, kaolin, feldspar, quartz sand, zircon, and toseki,
2. The inbetween industry, which includes the ceramic body materials, coloring materials and glaze, and
3. The downstream industry, which includes the pottery industry such as house ware and decoration pottery, also decorative ceramics such as tableware and gift items.

The three industrial groups mentioned above are located in four different locations, which are in Plered (West Java), Kasongan (Yogyakarta), Banyumulek (West Lombok), and Tabanan (Bali).

Like the footwear industrial cluster, the development of pottery and decorative ceramic industrial cluster also has targets which are divided into two different terms namely the middle-term targets (2010-2014) and the long-term targets (2010-2025).[312] The middle term targets for the development of pottery and decorative ceramics industrial cluster are:

a. The establishment of a decorative ceramic industrial cluster that can drive the development of other pottery and ceramic industry by a rate of 3.79 percent annually or 1,243 new business units per year, the increasing number of workforces in this sector by a rate of 3.68 percent annually or 5,219 new employees per year, and the increasing amount of production value by a rate of 6.49 percent annually or IDR 6.863 billion per year,
b. To provide raw materials not only from the company itself but also from the technical services unit in the potential sectors so that craftsmen and SMEs can perform better and create high quality products,
c. To create at least five potteries and decorative ceramic companies that apply the CE-Marking[313] dan 10 companies that apply ISO

312 Cf. Departemen Perindustrian 2009b, p. 75-76.

313 CE-Marking is a sign that the product is produced in accordance with trade regulations in the EU and the product is allowed to be sold in the EU region.

9000[314] to improve the productivity and to enter their potteries and ceramics into European market,

d. To create a Product Quality Control (*Gugus Kendali Mutu Produk*) in 30 export-oriented pottery and decorative ceramic companies (elected company is carefully selected).

Meanwhile, the long-term targets for the development of pottery and decorative ceramic industrial cluster are:

a. Forming a pottery and decorative ceramic cluster industry's system with a solid business network and is supported by strong subsystems. It is expected that until 2025, the total number of business will increase in average of 8.34 percent or 3,045 business units per year, an increase of the total employment by 5.2 percent or in average 10,212 people per year, and the average of production of 18.4 percent per year,
b. The availability of raw materials by the technical service units or other private companies in the 41 potential potteries and decorative ceramic's sentra,
c. The realization of national pottery and decorative ceramic that can compete in the domestic and international market so that there will be an increase in the value of export of the pottery and ceramic by 23.49 percent or up to USD 11,013,403 per year,
d. The establishment of at least 30 companies that apply CE-Marking and 55 companies that apply ISO 9000 as well as the establishment of a Product Quality Control for as many as 225 small medium enterprises in collaboration with large industries.

To achieve the above objectives, it is necessary to design a strategy and policy for the development of pottery and decorative ceramic industrial cluster.[315] These strategies and policies are based on the vision of the pottery and decorative ceramic industry, which is to build pottery and decorative ceramics industry nationwide which has national and international competitiveness and a high value added in 2025. To achieve these objectives, the strategy and policy for a cluster development of pottery and dec-

314 ISO 9000 is a standard management system designed to help a company in order to meet the interests of buyers and other stakeholders.

315 Cf. Departemen Perindustrian 2009b, pp. 77-80.

orative ceramic is focused on an increasing value added of these products by strengthening the value chain in all industries from upstream industry, inbetween industry, to downstream industry. There are seven stages of the implementation of those strategies and policies which focus on: a stage of cluster development and decorative ceramic pottery (which is done by implementing diagnosis, socialization, collaboration, implementation, and monitoring patterns), a stage of development of the business groups (which is done to ease the empowerment of existing business units), a stage of cooperation between stakeholders and business community (which is done to create synergies and cooperation by promoting coaching and development programs), a stage of increasing the capability of human resources in pottery and decorative ceramic's small industries (which is done through training to improve skills in technical aspects of the production, design, and production management), stage of modernization of machinery and equipment (to increase the quality and quantity of the product), a stage of strengthening development and institutional capability (to improve access to capital and market as well as to gain a better bargaining position in the market), and a stage of developing networking (which is done by the synchronization and harmonization of policies and programs across sectors to develop pottery and decorative ceramics industry nationwide).

In the Regulation of the Minister of Industry, it is also regulated programs and medium-term action plans (2010-2014) and long-term action plans (2010-2025) to develop pottery and decorative ceramics industry nationwide.[316] The medium-term action plans are focused on:

1. Promotion and marketing, which includes: facilitating the promotion and marketing through exhibitions at home and abroad, developing (potential) market which is associated with tourism activities, building a portal system for the purposes of widening information on the international (export) market, making a comparative study involving entrepreneurs and craftsmen abroad, promoting local products through print media (leaflets and catalogs) and electronics, joining the design competition abroad, as well as preparing directory of the national pottery and decorative ceramic,
2. Production Technology, which include: improving the quality management system, raising awareness to implement IPR, dis-

316 Cf. Departemen Perindustrian 2009b, pp. 81-84.

seminating and implementing of the CE-Marking and ISO 9000 systems to the business units, establishing the national product quality control as well as strengthening the role of universities and research centers in production techniques,

3. The strengthening of the business structure, that includes: increasing partnerships with major companies to pioneer the export market and to implement a transfer knowledge, conducting partnerships with suppliers/producers of raw materials, facilitating partnerships with relevant agencies in order to utilize insurance and export financing, conducting a collaboration with countries that have excellence in design and models as well as mapping the potential types of raw materials and their utilization,
4. Human resources, which includes: increasing human resource capacity building in the field of design, increasing the ability of conducting export-import activity and negotiation techniques, increasing knowledge in the area of product quality, and increasing the ability and knowledge of utilizing websites and e-commerce to promote their products,
5. The improvement of facilities and infrastructure, which includes: modernizing machinery and equipments in the technical services unit, providing assistance as well as machinery and equipment to potential business groups, providing assistance to build information networking, and regulating the role of organization and technical services unit,
6. The development of supporting institutions and organization that includes: building a direct service unit (*unit pelayanan langsung*, UPL) and revitalizing technical services unit in the potential *sentra*.

Meanwhile, the long-term action plans are focused on:

1. Marketing sector, which includes: the development of specific market for pottery and decorative ceramic products, improving mapping capabilities for market penetration and expansion of international markets, the development of showroom/outlet in the tourist centers in and outside the country as well as promoting collaboration with hotels and location of tourism to market their products as souvenir items,
2. Technology sector, which includes: the development of production machinery and equipment to process potteries and ceramic

crafts, establishing a pottery and ceramic certified qualification agency at the potential *sentra* to fulfill the CE-Marking, and improving product designs by computerized system,

3. *Sentra* of production (production center), which includes: strengthening the agency of pottery and ceramic producer groups (such as associations, cooperative, and business groups), developing communication and business networking through internet and e-commerce, and promoting *sentra* as a tourism shopping destination and study sites,
4. Cooperation with the stakeholders, which includes the development of SMIs' networking with universities and research institutions for technology development and product design as well as technology development and standardization of raw materials and products in collaboration with the Center for Ceramics and regional/local technical service units (*unit pelayanan teknis daerah*, UPTD).

There are many institutions, both government and non-governmental institutions, that are involved in running the strategies of the pottery and decorative ceramic industry development. They are: the Ministry of Industry, the Ministry of Cooperatives and SMEs, the Ministry of Finance, the Ministry of Education and Culture, the Ministry of Manpower and Transmigration, the Ministry of Justice and Human Rights, the Ministry of Trade, the Ministry of Public Work, the Ministry of Transportation, the Ministry of Foreign Affairs, the Ministry of Research and Technology, the Ministry of State-owned Enterprises, the Ministry of Energy and Mineral Resources, the Ministry of Forestry, the National Development Planning Agency (*Badan Perencanaan dan Pembangunan Nasional*, Bappenas), Bank Indonesia (Indonesian Central Bank), the BSN, the BPPT, the LIPI, local governments (including related offices/agencies), and universities as well as research centers. Cooperation among the agencies above can be seen in more detail in the following table.

Table 5.3: The Development of Pottery and Decorative Ceramic Industry Cluster's Programs and Action Plans

No.	Programs	Action Plans	Stakeholder(s)
1.	Development of a conducive business environment.	a. Provide guidance and easiness in handling (business) license	Ministry of Industry, local/ regional government
		b. Provide fiscal incentives to support business units	Ministry of Industry, Ministry of Finance
		c. Provide guidance and easiness of the arrangement of intellectual property rights	Ministry of Industry, Ministry of Justice and Human Rights
		d. Provide market access to domestic market especially related to the security of pottery and ceramic products	Ministry of Industry, Bappenas, Ministry of Trade, Ministry of Cooperatives and SMEs
		e. Support the provision of easy credit financing scheme for SMIs	Ministry of Industry, Bappenas, Ministry of State-owned Enterprises, Ministry of Finance, Ministry of Cooperatives and SMEs, Bank Indonesia, and other private banks/non-bank financial institutions
		f. Provide easy availability of domestic raw materials for pottery and decorative ceramics industry	Ministry of Industry, Ministry of Trade, Ministry of Energy and Mineral Resources, Ministry of Forestry
		g. Provide support to develop institutions/ agencies to improve the competency of human resources for	Ministry of Industry, Ministry of Manpower and Transmigration, Ministry of Education and Culture, Ministry of

			industrial pottery and decorative	State-owned Enterprises, local/ regional governments
		h.	Support the development of research and development institution in the field of development of raw materials, technology, and design for pottery and decorative ceramics industry	Ministry of Industry, Ministry of Research and Technology, Ministry of Education and Culture, BPPT, LIPI, universities
2.	Development of Maketing and Promotion	a.	Facilitate the organization of exhibitions and participate in the exhibitions at home and abroad	Ministry of Industry, Ministry of Trade, Ministry of State-owned Enterprises, local/regional governments
		b.	Facilitate positioning and branding products of the decorative ceramic pottery industry	Ministry of Industry, Ministry of Trade, universities, business actors
		c.	Facilitate business meeting and partnerships with local and international potential buyers	Ministry of Industry, local/regional governments, business actors
		d.	Facilitate the expansion of the market through bilateral cooperation, regional, and multilateral export target countries	Ministry of Industry, Ministry of Trade
		e.	Facilitate intensive promotion for products produced by the pottery and decorative ceramics industry (through brochures, advertisements, and catalogs)	Ministry of Industry, Ministry of Trade, Ministry of State-owned Enterprises, local/regional governments

3.	Development of technology standards and product quality	a.	Facilitate the availability of experts to serve as mentors in applying product design and packaging according to the pottery and ceramic market potentials	Ministry of Industry, universities, business actors
		b.	Facilitate the availability of experts in mentoring the establishment of quality management system (CE-Marking dan ISO 9000)	Ministry of Industry, universities, business actors
		c.	Facilitate the availability of experts in mentoring the establishment of product standardization and production process standardization	Ministry of Industry, universities, business actors
		d.	Facilitate the availability of experts in giving guidance upon the utilization and treatment of efficient production technology	Ministry of Industry, universities, business actors
		e.	Facilitate the availability of experts in choosing and storaging raw and supportiing materials for the pottery and ceramic industry	Ministry of Industry, universities, business actors
4.	Development of human resources competency	a.	Facilitate training to improve capability in technology, business, entrepreneurship, and management	Ministry of Industry, Ministry of Trade, Ministry of State-owned Enterprises, Ministry of Education and Culture, Ministry of Manpower and Transmigration, lo-

				cal/ regional governments, universities
		b.	Facilitate internships and comparative studies within and outside the country	Ministry of Industry, universities, business actors
		c.	Facilitate the development of business incubators	Ministry of Industry, universities, Ministry of State-owned Enterprises, business actors
5.	Access to raw materials development	a.	Facilitate securing the supply of quality raw materials for SMIs	Ministry of Industry, Ministry of Trade, Ministry of State-owned Enterprises, local/regional governments
		b.	Facilitate encouraging the use of raw materials and auxiliary materials that are environmentally friendly	Ministry of Industry, Ministry of Research and Technology, BPPT, LIPI, logal/regional governments
6.	Financial access development	a.	Facilitate the capability to access financial institutions through supervision and advocacy in the preparation of proposal and improve the company's bookkeeping	Ministry of Industry, Ministry of Cooperatives and SMEs, Ministry of Finance, Bank Indonesia, local/ regional governments, universities
		b.	Facilitating business meetings with banks and financial institutions as well as state-owned enterprises	Ministry of Industry, Ministry of Cooperatives and SMEs, Ministry of Finance, Bank Indonesia, local/ regional governments, universities
		c.	Facilitate the creation of business profiles for SMIs to gain easy access to financing	Ministry of Industry, Ministry of Cooperatives and SMEs, Ministry of Finance, Bank Indonesia, local/ regional

				governments, universities
7.	Business institutional development	a.	Facilitate the development and improvements of ascociations, business groups, cooperative, and technical services unit for SMEs	Ministry of Industry, Ministry of Cooperatives and SMEs, local/ regional governments, universities
		b.	Facilitate the development and strengthening of supporting technical services unit and business development service (BDS) to act more as a center of excellence as a means of self-reliance and innovation of pottery and decorative ceramic industry	Ministry of Industry, Ministry of State-owned Enterprises, BPPT, local/ regional governments, universities
		c.	Facilitate the development of business center as a means of market testing and consumer behavior learning	Ministry of Industry, Ministry of Cooperatives and SMEs, Ministry of State-owned Enterprises, local/ regional governments, universities, business actors
		d.	Increase cooperation with universities, businesses, and practitioners to empower SMIs thr-ough the OVOP approach	Ministry of Industry, Ministry of State-owned Enterprises, Ministry of Trade, Bank Indonesia, Bappenas, BPPT, local/ regional governments, universities
8.	Improve the capability of research and development (R&D)	a.	Facilitate the development of eco-friendly raw materials	Ministry of Industry, Ministry of Research and Technology, Ministry of Education and Culture, BPPT, LIPI, universities

	b.	Facilitate the development of appropriate technological innovations that are more efficient, effective, and productive	Ministry of Industry, Ministry of Research and Technology, Ministry of Education and Culture, BPPT, LIPI, universities
	c.	Facilitate the development of innovation designed to anticipate global trends	Ministry of Industry, Ministry of Trade, universities, business actors
	d.	Facilitate the development of product standards and process standards of pottery and decorative ceramic industry	Ministry of Industry, Ministry of Trade, BSN, universities, business actors
	e.	Facilitate benchmarking products, trends, and market opportunities for SMIs	Ministry of Industry, Ministry of Trade, universities, business actors
	f.	Facilitate the exploration of the potential of small-scale industries of pottery and ceramics decorative medium in the region	Ministry of Industry, local/regional government, universities, business actors

Source: Data is modified from Departemen Perindustrian 2009b, pp. 89-93

Looking at Regulation of the Minister of Industry of the Republic of Indonesia No. 135/M-IND/PER/10/2009 on the Roadmap of the Development of the Pottery and Decorative Ceramic Industrial Cluster, the expected type of business cluster in Plered is the Enright's working cluster.[317] This is due to the location of this cluster which can be categorized as a remote area. According to Enright (1997), a working cluster is characterized by having companies that are connected to each other and operated collectively to produce more products. Thus, it is expected that this cluster can

317 Cf. Rosenfeld 1997, p. 10.

share information among SMEs/SMIs, ignite new ideas, make networking with medium and large enterprises, and promote new firm start-ups.

5.2 Profile of the Cibaduyut Footwear Industrial Cluster

The Cibaduyut Footwear Industrial Cluster is located in the southern part of the city of Bandung and is approximately 5 km away from downtown Bandung. The total area of this industrial cluster is around 14 km^2, and includes five villages in the city of Bandung and three villages in the regency of Bandung. The detail of this footwear industrial cluster area is comprised of: the sub-district of Kebon Lega, the sub-district of Cibaduyut, the sub-district of Cibaduyut Wetan, the sub-district of Cibaduyut Kidul, the sub-district of Mekarwangi, the village of Cangkuang Kulon, the village of Cangkuang Wetan, and the village of Sukamenak.

The birth of this cluster began in 1918 when several senior Cibaduyut residents learnt how to make shoes and worked in a shoe factory in Bandung. Since 1920, this area has emerged as a collection of small businesses (home industries) that produces shoes even with unskilled employees. The employees who worked in this business were not official employees, but are family members who got a lesson on how to make shoes autodidactly. These business units were initially produced only to fulfill shoe orders from the community and individuals. In 1920, there were around 15 official business units registered in the Cibaduyut region.

Since 1976-1977, the Cibaduyut Shoe cluster has received special attention from the central government. The government via the Ministry of Industry, the Office of the Ministry of Industry in the West Java Province and the Institute for Social and Economic Research, Education and Information (*Lembaga Penelitian Pendidikan Penerangan Ekonomi dan Sosial,* LP3ES) intended to develop this shoe cluster as a means of enlarging job opportunities and promoting the economic development in the area. The task carried by these three institutions was to conduct some research and development in order to guide and develop the Cibaduyut Shoe Industry.

Based on the results of such studies, the technical services unit for Cibaduyut leather products (*Unit Pelaksana Teknis (UPT) Barang Kulit Cibaduyut*) was formed. This service center facility aimed to provide guidance and training to increase the skill of the craftsmen in Cibaduyut as well as to develop the region of Cibaduyut as an industrial cluster. A concrete result of the service center facility (together with the Cooperative of Indonesian Leather and Shoes/KOPSI) was the establishment of two showrooms in Cibaduyut. The aim of these showrooms is to promote and to sell leather products made by the craftsmen to the public.

In 2003, the Service Center Facility for Cibaduyut Leather Products changed its name to the Office for Developing the Small and Medium-sized Shoe Industry in Cibaduyut (*Instalasi Pengembangan Industri Kecil Menengah Persepatuan Cibaduyut*). This office works under the supervision and coordination of the West Java Office of Trade. The focus of this office is to provide training to increase the quality and quantity of shoe production in the cluster. Therefore, the objectives of this office are to: (a) increase revenues of the businessmen and labor income; (b) increase productivity and the work efficiency of the shoemaker, (c) provide guidance and training that can add to the knowledge of the craftsmen not only about the shoe-making process but also about other insights to support their business; and (d) be a facilitator and an innovator for business actors in Cibaduyut.

Since 2006, the government has conducted a study to identify and map potential (core) footwear industries, supporting industries, and other related industries in West Java and West Java ultimately chose as one entry point to develop national footwear industrial clusters.[318] By 2008, there were about 867 business units in the Cibaduyut Footwear Business Cluster which employed 3,613 workers with a total annual production that reached 4,952,780 pairs of shoes.[319] The Cibaduyut Footwear Business Cluster has been known for a long time not only as a tourist area but also as a center of trade and shopping. Moreover, this region is also considered to have the potential to be a tourist area where educational institutions like schools and colleges could use this industrial area as a place to conduct research as well as to encourage vocational education.

There are several characteristics that are embedded in the Cibaduyut's SMEs. *First*, there is no clear division of work between administrative (the owner) and operational (the employees) levels. Individuals who work as an owner as well as an employee of the company manage most of these SMEs. Therefore, sometimes the owner disregards the separation of company and personal affairs. They often use the company's money for personal expenses and vice versa.

318 Cf. Departemen Perindustrian 2009a, p. 208.

319 Cf. Instalasi Pengembang Industri Kecil Menengah Alas Kaki/Persepatuan Bandung 2008.

Second, most of these SMEs have low access to formal financial institutions. Most of them rely heavily on their own money and savings or they borrow from relatives, other enterprises owners, or even illegal money lender (usurer) to finance their expenditures.

Third, most of these SMEs are categorized as informal economic units (illegal entities). Therefore, these SMEs find it hard to get loans/credits from financial services. In the city of Bandung, there were about 25,793 non-formal small enterprises which work in the industry and trade sector in 2008 and the number has increased to 101,264 non-formal small enterprises in 2009.[320] The percentages of these non formal small enterprises were 70.27 percent in 2008 and 92.08 percent in 2009.[321]

Fourth, these SMEs' products are generally categorized as a very labor intensive product. Since the employees have no formal education and entrepreneurial spirit, most of their products are characterized as a handmade product. The consequence is that their products occasionally have problems with precisions and are difficult to be standardized.

Tulus Tambunan added several characteristics of Indonesian SMEs that can be found in Cibaduyut as follows.[322] *First*, most of these SMEs are owned by local or indigenous people (the Sundanese and Javanese people). *Second*, another unique characteristic is the low participation of female entrepreneurs in CIbaduyut. The BPS stated that in 2010, the comparison of male and female workers in the leather, leather products, and footwear industries is 92,284 male workers to 22,211 female workers.[323] This shows that male workers are dominant in this sector by 80.6 percent.

5.2.1 The Importance of the Cibaduyut Footwear Industrial Cluster and its SMEs/SMIs to West Java's Economic Performance

Like other countries, the Indonesian government and the provincial government of West Java have the responsibility for promoting economic growth at national and local levels to increase people's welfare in general and the welfare of the West Javans in particular. In order to achieve this

320 Cf. Dinas KUKM dan Perindag Kota Bandung (n.d.).

321 The percentage is resulted from the number of non-formal small enterprises divided by the total number of enterprises including small, medium, large and non-formal small enterprises.

322 Cf. Tambunan 2008b, pp. 112-14, Tambunan 2009c, p. 1.

323 Cf. Badan Pusat Statistik 2010, p. 45.

goal, the president of the Republic of Indonesia, President Susilo Bambang Yudhoyono (SBY) said his concern is to overcome unemployment and poverty. His concern is then formulated into a triple track strategy: pro-growth, pro-jobs and pro-poor.[324] The *first* track is to increase economic growth by prioritizing the export sector and investments. The *second* track is to promote the real sector to create jobs. The last track is to revitalize agriculture, forestry, marine and rural economy to reduce poverty. Following President SBY's strategy, it is not surprising that SMEs/SMIs in the Cibaduyut Footwear Industrial Cluster should earn priority in the implementation of this strategy for a number of reasons.

First, SMEs in Cibaduyut play a vital role in the structure of West Java's and the city of Bandung's economic performance. In the city of Bandung, there are about ten potential industrial/business clusters.[325] They are: the Cibaduyut Footwear Industrial Cluster, the Cihampelas Jeans Cluster, the Suci T-shirt and Screen Printing Cluster, the Binong Jati Knitting Industrial Cluster, the Cigondewah Textile and Textile Products Business Cluster, the Cibuntu Tofu and Tempeh Cluster, the Kiaracondong Automotives' Spare Parts Cluster, the Muncang Puppet Products Cluster, and the Leuwipanjang Bag Cluster. The following table shows the (economic) potential generated by the Cibaduyut Footwear Industrial Cluster in terms of number of existing units, number of employees, number of annual shoe production, total investment, and the production value.

324 Cf. http://www.presidenri.go.id/index.php/topik/2006/12/21/44.html, accessed September 18, 2012.

325 Cf. "Surat Keputusan Walikota Bandung No. 530/Kep.295-DISKUKM.PERINDAG/2009", Dinas KUKM dan Perindag Kota Bandung, http://diskopukmperindagbdg.blogspot.de/p/profile.html, accessed September 26, 2012.

Table 5.4: Production Potential in the Cibaduyut Footwear Industrial Cluster

No.	Potential	Year			
		2005	2006	2007	2008
1.	Business Unit	845	828	847	867
2.	Worker	3,556	3,498	3,516	3,613
3.	Annual Production (pair of shoes)	4,046,700	3,310,800	4,546,300	4,952,780
4.	Investment (in thousand IDR)	23,720,675	14,570,160	14,507,168	14,669,123
5.	Total Production Value (in thousand IDR)	323,736,000	355,381,200	487,999,750	529,921,900

Source: Data from Instalasi Pengembang Industri Kecil Menengah Alas Kaki/Persepatuan Bandung (2008)

From the data above, it can be seen that the role of the Cibaduyut Footwear Business Cluster is to implement the government's triple track strategy in reducing unemployment and poverty. The data also shows two important elements which are embedded within these SMEs: (a) SMEs are very important as a provider of employment in Indonesia. In the midst of the economic crisis that hit the world and the rush of similar products into the Indonesian market, these SMEs are able to maintain employment for its workers; (b) from that table, it can be seen that SMEs has grown from year to year (except in 2006). In the period of 2006-2008, there was a growth of SMEs at a rate of 2.6 percent in terms of number of enterprises, at a rate of 1.6 percent in terms of employment rate, at a rate of 22.39 percent in terms of annual production, at a rate of 63.68 percent in terms of total production value. Even though there was a decrease in investment by 38.08 percent, it did not affect the growth of this area, especially looking at the high percentage of total production value.

Second, the presence of SMEs in the region has also led to the birth of several supporting industries as seen in Table 5.5. Unfortunately there is no official data related to the number of workers absorbed in these supporting industries, number of total investments, and the value of trade between these supporting industries and the SMEs.

Table 5.5: Supporting Industries in Cibaduyut

No.	Types	Number of Units
1.	Showroom/oulet/store	176
2.	Shopping Centers	4
3.	(Raw) Materials Stores	38
4.	Spare Parts Industry	3
5.	Packaging Industry	15
6.	Rubber Soles Stores/Industry	5
7.	Other Industries	8

Source: Data from Instalasi Pengembang Industri Kecil Menengah Alas Kaki/Persepatuan Bandung (2008)

Third, the role of these SMEs in the regional economy can also be seen from their contribution to the GRDP. Table 5.6 shows the contribution and proportion of the GRDP of SMEs to Bandung's economy.

Table 5.6: Contribution and Proportion of Textile, Leather Products, and Footwear Industries to the City of Bandung's Gross Regional Domestic Product in 2008-2009

Industry	Current Prices (based on 2000 prices)				Constant Prices (based on 2000 prices)			
	Contribution (in million IDR)		Proportion (in percent)		Contribution (in trillion IDR)		Proportion (in percent)	
	2008	2009	2008	2009	2008	2009	2008	2009
Textile, Leather Products, and Footwear	9,271,085	9,825,658	15.34	13.98	4,906,714	4,936,212	27.96	26.66

Source: Data is modified from Badan Pusat Statistik Kota Bandung (n.d.)

Looking at the data above, the textile, leather products, and footwear industries have contributed well of the total GRDP of the city of Bandung between the years 2008-2009. In terms of current prices, these SMEs contributed 15.34 percent in 2008 and 13.98 percent in 2009 while in terms of constant prices, they contributed 27.96 percent in 2008 and 26.66 percent in 2009 (more than one fourth of the total contribution). It ranked number two after the big retail trade sector as the biggest contributor to the GRDP. Unfortunately, there is no exact number on the contribution of the footwear industries in Bandung to the city's GRDP.

5.2.2 The Implementation of the Cluster Concept in Cibaduyut

The previous chapter has indicated that to understand a cluster, we need to analyze the six attributes of Porter's diamond theory to promote a competitive advantage of a firm. However, in viewing the implementation of business clusters in Indonesia, the researcher will only describe the four main attributes which are firm strategy, structure, and rivalry, factor conditions, demand conditions, and related and supporting industries. While the other two attributes (chance and government's role) are seen as supporting attributes in a cluster. Below, the researcher will describe the four attributes that are embedded in Cibaduyut.

Firm Strategy, Structure, and Rivalry

As mentioned in previous chapters, what is included in this attribute are: goals, strategies, and ways of organizing firms in industry as well as domestic rivalry. In Cibaduyut, the growth in the number of business units engaged in the production of footwear has increased from year to year. Data from the Office for Developing the Small and Medium-sized Shoe Industry in Cibaduyut stated that in the period of 2005-2008 the number of business units has increased from 845 to 867 (or growing at rate of 2.6 percent).[326] Interviews and observations conducted by the researcher in the period of 2011-2012 found that almost all business units (business owners) have business goals and objectives. Some business objectives that can

326 Cf. Instalasi Pengembang Industri Kecil Menengah Alas Kaki/Persepatuan Bandung 2008.

be summarized are: to continue family/parent's business, to earn income to support the family expenses (including education), to dominate the local shoe market (including Java and outside Java), to conduct export activities to enter the international market, and to develop a personal brand. While the consumer's target to be reached by these SMEs/SMIs are divided into: consumers in the city of Bandung and surroundings, consumers in the Province of West Java, national consumers (Java and outside Java), and international customers such as Malaysia, Vietnam, the United States, and Europe.

Interviews with staff from the Office for Developing the Small and Medium-sized Shoe Industry in Cibaduyut also found that most (unfortunately there is no official data) SMEs/SMIs in Cibaduyut is a family business and is informal.[327] Most of these SMEs are managed by individuals who work as an owner as well as an employee of the company. In conducting their business, the owner is assisted by four to five workers with weekly payments' method.

In terms of domestic rivalry, what is mentioned by Porter (1998) that rivalry will push companies to improve and innovate is not clearly seen in Cibaduyut.[328] Observations and interviews conducted by the researcher in Cibaduyut found that cooperation is more dominant than competition amongst SMEs/SMIs. The following illustrates the pattern of cooperation between SMEs in Cibaduyut. *First*, there is a clear division of jobs (especially in micro and small enterprises) among SMEs such as cutting leather materials into pieces and manufacturing of rubber soles for footwear materials. *Second*, this semi-finished material will be passed to other SMEs which combines leather with rubber footwear in the first phase above. *Third*, the finishing process will be carried out either by other SMEs or back to the first SMEs (in the first phase) before sold to the market. This type of cooperation is what Marijan (2005) calls a joint action.[329]

Another method is the cooperation undertaken by large enterprises that subcontract their production to smaller firms. In this case, to meet the quantity of shoes that will be sold (usually exported); these large compa-

---

327 What is meant by informal business is that there is no formal management structure of the company such as director, head of production, secretary, treasurer and other elements of a formal organizational structure. In an informal structure, there is no clear division of work between administrative (the owner) and operational (the employees) levels.

328 Cf. Porter 1990, p. 118.

329 Cf. Marijan 2005, pp. 221-22.

nies subcontract the manufacture of shoes to local SMEs. This large enterprise simply gives an example of the desired shoes to the SMEs, offers a number of target (number of shoes), and proposes work deadlines. This type of cooperation is called horizontal cooperation according to Tambunan's internal networks.[330] Usually, each SME (with limited number of workers and technology) is only able to make between 30-100 pairs of shoes.

However, competition also occurs among SMEs (mainly medium-sized enterprises) in Cibaduyut. Looking at marketing strategy conducted by these SMEs, it is obvious how they compete to attract potential buyers (either online or direct buyers) through the website (e-commerce). This, as mentioned by Porter (1998), can be a start of innovation.[331] There are many websites that offers online purchasing for Cibaduyut shoe products.[332] With the example of the shoes displayed in the website, a firm must always keep an eye on its competitors' website so that there is always an effort to make improvements and innovation (or even just imitating) of its products. There is no denying that the development of technology has an influence on the pattern of competition to make improvement and innovation in Cibaduyut. However, in addition to competition, SMEs also cooperate in marketing their products. Few small firms work together (not only in term of creating and running a website) to offer their products in one website. So what was mentioned by Porter (1998) that inside a cluster there would be a form of cooperation and competition is proven in Cibaduyut.[333]

Not only competition among SMEs inside the cluster, competition also occurs between SMEs in the cluster with the shoe stores outside the cluster. Many shopping centers (like malls) sell shoes including shoes from Cibaduyut. The advantage of shopping at the malls is that buyers can shop with the concept of '*one-stop shopping*' that saves time, effort and cost. This gives pressure to SMEs/SMIs in creating marketing strategy to keep attracting potential buyers to visit Cibaduyut.

330 Cf. Tambunan 2005, pp. 140-41.

331 Cf. Porter 1998a, p. 213.

332 See for example http://www.cibaduyutshoes.com, http://www.boss-sepatu.com/, and http://sepatucibaduyut.web.id/toko.

333 Cf. Porter 1998a, p. 79.

Factor Conditions

There are several items that are included in the factor conditions such as a pool of (skilled) human resource, raw material sources, the availability of capital or funds, and good infrastructure facilities such as roads, and so forth. In terms of human resource, there are about 3,613 workers conducting shoe production in Cibaduyut. In general, the Cibaduyut workers are local people living in Cibaduyut with the average level of education is high school.[334] This industrial cluster also offers an opportunity for the internship of vocational high school students in not only studying the production's technique but also sharing the knowledge (production's techniques) acquired in school to the workers in Cibaduyut. Based on the interviews and observations at the research site, it is discovered that the skills acquired by the shoemaker and the craftsmen are obtained by independent learning from other workers without any formal education or training of the shoe manufacturing process.[335] This causes a poor design and poor quality of products. In terms of raw material sources, usually the raw materials (leather) are sent form the animal farms in Garut dan Tasikmalaya, West Java. Some SMEs' owners buy raw materials from local markets as well as from neighboring countries like Malaysia.

In terms of the availability of capital and funds, there are many banks and non-bank institutions that offer loans to SMEs in Cibaduyut. Examples of such loans are provided by the Microcredit Program of Bank Jabar and Microfinance Fund of Bank Danamon.[336] The government also provides loans to help these SMEs such as the program of KUR. In regards to basic infrastructure, the infrastructure facilities in Cibaduyut are quite complete. *First,* the Cibaduyut Footwear Industrial Cluster is located in the southern part of the city of Bandung and is approximately 5 km away from downtown Bandung. This cluster is located in Jalan Cibaduyut Raya

---

334 Cf. Dinas Perindustrian dan Perdagangan Pemprov. Jawa Barat dan PT. Nusantara Citra Konsultan 2007, p. 28.

335 Interview with W.D. from the Office for Developing the Small and Medium-sized Shoe Industry in Cibaduyut in Bandung on September 19, 2012, conducted by Lukas Tambunan. Unfortunately, there is no official data on the number of skilled and unskilled workers in Cibaduyut.

336 For further details see http://www.bankbjb.co.id/id/4/117/155/261/bjb-Kredit-Mikro-Utama.html and http://www.danamon.co.id/Home/GrowingYourBusiness/Financing/Microfinance/tabid/105/language/id-ID/Default.aspx, accessed January 6, 2014.

which has a length of 2 km. To get to this industrial area, visitors can pass through Jalan Soekarno Hatta. As a sign of the location of the cluster, the local government built a shoe's sculpture at down the street of Jalan Cibaduyut Raya. The location of this industrial cluster is only about 2 km away from the bus terminal of Leuwipanjang. The proximity to the bus terminal gives some benefits to this area namely the easiness of the transportation activity for the purposes of transporting of raw materials, distributing products, and marketing. Not only that, this proximity to the bus terminal also eases potential buyers to Cibaduyut by using public transportations. There are several modes of public transportation (other than a private vehicle) to go to Cibaduyut, namely small minibus (*mikrolet/ angkutan kota*), taxis, and rickshaws. *Second*, this location is also supported with good communication facilities (telephone and internet networks), the availability of (clean) water, and electricity networks. *Third*, there is a local post office to assist the distribution of products and to conduct correspondences.

Demand Conditions

What is meant by demand condition is the nature of local markets and local demands. During fieldwork in the shoe industry Cibaduyut, West Java, it was found out that there are two types of consumers in Cibaduyut. The *first* one is classified as people looking for a high quality product without questioning the price of the product. For these people, they prefer to buy a high quality of shoes so that it can last for longer wear. This type is also divided into two buyer categories namely adult buyers and younger buyers. Adult buyers are usually not concerned with the shoe design as long as it is a good quality product. Younger buyers are usually very demanding, especially about the design and color of the shoes. These buyers usually take an example (model/image) shoes obtained from magazines or websites and then ask the local craftsmen to produce (imitate) such shoes. The *second* type, are people who look for a cheaper price. These people consider the quality of the product but would prefer buying the product if sold at a lower price; these people have to do so because of financial constraints as well as other important needs outside of buying shoes that must be considered. With the flood of Chinese products (especially after the implementation of ASEAN-China Free Trade Agreement, January 2010), consumers have many choices of whether to buy shoes with high quality and high prices or to buy cheaper products (mostly local production and

Chinese) with a lower quality. In addition, female buyers play crucial roles in improving the quality of design and product of Cibaduyut's shoes. Female buyers are a type of sophisticated (and demanding) buyer. This buyer always wants the latest model because of the promotion and product information through printed and electronic media. The vigorous promotion and demand makes the shoe craftmen constantly monitor the development of the latest model as well as improve the design of their footwear products according to market taste.

The Presence of Related and Supporting Industries

The presence of related and supporting industries is essential for promoting competitive advantage of firms or clusters as mentioned in the previous chapter. In Cibaduyut, there are several related and supporting industries. Looking at Table 5.5 above, there are at least 249 related and supporting industries exist in Cibaduyut such as showrooms, shopping center, raw materials stores, spare part industries, packaging industries, rubber soles stores, and other industries. Not only that, the establishment of technical service unit in 1977 also supports the existence of this cluster. This unit acts as both a trigger and a promoter of business development in Cibaduyut. This unit offers a variety of facilities such as managerial training and production engineering training to support the growth and development of footwear products. It is expected that SMEs in Cibaduyut can produce high-quality products, a wide variety of products, and affordable price so that it can enter the market among all segments.

The presence of research centers and universities is also an advantage of this cluster. There are many universities in nearby areas that are used to help the technical service unit and the local government to conduct trainings and researches such as Bandung Institute of Technology, Padjajaran University, University of Pasundan, Parahyangan Catholic University, and research institutes under those universities. Outside the region, there are several institutions that have a relationship with this cluster such as the Yogyakarta Leather Technology Academy (*Akademi Teknologi Kulit*, ATK), the Yogyakarta Center for Leather, Rubber, and Plastics (*Balai Besar Kulit, Karet, dan Plastik Yogyakarta*, BBKKP), Gadjah Mada University (Yogyakarta), the LIPI, and the BPPT.

Inside the cluster itself, there are many associations which function as a means of communication and information among SMEs in Cibaduyut such as the Businessmen Association of Cibaduyut (*Asosiasi Pengusaha*

Cibaduyut, APACI), the Association of Shoe Businessmen in Cibaduyut (*Asosiasi Pengusaha Sepatu Cibaduyut*, APSC), the Working Health Committee (*Komite Kesehatan Kerja*, K3), the Communication Forum for Shoe Businessmen in Cibaduyut (*Forum Komunikasi Pengusaha Sepatu Cibaduyut*, FKPSC), and the Cibaduyut Community Care Forum (*Forum Peduli Masyarakat Cibaduyut*).[337] In addition, there are also four big parking spaces (provided by Oval, Diana, Grutty, and Pormil's stores) inside the cluster to accomodate the arrival of private cars, minibus, and bus in Cibaduyut.[338]

5.2.3 Challenges in the Globalization Era

Looking at the general overview in the Cibaduyut Footwear Business Cluster, we can then figure out several problems faced by SMEs in Cibaduyut. The problems can be defined as follows.

The *first* is related to the aspect of human resource including the worker, the craftsmen, and the entrepreneur (owner). The skills acquired by the shoemaker and the craftsmen are obtained by independent learning from other workers without any formal education or training of the shoe manufacturing process as mentioned above. Therefore, there is almost no formal training obtained by these workers that result in the poor design and poor quality products. This limitation creates difficulties to Cibaduyut shoe products to compete with its competitor products especially those from abroad. Most craftsmen and workers in Cibaduyut do not understand the shoe-making techniques. According to WD, a pair of shoes should have not only a good quality in its raw material but should also consider the convenience of the shoes.[339] Most craftsmen in Cibaduyut are able to produce good shoes but only few of them understand in producing a comfortable shoe. This has led to the decrease in the quality of products, which makes the number of requests or orders also decrease and push many businesses out of business.

---

337 Cf. Dinas Perindustrian dan Perdagangan Pemprov. Jawa Barat dan PT. Nusantara Citra Konsultan 2007, pp. 38-39.

338 Cf. ibid., pp. 43-44.

339 Interview with W.D. from the Office for Developing the Small and Medium-sized Shoe Industry in Cibaduyut in Bandung on September 19, 2012, conducted by Lukas Tambunan.

Looking at the salary or honorarium received by the workers and craftsmen, it can be said that their salary does not meet with the standards of the regional minimum wage in the city of Bandung. According to the Decree of the West Java Governor, the regional minimum wage in the city of Bandung is IDR 1,118,000 per month.[340] There are two things that can answer the question why their salaries are still far from the minimum standards. Firstly, almost all employees or workers in the area of Cibaduyut are categorized as informal workers. A survey conducted by BPS found that in 2010, there were 6,447,260 workers in the SMEs sector.[341] Out of this number, it is found out that as many as 4,296,161 (or approximately 66.64 percent) of workers do not receive a salary (unfortunately, there is no accurate data on the number of both formal and informal workers in the Cibaduyut's Footwear Business Cluster). This indicates that most of the enterprises is a family-oriented business and has no business administration record. This also means that there is only a monthly salary (for workers stores) or weekly wages (for the shoemaker) without any other allowances such as transport or health benefits. As an illustration, most of the SMEs in Cibaduyut consist of four to five workers.[342] Usually they get an order to produce as many as 40-60 pairs of shoes per week. The owner will be paid IDR 10,000 per pair of shoes. The owner usually takes 40 percent of the money and the remaining 60 percent is given to the craftsmen or the workers. So from that illustration, SMEs in Cibaduyut cannot implement the regional minimum wage in the city of Bandung. Secondly, other than a low salary of the workers, the payment system between the owner and the potential buyers is still an issue.[343] Potential buyers tend to do the payment with the bank gyro transfer. This method of transferring money usually is done when all products are sold. This potential buyer usually gives about 40 percent down payment of the total value. Because of this system, many SMEs' owners complain because the rest of the

340 Cf. Keputusan Gubernur Jawa Barat No. 561/Kep.1665-Bangsos/2009.

341 Cf. Badan Pusat Statistik 2010, p. 20.

342 Interview with W.D. from the Office for Developing the Small and Medium-sized Shoe Industry in Cibaduyut in Bandung on September 19, 2012, conducted by Lukas Tambunan.

343 Who are meant by potential buyers are those big entrepreneurs who own big stores or outlets and focus its sales on overseas markets. Many of these entrepreneurs do not have workers or craftsmen (if any, the number of workers is not that many). Therefore, they rely on small and medium enterprises (entrepreneurs) to fulfill orders from abroad or to sell a big number of pair of shoes to the local market either in nearby market or to other islands in Indonesia.

payment settlement takes a long time. These are two explanations why the number of SMEs producing shoes in Cibaduyut decrease every year.

Another problem that is related to the aspect of human resource is that most entrepreneurs have a low level of entrepreneurial spirit. Table 5.7 shows the level of education of the SMEs' owners (entrepreneurs) in the footwear industry in Indonesia in 2010. Looking at the table below, it is discovered that the percentage of entrepreneurs with a university background was only 0.08 percent while the largest portion is on the level of basic (primary) education that is 37.71 percent.[344] This figure shows the low quality of human resource of SMEs especially in the footwear industry in Indonesia. It is not surprising that these entrepreneurs struggle to develop their business. This means that these entrepreneurs do not know how to improve their product quality, how to market their products abroad, and how to create innovation to win tight competition. This is even worse when dealing with low-skilled labor. Most SMEs have low-skilled labor to produce their products. Of course, when competing with imported goods, these SMEs must create new innovation and it is impossible to create new innovation without having high-skilled labor and appropriate technology.

Table 5.7: Level of Education of the SMEs' Owners in Indonesia in the Footwear Industry, 2010

Level of Education	Number of People
Not completed elementary school	4,534
Completed elementary school	12,413
Completed junior high school	8,320
Completed senior high school	7,187
Completed academic level education (D I/II/III)	160
Have university diploma	296
Total	32,910

Source: Data is modified from Badan Pusat Statistik (2010)

344 In elementary school, junior high school, and senior high school, there is no subject that focuses on entrepreneurial spirit.

The *second* is the managerial aspect. The family management system run by most of the business industry in Cibaduyut makes this industrial cluster difficult to develop. The composition of the family members dominates the structure of the company. There are many cases where the owners of small business units put themselves not only as the owner or the leader of the company but also as the workers and the salesman. There is no clear vision, mission, and objectives of their business so usually they run their business for fulfilling their basic objectives: to be able to eat for today and to be able to send their children to school. As for the medium business units, even though they notice the importance of the managerial aspect (characterized by a clear and well-managed division of labor and the recruitment of the worker based on skill), but they do not yet fully run a good enterprise's management system. This can be seen from the absence of the quality control management where many of their products are rejected by potential buyers because the products do not meet with the minimum standard of product required by the potential buyers. Table 5.8 shows the number of SMEs in the footwear industry in Indonesia with its workers receiving business advisory in 2010.

Table 5.8: Number of SMEs in Footwear Industry with its Workers Receiving Business Advisory

Number of Enterprises		**32,910**
Not Receiving Business Advisory		27,922
Receiving Business Advisory		4,988
Type of Business Advisory	Managerial	219
	Production Technique Skill	3,583
	Marketing	377
	Others	823

Source: Data is modified from Badan Pusat Statistik (2010)

Looking at the table above, it can be seen that the percentage of SMEs that received business advisory was only 15.15 percent while the rest (around 84.85 percent) has never received any type of business advisory. Of those SMEs, only 0.06 percent has received the managerial trainings. This figure shows the low quality of managerial aspect of SMEs especially in the footwear industry in Indonesia. This becomes another cause on why these entrepreneurs struggle to develop their business.

The *third* is related to the capital issue. Some entrepreneurs or SMEs in Cibaduyut have experienced how difficult it is to get fresh money (loans)

to finance or even to increase their business activities due to their status as informal economic units (illegal entitities). Sandiaga Uno, vice chairman of the KADIN for SMEs and Cooperatives, stated that in 2010 almost 80 percent of SMEs do not have legal entity.[345] Therefore, these SMEs find it hard to receive loans/credits from financial services. This situation certainly creates problems for both SMEs and the government. For SMEs, by having no legal entity, they would have difficulty in accessing banking facilities. On the other hand, with many SMEs having no legal entity, state revenue through taxes would not be optimal.

Statistics Indonesia recorded that in 2008 only 19 percent of all SMEs received loans from the banking sector.[346] The government offers many loan mechanisms in order to support SMEs, however when in direct contact with the bank administration there is a different story. Some of these SMEs decide not to go further with their application for loans due to complicated administration processes of the banks or because their business is unsuitable to be funded by the bank. In fact some of these SMEs have never heard that the government provides any type of loan mechanisms. Hence, most entrepreneurs and SMEs depend on their own money and savings (or borrow from their relatives) to finance their business activities. Another problem is that many of these SMEs are labeled with no legal entity. The KADIN (2010) found out that there are several reasons why Indonesian SMEs remain not formalized: the cost to legalize company documents is too expensive, the process of issuing business trading license and company registration by local authorities takes several days (it is up to 16-21 working days),[347] most of them have lack of capital, and these entrepreneurs do not see the benefit of having their business formalized (e.g. in order to get credit from financial institutions). In their mind, to develop the company would increase the risk to be carried out by the owner of the company such as the need to appoint permanent staffs and workers, the

345 Cf. http://us.finance.detik.com/read/2010/09/03/121518/1434289/4/4716-juta-unit-umkm-belum-berbadan-hukum, accessed September 14, 2012.

346 Report on the Impact of the People based Small-Business Loans, Deputy for the Study of Empowerment of SME (Laporan Hasil Kajian Dampak Kredit Usah Rakyat 2009, Deputi Bidang Pengkajian Sumberdaya Koperasi dan UKM).

347 For further explanation see Indonesian Chamber of Commerce and Industry (KADIN) (2010). Key Challenges Faced By Entrepreneur: Indonesia. Paper presented at the Workshop on Reducing Start-Up and Establishment Time of Business. Hiroshima, http://aimp.apec.org/Documents/2010/EC/WKSP1/10_ec_wksp1_006.pdf, March 1-2, 2010.

obligation to provide health benefits, bonuses, and allowances to their workers, and the obligation to have good financial management related to the payment of taxes to the government, and other things. On the other hand, by having no legal entity of course they cannot submit their application to the banking services to get loans. Besides, banks and other financial services are often hesitant in helping SMEs get loans (Hill, 2001). The reason is the lack of sufficient guarantees provided by SMEs when they borrow funds to the bank as well as to minimize the financial risks due to a high number of non-formal SMEs. As a result, SMEs are forced to find sources of other funding services (usually illegal moneylenders) or are forced to close down their business. Table 6 shows the number of SMEs in the leather industry, leather goods, and footwear products in Indonesia that received loans from the financial institution.[348] Then, the following tables (Tables 5.9, 5.10, and 5.11) illustrate how many (as well in percentage) SMEs in the footwear sector in Indonesia that received a loan from the bank, how many of them get loans from the non-bank sources, and the reasons for taking loans from non-bank sources.

Table 5.9: Number of SMEs that Received Loans

Number of Enterprises	**Number of Enterprises that Received Loans**	
	From Banks	From Non-bank Sources
14,117	2,085	12,032

Source: Data is modified from Badan Pusat Statistik (2010)

The data above shows the comparison between SMEs which take loans from the banks and SMEs that do not borrow from the banks. There is a big gap between these two categories which is 14.76 percent of SMEs receiving loans from the banks compared to 85.24 percent of those receiving loans from non-bank sources. This shows not only the difficulty of SMEs

348 Statistics Indonesia published a book titled: Profile of Micro and Small Industries in 2010. It divided several industries into the Indonesian Standard Industrial Classification where the footwear industry is classified under the leather industry, leather goods, and footwear products. Unfortunately, there is no official data or survey ever conducted in the Cibaduyut Footwear Industrial Cluster regarding financial/capital issues.

in getting loans from the banks but also their own unpreparedness in applying for loans to the bank due to the incompleteness of the administrative procedures or other things. The next table illustrates the sources of capital (loans) obtained by SMEs. Table 5.10 shows the percentage of sources of main loan by SMEs in footwear industry in Indonesia in 2010.

Table 5.10: Percentage of Sources of Main Loan

Sources of Main Loan[349]						
Bank	Cooperatives	Non-bank Financial Institutions	Venture Capital	Individual	Family	Others
14,76	3,7	1,13	--	15,44	9,71	55,26

Source: Data is modified from Badan Pusat Statistik (2010)

Looking at the table above, it is obvious that most of the SMEs have to finance their own business. Approximately 25.15 percent of SMEs use their personal money or borrow from their families and relatives; while 55.26 percent of them did not state clearly the source of their loans (they might get a loan from a lender with a high interest rate that can feel like being strangled in the neck). Once again, the above data shows that funds from personal and family sources are still considered as a major source of funding their activities. There are several reasons of these SMEs for not applying loans to the banks or other formal financial institutions. Table 5.11 shows the number of SMEs in the leather industry, leather goods, and footwear products that had loans from other non-bank sources and their main reasons for not applying loans to the banks or other financial institutions in 2010.

349 The percentage at Table 5.10 is calculated by the writer from data on the Number of Micro and Small Scale Establishments, taken from Profil Industri Mikro dan Kecil 2010.

Table 5.11: Main Reason of SMEs for not Applying for Loans

Number of Enterprises		**30,698**
Main Reasons for not Applying to the Bank	Not Knowing Procedure	2,420
	Difficulty of Procedure	2,682
	Not Having Collateral	4,643
	High Interest Rate	1,918
	Proposal Rejected	168
	Not Interested	18,867

Source: Data is modified from Badan Pusat Statistik (2010)

Out of 30,698 SMEs, it was found that 61.46 percent expressed their apathy to take out a loan from the bank. There is no clear argumentation why they were not interested in borrowing from the banks, but the interviews conducted by the author to the owners of SMEs in Cibaduyut actually found that their disinterest because of the things mentioned earlier such as a lack of proof of a good administrative and financial statements as well as a lack of desire to formalize their businesses (as a condition of getting a loan from the bank).[350]

The *fourth* is the technological aspect. Generally, the technology and machinery used by the shoemakers and the craftsmen is an outdated technology that is not economical, requires high maintenance costs, and a decline in the machine's accuracy. The result is low quality of products produced by the SMEs.[351] This is also worsened by the limited number of workers who have at least basic knowledge of shoe-making production. It was discovered that most SMEs' owners in Cibaduyut do not have their own shoe-making machines. Usually they use existing production machinery facilities in the Office for Developing the Small and Medium-sized Shoe Industry in Cibaduyut in their shoe-making process. This causes the design and models of their shoes to be very limited and often not in line with the wishes of the market and consumers. According to former Indonesian Minister of Trade, Marie E. Pangestu (2011), if the shoe industry in Cibaduyut (West Java) wants to compete and be accepted in the international market, it is necessary to improve the standardization and quality of

350 Interviews conducted during the fieldwork in Cibaduyut in 2010.
351 Cf. Aspiranti et al. 2008, p. 1.

their products.[352] However, due to the limited skills of the labor force, it is difficult for this industry to increase the quality of its product as mentioned by HD (one of the business actors in Cibaduyut, West Java).

The *fifth* is the marketing aspect. Marketing SMEs' products is not an easy task for most entrepreneurs as well as the entrepreneurs in Cibaduyut. The main problem is that these entrepreneurs do not have the capacity to locate potential markets. The difficulty to find potential markets abroad are usually associated with four things. Firstly, with low education levels, these entrepreneurs do not understand the use of internet or other means of communication to find potential buyers or to promote their products. This is also shown by the result of the Indonesian Statistics' survey in the following table.

Table 5.12: Number of SMEs and the Use of Computer and Internet Networks

Number of Enterprises	**Using a Computer**	**Not Using a Computer**	**Making Use of Internet Networks**	
			Making Use	Not making Use
32,910	1,055	31,855	751	32,159

Source: Data is modified from Badan Pusat Statistik (2010)

Looking at the table above, it can be concluded that most of the SMEs do not have computers to support their business (as well as a means of good administration filing system). They prefer to use a conservative method to record all their business activities and transactions such as writing by hand in a small pocket book. Moreover, because most entrepreneurs do not have good managerial skills due to a low education level, they rely their marketing system on their inner circle within the area (with other SMEs) or through other retailers. This is shown by the low number of business units that utilize the internet networks to market their products.

Secondly, most of these entrepreneurs also do not understand how to run the marketing techniques, create business plans and implement business strategies in order to enter the global market. Thirdly, SMEs often do not receive assistance from the government (central and local), industry

352 Cf. http://www.antaranews.com/berita/245873/mendag-industri-sepatucibaduyut-miliki-potensi-internasional, accessed September 14, 2012.

associations, and research centers in finding potential markets (because many SMEs do not have a legal entity). Fourthly, because of the use of low-tech equipment, products of SMEs usually do not meet the global standards (as mentioned earlier). At the end, these entrepreneurs simply sell their products in domestic markets. The table below shows the number of the leather industry, leather goods, and footwear products in Indonesia which sells their products to the domestic markets and to the international markets. Most of them (99.1 percent) decided to sell their products in the domestic markets rather than the international markets. There were only six enterprises which sell their products overseas and 281 enterprises that sell their products both in the domestic and international markets.

Table 5.13: The Marketing Area of the Leather Industry, Leather Goods, and Footwear Products in Indonesia

Number of Enterprises	**Marketing Area**		
	Domestic	International	Both
32,910	32,623	6	281

Source: Data is modified from Badan Pusat Statistik (2010)

Not only that, the difficulty in selling their products abroad is due to some simple problems on the quality of their product. First, they have difficulty in obtaining high quality raw materials so the result is that their quality of products cannot compete in the global market. The result of the Indonesian Statistic's survey indicates that there are two major reasons of the difficulties in obtaining raw materials namely: the price is too expensive (50.4 percent) and the difficulty to get raw materials (43.8 percent).

Table 5.14: Kind of Main Difficulty with Raw Materials

Number of Enterprises Having Difficulties with Raw Materials	**Kind of Main Difficulty**			
	Scarcity	Prices	Distance	Other
3,764	1,651	1,898	96	119

Source: Data is modified from Badan Pusat Statistik (2010)

Second, in general the packaging products of SMEs are not attractive to consumers. The main reason is the limited capital and human resources that creates difficulties in a more attractive packaging.

The *sixth* is the infrastructure aspect. One of the requirements to support the existence of the Cibaduyut Footwear Business Clusters is the infrastructure provided by the government. There are a number of problems that are still being faced by SMEs in Cibaduyut.[353] These problems are: Firstly, the existing roads in the region are relatively small which causes frequent traffic jams. This is exacerbated by the not well-organized of the street vendors and the low discipline of public transportation drivers who are careless in picking up, dropping off, and waiting for passengers.[354] It discourages the visitors' interest to shop due to traffic jams and discomfort in shopping. Secondly, flooding is frequent in this region due to poor drainage systems and a high amount of waste disposed carelessly by the indiscipline society. This gives a negative impact to the region, especially during the rainy seasons which results in the declining number of tourist arrivals and prospective buyers.

Related to the supporting industries in the Cibaduyut Footwear Business Cluster, there are two main problems that are still being faced by the SMEs' owners and the craftsmen. Firstly, there is only one government agency in the region which focuses only on the development of product design and product quality of the SMEs in the region. This limitation is also coupled with the low interest of the SMEs' owner and the craftsmen to get assistance from the Office for Developing the Small and Medium-sized Shoe Industry in Cibaduyut. Secondly, the lack of synergy among stakeholders such as SMEs' owners and the craftsmen, related industries, bureaucracy, professional associations, universities and research centers, and financial institutions in helping to solve problems faced by SMEs as already mentioned above. It is common that these stakeholders create their own programs or assistance to help the SMEs in Cibaduyut independently without having any coordination with each other to avoid the overlapping of similar programs and assistance.

Looking at current conditions and problems faced by SMEs/SMIs in Cibaduyut, this cluster can be categorized as Tambunan's active cluster, which is characterized by an improvement in terms of production system, human resources skill, and marketing networks. Therefore, there are many

353 Cf. Soekarni/Suryanto 2009, p. 28.

354 In almost all areas in Indonesia, the public transportation system does not have a regular departure and arrival time schedule. It is up to the driver to decide whether to wait for passengers or to move to other stops.

improvements needed to achieve a type of industrial cluster (or at least a dynamic cluster) in Cibaduyut as mentioned earlier.

5.3 Profile of the Plered Decorative Ceramic Industrial Cluster

Plered (also known as Palered) is a district in Purwakarta regency, West Java, with an area of 91.1 ha. Plered history cannot be separated from the history of ceramic which includes the old town or village in the district of Purwakarta such as Plered, Cirata, Gandasoli, and Citalang. Plered ceramic is the result and a product of the people of Plered that is derived from one generation to the next. Ceramic business in Plered began in the early 1900s. At that time, ceramic tiles produced by the craftsmen at Plered were simple products like jars, flower pots, and piggy banks although there were also ceramic products other than those three products. Plered ceramic can easily be found because it is displayed and is sold along the row of people's houses and on the edge of the road in Purwakarta.

Ceramic as a craft, have appeared since the Dutch colonial era around the year of 1795 in the area of Citalang where there are many *lio-lio* (a place to make roof tiles and bricks).[355] At that time, there were many original houses that had thatched roofs, shingles, palm leaves, and reeds which later turned into rooftile houses. The area around Citalang such as Anjun (Panjunan) was the location of many pottery-making businesses. Beginning in 1935, the pottery product became a home industry for the people of Plered. In the same year, there was also a big Dutch factory named Hendrik De Boa in Warungkandang, Plered that produced pottery.

In the Japanese colonial era, pottery industry has deteriorated as most craftsmen were forced to be a *romusha*[356] by Japanese soldiers while the factory of De Boa was taken over by the Japanese soldiers and changed its name to Kaki Kojo. Nevertheless, the company still operated and produced pottery. During the struggle for independence against the Japanese, pottery production was almost at a standstill because of the involvement of the people (including the craftsmen) in the fight. Ceramic industry in

355 Cf. http://purwakartakab.go.id/sejarah-dan-perkembangan-keramik-plered, accessed September 3, 2012.

356 Romusha can be defined as an employee who was forcibly recruited by the Japanese government to carry out development projects during the Japanese occupation of Indonesia from 1942-1945.

Plered rose again especially since Indonesian Vice President Hatta officially opened the ceramic industry in the area of Gonggo, Plered in 1950. At that time, many imported machines from Germany were sent to this area in order to help and foster the development of the ceramic industry. As a result, this ceramic industry was successful in guiding the domestic industry to grow rapidly. Successful examples of this industry were: (a) the manufacture of a large barrel that is 170 cm tall and has a diameter of 150 cm that were specially made to welcome the opening of the Games of Emerging Forces (The Ganefo) in Jakarta on November 10, 1963 and (b) the construction of Istiqlal Mosque in Jakarta in which the body and its minaret are made of small bricks produced by the ceramic industry (the nature of the sticky and solid Plered's clay makes it good for building mosques).[357]

Unfortunately in 1965, the development of ceramic production in Plered decreased both in quality and quantity due to a flood of similar products made from plastic. In 1974, with the decline in the quality and quantity of ceramic Plered, the local government of Purwakarta together with the Office of Industry and Cooperatives and the Ceramics Research Institute (now is called the Center for Ceramic) formed a Consultative Body of Plered Ceramics to revive the ceramics industry in Plered. In 1976, the Ministry of Industry through the BIPIK established a pilot unit that served as a means for developing the craftsmen in Plered under the supervision of the Center for Ceramic in Bandung. As a follow up of the BIPIK, in the year of 1979/1980 the Ministry of Industry established the Technical Services Center in Plered and commenced its operation on July 8, 1981. In 1983, the Technical Services Center changed its name to the Plered Ceramic Technical Services Unit which its main task is to implement several tasks of the Directorate General of Small Industries in developing and empowering small industries by utilizing existing infrastructures in Plered. Because of support from this technical services unit and the government, since 1985 the Plered Ceramic Industry began to rise marked by receiving an award from the President of the Republic of Indo-

357 Cf. Dinas Tata Ruang dan Bangunan Pemerintah Kabupaten Purwakarta 2003, p. 44.

nesia and the United Nations due to an increase in quality and quantity of ceramic products in the Plered Ceramic Industry.[358]

The ceramic industry in Plered has significantly contributed to the economic structure of the Regency of Purwakarta. There are two positive contributions from the existence of SMEs/SMIs and industrial ceramic in Plered. *First*, there are about 286 business units in the Plered Ceramic Industry. Since 2010, there were approximately 286 business units in Plered that are producing ceramic (including tiles).[359] This number is then divided into four groups which are the crafters for processing raw materials (10 units), the crafters for production (200 units), the suppliers and traders (50 units), and the exporters (26 units). From this number, they were able to absorb the labor force of 3,000 workers (although it is not known exactly the number of formal and informal workers).[360] The total production capacity of all business units in Plered reached 7.2 million units. While the production value in this industry was IDR 17.5 billion and the total value of exports reached IDR 9.5 billion.[361] Moreover, if we look deeply into those SMEs focusing only on ceramic production, there were only 126 business units that focus on producing ceramics.[362] These business units are able to absorb 1,102 labor forces (out of 6,765 workers in all sectors in Purwakarta), have a value of IDR 946 million of investment (out of IDR 11.0442 billion of the total investment in Purwakarta), have an annual production value that reached IDR 16.26 billion (out of IDR 50.87669 billion of the total production value in Purwakarta), and the annual production capacity of 1,500,000 pieces of ceramic. These figures illustrate the contribution of the Plered ceramic industry to the economic structure of Purwakarta as well as the contribution of these SMEs to provide employment in the region.

---

358 Cf. UPTD Litbang Keramik Disperindag & PM Kabupaten Purwakarta, Dinas Perindustrian, Perdagangan, dan Penanaman Modal Kabupaten Purwakarta 2006/2007.

359 Unfortunately, there is no official data about the number of business unit in 2010-2012. Based on the interview with the head of the UPTD Litbang Keramik Plered, the number has not changed much until today.

360 Most of these SMEs are categorized as informal economic units (illegal entities). Therefore, it is common to use informal workers as well as family members to run the business.

361 Cf. UPTD Litbang Keramik Dinas Koperasi, UMKM, Perindustrian, dan Perdagangan Kabupaten Purwakarta (n.d.).

362 Cf. Badan Pusat Statistik Kabupaten Purwakarta 2010, pp. 225-26.

Second, the Plered ceramic products are usually sold both in local and international markets. Types of ceramic that are produced by the SMEs in Plered are usually various ready-to-use decorative ceramics such as vase, pots, jars, ceramic stove, piggy banks, etc. Looking at its ceramic types, there are three types of ceramic products produced in Plered: (a) Traditional pottery/ceramic such as urns and other traditional tools made of ceramic, (b) Construction materials such as bricks and tiles, and (c) Decorative ceramic, such as jars and other decorative ceramic. Plered ceramic can be found in almost all regions of Java (including Jakarta), Bali, West Nusa Tenggara, East Nusa Tenggara, Sumatera, Sulawesi, and North Maluku. While in the international market, these ceramics are exported to the United States of America, Canada, the United Kingdom, Italy, Spain, Germany, Netherlands, France, Australia, New Zealand, South Korea, Taiwan, Japan, Saudi Arabia, United Arab Emirates, and countries in Latin America. The sale of ceramic to various locations at least guarantees the survival of craftsmen in Plered as well as a promotional tool to promote the region of Plered to attract local and international tourists and consumers.

Aside from those contributions, Plered is also known of its clay's quality and variations. Clay as raw material for making ceramic in West Java is famous for its quality and variations. This clay can be found in industrial ceramic areas such as Plered (Regency of Purwakarta), Sitiwinangun (Cirebon), Gunung Guruh (Regency of Sukabumi), and Kadang Haur (Indramayu).[363] A research conducted by the Bandung's Center for Ceramic found that clay reserves in Plered as the main material in the ceramic production will be inexhaustible within the next 50 years and if it runs out in Plered there are still available reserves in other areas.[364] Data from the Plered Center for Innovation Ceramic found that the potential of clay reserves in Plered ranges from 255,000 to 420,000 tons within an area of 11 acres in the block villages of Batutumpang and Pamoyanan.[365] Not only good for ceramic production, the white clay in Sukabumi is also sought by the craftsmen to be used as raw material for the manufacture of porcelain.

---

363 Cf. Ridwan 2009.

364 Cf. Dinas Tata Ruang dan Bangunan Pemerintah Kabupaten Purwakarta 2003, p. 30.

365 Cf. Antara 2009.

5.3.1 The Implementation of the Cluster Concept in Plered

As mentioned earlier, the researcher will describe in detail the four attributes that are embedded in the Plered Decorative Ceramic Cluster. Those attributes are: firm strategy, structure, and rivalry, factor conditions, demand conditions, and related and supporting industries.

Firm Strategy, Structure, and Rivalry

In this attribute, there will be at least four items to be described. They are: goals, strategies, firm's structure, and domestic rivalry. In Plered, the growth of business units in Plered has increased from year to year. Data from the UPTD Litbang Keramik Plered stated that in the period of 2005-2011 the number of business units has increased from 268 to 286 (or growing at rate of 0.06 percent).[366] The field research conducted by the researcher in March-April 2012 found that almost all business units (business owners) have business goals and objectives.[367] Some business objectives that can be summarized are: to continue family/parent's business, to earn income to support the family expenses (including education), to sell their products to local market (including neighboring market such as Bandung and Jakarta), and to export their products tointernational markets. While the consumer's target to be reached by these SMEs are divided into: consumers in the city of Plered and surroundings, consumers in the Province of West Java, national consumers (Java and outside Java), and international customers such as Vietnam and European countries (mostly to Germany).

Based on the survey conducted during the field research in Plered, it is found out that most (unfortunately there is no official data) SMEs in Plered is categorized as a family business and is informal. Most businesses in Plered even still have brotherly ties with each other. Yuni (2012) found out that in conducting their business, the owner is mostly assisted by five

366 Cf. UPTD Litbang Keramik Disperindag & PM Kabupaten Purwakarta, Dinas Perindustrian, Perdagangan, dan Penanaman Modal Kabupaten Purwakarta (2006/2007), interview with AN, from the UPTD Litbang Keramik Plered on March 7, 2012 in Plered, Purwakarta.

367 The researcher has surveyed about 50 SMEs in Plered with a simple random sampling method in March-April 2012.

to ten workers.[368] Usually they receive their payment (salary) either daily or weekly depending on the status of the workers.[369]

In terms of business competition and cooperation, it is not clear the pattern of competition among SMEs in Plered. Observations and interviews conducted by the researcher in Plered found that cooperation is more dominant than competition amongst SMEs. In Plered, there is a common division of labor in the process of making decorative ceramics. That means there are enterprises which focus on doing a specific task. This division of task is divided into: the formation of (raw) ceramic, the decoration, the burning process, and the finishing touch. It is common in Plered that there are enterprises that perform one or two tasks as mentioned above. This is due to many enterprises that have limited capital so that they cannot conduct all process (forming of raw material, decorating, burning, and finishing process) by themselves. Thus, they prefer to focus on one or two tasks only. However, the influence of local culture (will be explained in the next chapter) also plays an important role. In order to minimize the production costs, there are many enterprises that share the cost of burning ceramics. This action occurs because not all SMEs have a ceramic combustion engine. This shows a collective action (cooperation) in producing ceramic in Plered or a joint action as mentioned by Marijan (2005). With the close (kinship) relationships among SMEs, this pattern is common by SMEs in Plered.

Looking at business activity in this cluster, it is quite hard to see a pattern of competition among SMEs. Based on observations, competition occurs only in the process of selling ceramic products in stores located in Plered. In that sense, competition occurs mainly to attract as many potential buyers to visit their stores. This is done simply by displaying their decorative ceramics in order and as neat as possible.

Factor Conditions

There are several items that are included in the factor conditions such as a pool of (skilled) human resources, raw material sources, the availability of capital or funds, and good infrastructure facilities such as roads, and so

---

368 Cf. Astriani 2012, pp. 60-61.

369 Data on payment method is collected during the field research by the researcher in Plered.

forth. In terms of human resources, there is about 3,000 employees (mostly informal) working in Plered. Research conducted by Yuni (2012) found out that these workers usually come from their family members, relatives, and neighbors.[370] Most of these workers have only completed elementary school and junior high school.[371] Based on interviews and observations in the research site, the researcher found that the skills acquired by the workers are from: an independent learning, learning from their parents (due to the need of continuing the family business), or learning from other workers independently i.e. without any formal education or training of decorative ceramic manufacturing process.[372] This cluster also used to be one of the locations for student internships. One example of an internship is conducted by Bandung Institute of Technology's students majoring in Kria.[373] In terms of raw material sources, materials for making ceramics can be easily obtained from the areas surrounding this cluster such as in Block Village of Batutumpang (with reserves of clay 135,000-270,000 tons) and Block Villages of Pamoyanan (with clay reserves at 120,000-150,000 tons).[374] Not only that, other raw materials such as kaolin, ball clay, feldspar, zeolite, and quartz sand can be found in the district of Pamokolan (Tasikmalaya), the district of Cicantayan (Sukabumi), the district of Parungpanjang (Tangerang), the district of Cikidang (Sukabumi), the district of Cikembar (Sukabumi), and the district of Cisaat (Sukabumi).[375]

Demand Conditions

Looking at the nature of the demands in Plered, there are two types of potential buyers. *Firstly*, local buyers who look for household and decoration purposes, and, *secondly*, foreign buyers. For local buyers, they usually buy ceramic items for household use such as flower pots or for decoration purposes such as jars, piggy banks, and decorative plates. Because the items

370 Cf. Astriani 2012, p. 61.
371 Interview with A.N. from the UPTD Litbang Keramik Plered on March 7, 2012 in Plered, Purwakarta.
372 Ibid.
373 Cf. "Kuliah Lapangan Mahasiswa Kriya Keramik ke Sentra Keramik Plered Pada 29 November 2012". http://www.kria.fsrd.itb.ac.id/?p=541, accessed January 15, 2014.
374 Cf. Antara 2009.
375 Cf. Subari 2010.

purchased are not primary needs, the buyer usually does not question the quality of the product. It is just that they are very concerned with the appearance and color of the ceramic products. For foreign buyers, instead of the appearance, they are also concerned with the quality of the product especially with similar products coming from China and Vietnam in international markets. Usually the ways the craftsmen produce a better (or at least imitate) product (in terms of quality and appearance) than the product of China and Vietnam are by seeking information through magazines, websites, and by following international exhibitions. Buyers in international exhibitions usually give inspirations to produce products that are completely new or at least make an improvement from the old ones.

The Presence of Related and Supporting Industries

The presence of related and supporting industries is essential for promoting improvements and innovations in a cluster as mentioned in the previous chapter. In Plered, there are several related and supporting industries. Based on interviews and observations in Plered, those industries are comprised of: raw materials (clay) industry, the UPTD Litbang Keramik Plered, production facilities (workshop production) of the UPTD Litbang Keramik Plered, and the Plered Ceramic Gallery. The UPTD Litbang Keramik Plered is actually directed as a provider of qualified raw materials to SMEs in Plered as well as a means of conducting trainings especially on production techniques, while the Plered Ceramic Gallery is intended as a promotional tool to show the types of Plered decorative ceramics Plered to the public.

Other supporting industries are the presence of universities and research centers in Plered. They are the Bandung Institute of Technology, University of Indonesia, the Bandung Ceramic Center, the LIPI, and the BPPT. Unfortunately, none of these universities and research centers is located in Plered. The ways these industries help SMEs in Plered are by conducting the internship program (Bandung Intitute of Technology for example), visiting Plered to conduct trainings, and inviting the craftsmen to come to Bandung Ceramics Center for taking trainings.

5.3.2 Problems Faced by SMEs and the Ceramic Cluster

Looking at the potential of these SMEs in the Plered Ceramic Industry, the government should give special attention and assistance so that these SMEs can continue to survive and develop themselves in the swift currents of globalization. There are several problems that hinder SMEs to grow and continue to contribute to the economy of Purwakarta.

The *first* is related to the aspect of human resource. A common problem that occurs to the SMEs in Plered (as well in Indonesia) is a '*one-man show*' business activity.[376] This business method means that there is no clear division of work between administrative (the owner) and operational (the employees) levels. Most of Indonesian SMEs are managed by individuals who work as an owner as well as an employee of the company. Therefore, sometimes the owner disregards the separation of company and personal affairs. They often use the company's money for personal expenses and vice versa. Not only that, they often include their relatives in running the enterprise. Based on an economic survey conducted by the Central Bureau Statistics (BPS) in 2006, the survey found out that in 2006 from the total of 22,513,552 micro and small enterprises (not including agricultural enterprises and medium enterprises), there are 43,911,721 employees work for these micro and small enterprises.[377] From that number, only 12,674,094 employees get paid. The rest did not get paid since they work to help the owners run their business. It also occurs in Plered ceramic industry where many SMEs involve their family members as employees. During a fieldwork in Plered, the writer interviewed three business owners in order to understand the reasons of recruiting family members in their businesses.[378] *First*, these business owners try to reduce the cost of production by recruiting their family members in their business production/activity. Due to its status as a member of the family, the owners are then not required to pay the workers' wages. *Second*, business owners feel

---

376 Cf. Dipta (n.d).

377 Cf. Suherman 2006.

378 The writer spent three months (March-May 2012) in Plered to collect the data on the Plered Decorative Ceramic Industrial Cluster, to interview the head of the UPTD Litbang Keramik Plered in order to observe the activity of the SMEs in the region as well as the problems faced by the UPTD Litbang Keramik and the SMEs towards their daily business activity, to interview business owners related their business activity, and to meet the representatives of the UPTD Litbang Keramik Plered.

more comfortable and confident in family members than workers who are not members of the family. Of course this can cause problems in the future such as difficulty to determine fixed working hours for the workers, the reluctance to warn employees if doing production errors, and the lack of good (standard) financial statements, especially if it is associated with the tax payment. The recruitment of family members regardless of sufficient ability to make decorative ceramic becomes one of the causes of low quality ceramic products in Plered.

AN, from the UPTD Litbang Keramik Plered, added that there are two main problems related to this matter within SMEs/SMIs in the Plered ceramic cluster.[379] *First*, the actors in Plered still view producing ceramic as means to support their daily finances rather than viewing this as a long-term business potential (in terms of getting bigger and better). Based on the survey that was conducted in March-April 2012, the writer found that the majority of the business actors in the Plered Decorative Ceramic Industrial Cluster produce decorative ceramics or other ceramic products without a production target or sale. It means that the actors produce the ceramics as a daily routine. Furthermore, there have been difficulties in encompassing potential consumers that has declined drastically since the opening of the Purbaleunyi toll road. That has caused ceramic production to decline as well hence impacting the profit of the businesses. *Second*, the production process that still mixes housing (the kitchen) as its production facility. The lack of production space has caused almost all the business actors of Plered ceramic industry to carry out the production process in their own homes. It cannot be denied that limitation of land and lack of capital to purchase facility space has caused houses to be transformed as an alternative place to produce ceramics. As a result, there is no sanitation in the houses of these actors and therefore threatens their health along with the health of their family members.

Pakpahan (2010) also added that the biggest problem in the management of SMEs in Indonesia (and Plered) is the low level of entrepreneurial spirit.[380] This means that these entrepreneurs do not know how to improve their product quality, how to market their products abroad, and how to create innovations to win tight competitions. This is even worse when dealing with low-skilled labor and workers who have specialization in de-

379 Interview with A.N. from the UPTD Litbang Keramik Plered on March 8, 2012 in Plered, Purwakarta.

380 Cf. Pakpahan 2010.

sign.[381] Most workers in the ceramic industry Plered obtain knowledge in the production and design of ceramic by independent learning from other (senior) workers or passed down from one generation to the next without any formal education or trainings. Therefore, there is almost no formal training obtained by these workers which results in the poor design and poor quality products. Hence, most of their products have problems with precisions and are difficult to be standardized. A research conducted by Yuni Astriani (2012) on the welfare of the craftsmen in the Plered Decorative Ceramic Industrial Cluster found that education level of and skills acquired by the business owners and workers vary widely.[382] At the level of the business owner, 51.86 percent of business owners have a high school diploma while the rest are scattered in primary education (22.22 percent), middle school (22.22 percent), and university levels (3.7 percent). While at the level of the workers found that 50 percent of workers have only primary school diploma while the rest have a junior diploma (37.5 percent) and a high school diploma (12.5 percent). Related to the skills (of making/producing ceramic) acquired by the business owners and workers, Astriani categorized her finding into three categories. The *first* are those who are acquired the skills to make pottery from their parents. At the level of business owners, it is found out that 29.63 percent of business owners learned to make ceramic from their parents while at the level of the workers the percentage is 41.67 percent. The *second* are those who acquired their skills on their own (self) on how to make ceramic. At the level of business owners, it is found out that 55.56 percent of them are acquired the skills by independent learning while the level of worker, the percentage is 52.08 percent. The *third* are those who gain the skills by asking their fellow crafters. It is found out that 14.81 percent of business owners and 6.25 percent of workers get their skills by asking from other crafters. These findings explain how low the entrepreneurial spirit and skills of business owners and workers in the Plered's Ceramic Industry. It is not surprising that the quality of their products is not optimal.

The problem in the quality of human resource does not happen only to the SMEs, the same problem also occurs to the government agency in the area. The UPTD Litbang Keramik Plered is the government's representative in Plered. Its main function is to conduct research and development programs on designs, technology, and marketing. Based on an interview

381 Cf. Ridwan (n.d.).
382 Cf. Astriani 2012, p. 56.

with AN, it is found that his office has only ten staffs including himself and his deputy (i.e. the chief sub-section who deals with the administration matters). According to AN, this number has not been ideal in handling all the needs of SMEs and the development of this ceramic industry. Another problem that is related to the existence of this office is the absence of the regular budget and adequate supporting facilities. Sometimes to conduct research and development programs, the staffs work independently to resolve problems and the needs of SMEs.

The *second* problem is related to the work ethic and technology issues.[383] According to the UPTD Litbang Keramik Plered, there are many efforts to improve the quality and value-added ceramic products. An example of such program is the pilot programs for the SMEs and business owners either directly or indirectly. The Purwakarta's Office of Industry and Investment has given technical assistances on how to process raw materials to be good materials and to make tiles and ceramic tiles from those materials. However, due to the local work ethics and culture issues (to produce fast and cheap), these SMEs tend to ignore such procedures. For example, the cultivation of land (materials) that requires 20 percent of a mixture of silica (SiO2) and limestone (CaCO3) is given only 12-15 percent by the workers (SMEs). Another example is that sometimes the workers do the process of drying and burning the soil (materials) in a hurry so that most of the products are damaged and broken. Looking at Plered's clay, the perfect drying process should take 36 hours (or about three days) and the perfect burning process should use a 950 degrees Celsius burning-machine.[384]

Meanwhile, because of the traditional burning machine (furnace) with no heat measuring instruments used by the SMEs, the quality of their product are not that good. This is also worsened by the use of different burning machines with varying measurements (800 degrees, 850 degrees, and 900 degrees) that degrades the quality of the ceramic. In addition, the use of traditional combustion engines (using firewood as the primary fuel) is still widely used by SMEs in Plered. The use of the traditional machine is of course highly dependent on the availability of firewood. Usually, this machine uses the rambutan's wood from the area of Garut and Tasikma-

---

383 Dinas Tata Ruang dan Bangunan Pemerintah Kabupaten Purwakarta 2003, pp. 45-47.

384 Interview with AN from the UPTD Litbang Keramik Plered on March 8, 2012 in Plered, Purwakarta.

laya, West Java. Of course, the use of firewood cannot provide an exact measure of the combustion quality (as mentioned earlier) and therefore leads to a poor ceramic production. Many of these SMEs and business owners feel that they already know almost everything since they run their business quite long and has been carried down from generation to generation, therefore they usually do not pay attention to the programs offered or given by the government officials.

Not only that these SMEs often lose trust from the customers because of their difficulty to meet production deadlines and to maintain the quality of their products delivered on a large scale. This is due to their ability of the workers and their capability of the machines. It is not a surprise if they sometimes lose big orders from their customers.

The *third* problem is the increasing number of foreign competitors and imported products coming into Indonesia (especially from China) not to mention that some of these products have better quality at cheaper prices.[385] It is undeniable that the flood of Chinese ceramics in the Indonesian market (as well as international markets) has put Plered SMEs' products in danger. The quality of (raw) materials and attractive designs are major threats to the Plered ceramic. The difficulty in competing with foreign products is not only related to the quality and price of goods but also the difficulties in reaching markets outside Plered. The opening of new toll road Purbaleunyi (Purwakarta - Bandung - Cileunyi) makes the Plered ceramic cluster became marginalized. Before there were highways, Plered ceramic cluster can still attract consumers who are headed Jakarta through the Plered's main street, but since the opening of freeway access, most people choose the toll lanes to cut travel time. The outcome was the fall in potential buyers to the region and the reduction Plered craftsmen's income and total sales.

Other difficulties in selling their products (to the local and international markets) are due to several simple problems on the quality of their product.[386] *First*, they have difficulty in obtaining high quality raw materials so the result is that their quality of products cannot compete in the global market. *Second*, natural gas supply as a fuel source for modern burning-machines for producing ceramic is not a long-term guarantee from the government. The head of the Bandung Center for Ceramic, Lintong Supandi Hutahean and Director of the downstream chemical industry of

385 Cf. Ridwan (n.d.).
386 Cf. Ridwan (n.d.).

the Ministry of Industry, Toety Rahajoe, stated that the biggest problem in the ceramic industry is the availability of fuel gas.[387] The problem is not just the availability of fuel gas, but also the allocation and realization of gas supply which is inconsistent. Regulation on the allocation and utilization of natural gas for the fulfillment of the domestic needs has regulated in the Ministry of Energy and Mineral Resources Decree No. 3/2010. However, many people say that there is a need to revise that decree especially in article 6. It is stated in article 6 that the determination of allocation and utilization of natural gas should be implemented to the priority of [increasing the production of] national oil and gas, the fertilizer industry, the supply of electric power, and other industries. In other words, the allocation of natural gas to the industrial sector is the last priority. *Third*, natural gas price is pegged to the U.S. Dollar (USD); therefore, if the value of the rupiah (IDR) depreciates then there will be an increase in the cost of production. *Fourth*, the industry of ceramic raw materials processing is limited so several areas have to import raw materials with good quality. *Fifth*, the mastery of research and development is still weak. *Sixth*, human resources in the design scope are weak as well.

Looking at current conditions and problems faced by SMEs/SMIs in Plered, this cluster can be categorized as Altenburg and Meyer-Stamer's survival cluster of micro and small-scale enterprises, which is the collection of local firms located in small areas producing low-quality goods for local markets or Tambunan's artisanal cluster, which is characterized by low levels of productivity due to the low quality of human resources and the use of technology as well as the lack of specialization and linkages among SMEs. Therefore, there is still a long way to go and many improvements needed to achieve a type of working cluster in Plered as mentioned earlier.

387 Cf. Solusi Magazine 2012a, p. 38, Solusi Magazine 2012b, p. 48.

6. Factors Affecting the Implementation of Business Clusters in Indonesia

This chapter will examine the implementation of the concept of business clusters in Indonesia by looking at the two business clusters (in Cibaduyut and Plered, West Java) as a case study. While Porter's diamond theory is used to explain the implementation of business cluster in Indonesia, there are number of further factors that require consideration. In the previous chapter, the researcher has already described the profile of two case studies in implementing the concept of business clusters and problems faced by them. The implementation of the concept of business clusters in Indonesia does not automatically provide the advantage of increasing firm's competitiveness and product innovation. This is due to factors that affect the implementation of that concept in Indonesia, namely: decentralization and the influence of culture. Looking at the implementation of the business cluster in the two research sites, there are three main concerns that attracted the attention of the researcher and will be discussed in this chapter. *First*, the application of decentralization (local autonomy) in Indonesia as stipulated in Law No. 32/2004 on Regional Government. *Second*, the influence of national and local cultures in a way people conduct business activity such as the national principle of working together (*gotong royong*), the Javanese principle of togetherness i.e. "it is unimportant to have food on the table, the most important is to get together" (*mangan ora mangan anggere kumpul*), and the Sundanese principles of comforting, educating, and caring toward each other (*silih asih, silih asah, silih asuh*). *Third* is the family business ownership that can be found in many SMEs/SMIs inside the cluster in Indonesia. According to the researcher, those three concerns above are the main obstacle that impedes the implementation of business clusters in Indonesia.

6.1 The Implementation of Decentralization (Local Autonomy) in Indonesia

The need to understand the concept of decentralization is important in this research. According to Rondinelli and Nellis (as cited in Rondinelli et al., 1989), decentralization is

> "the transfer of responsibility of planning, management, and the raising and allocation of resources from the central government and its agencies to field units of government agencies, subordinate units or levels of government, semi-autonomous public authorities or corporations, area-wide, regional or functional authorities, or non-governmental private or voluntary organizations".[388]

In short, decentralization is about transferring of some central government's authorities to the local governments i.e. the right of regional government to organize regional (local) affairs independently (or autonomy). However, using the Indonesian context, decentralization does not include the transfer of responsibility to the non-governmental private or voluntary organizations. According to Abdul Gafar Karim (as cited in Jati 2012, 747), autonomy, as a manifestation of democracy, applies the concept of '*areal division of power*' that divides a country's power vertically between the central government and local governments.[389] Related to this research, this concept is important because the implementation of a business concept cluster in the two research sites (Cibaduyut and Plered) firstly came from the central government's initiative. Here, the formation of the two clusters formally outlined in the regulation of the minister of industry (as a representative of the central government) and then implemented locally by the local governments. The concept of decentralization in Indonesia is actually enacted by Law No. 32/2004 on Regional Government as an improvement of Law No. 22/1999 on Regional Government. In this law, the local government is authorized to regulate and manage its own affairs in accordance with the principle of autonomy and assistance.[390] Granting broad autonomy to the region is basically aimed to accelerate the realization of public welfare through improvement of services, empowerment, and community involvement. Besides extensive autonomy, the region is expected to improve its competitiveness with regard to the principles of democracy, equality, justice, privilege and specificity as well as the potential and diversity of the regions in the framework of the Unitary Republic of Indonesia.[391] The local government is given discretion to manage its own affairs except specific matters related to the issues of: foreign policy,

388 Rondinelli et al. 1989, pp. 58-59.
389 Cf. Jati 2012, p. 747.
390 Cf. the consideration section of Law No. 32/2004.
391 Cf. Article 2 Paragraph 3 of Law No. 32/2004.

defense, security, legal system, monetary and fiscal policy as well as religion.[392]

While other affairs that are not included in the jurisdiction of the central government, the central government can organize those affairs together with the local governments (in this case provincial, city, and regency governments) or can delegate those affairs to the local government.[393] Referring to Government Regulation No. 38/2007 on the Division of Government Affairs Among the (Central) Government, the Provincial Government, and the City/Regency Governments, there is a division of government affairs consisting of: (a) those which are fully under the authority of the central government and (b) those which are shared between the levels and/or levels of government.[394] In this law, the government affairs which are shared include the affair of cooperatives and SMEs, trade, and industry.[395] Talking about shared affairs, we have to of course deal with different levels of government agencies.[396] That includes not only the relationships between the central government and the local government(s), but also the relationship among local governments as well as the relationship among their local agencies (such as regional office, regency, city, and village for example).

In the context of promoting regional development (in order to increase regional's public welfare and competitiveness), the concept of decentralization is clearly needed. In Indonesia, the concept of decentralization is applied as a form to accommodate local (regional) desire that demands changes in the economic relations between central and regional government.[397] It is believed that in the past (before the issuance of Law No. 22/1999 on Regional Government), the economic relations between central and regional governments were more favorable for the central government. Moreover, Baier et al. (2013) state that central government policies sometimes cannot answer the interest of the regional level because of its policy interests are addressed in general (to support the whole economy).[398] Hadiz (2004) said that to support the (regional) development program, the involvement of local communities in decision-making should be

392 Cf. Article 10 Paragraphs 1 and 3 of Law No. 32/2004.
393 Cf. Article 10 Paragraph 5 of Law No. 32/2004.
394 Cf. Article 2 Paragraph 1 of Government Regulation No. 38/2007.
395 Cf. Article 2 Paragraph 4 of Government Regulation No. 38/2007.
396 Cf. Clark 1984, p. 196.
397 Cf. Jati 2012, pp. 762-63.
398 Cf. Baier/Kroll/Zenker 2013, p. 2.

encouraged.[399] He added that decentralization will also lead to bigger prioritization of local needs in development policy.[400] In the context of economic development, decentralization provides more flexibility to design a regional economic policy based on the potential of natural resources and the uniqueness of the region. There are several advantages of decentralization, which includes: the aspirations of local (regional) communities can be accommodated, reduce the bureaucracy and complicate procedures, better '*penetration*' toward rural areas (where the central government plans are often not understood by local communities or inhibited by local elites, and thus the support for the government's program is limited), and local governments cannot escape from responsibility for (almost) all policies that are designed by local governments and therefore the supervision of regional programs become more optimal.

There are at least two points with regards to decentralization and clustering in West Java. *First*, the lack of coordination among government agencies which happens not only between the central government and local governments but also between local governments and sub-regional governments (in this case the city and regency governments). Hadiz (2004) supports this finding by stating that decentralization sometimes makes coordination of national programs become more complicated.[401] *Second*, the failure of policy implementation at the regional level i.e. the program that is designed by the central government is sometimes not carried out properly at the level of local and sub-regional governments. This is what LaPalombara (1971) described as a penetration crisis.[402]

The *first* point is related to the coordination between government agencies. Looking at the development of SMEs/SMIs in West Java, there are two governmental agencies and four regional agencies in charge for the development of the SMEs/SMIs' sector. The two governmental agencies are the Ministry of Cooperatives and SMEs and the Ministry of Industry. While in the regional level, the first two are in the provincial level which is the Office of Cooperatives and SMEs and the Office of Industry and Trade. The other two are in the level of city and regency level which are the Office of Cooperatives, SMEs, Industry, and Trade of the city of Bandung and the Office of Cooperatives, SMEs, Industry, and Trade of the re-

399 Cf. Hadiz 2004, p. 700.
400 Cf. ibid.
401 Cf. Hadiz 2004, p. 705.
402 Cf. LaPalombara 1971, pp. 207-08.

gency of Purwakarta. To give more focus on this research, there are also two technical service units that are responsible to provide assistances to two research sites: the Office for Developing the Small and Medium-sized Shoe Industry in Cibaduyut and the Ceramic Technical Services Unit in Plered. The Office for Developing the Small and Medium-sized Shoe Industry in Cibaduyut is under the coordination and supervision of the West Java Office of Industry and Trade[403] while the Ceramic Technical Services Unit in Plered is under the coordination and supervision of the Office of Cooperatives, SMEs, Industry, and Trade of the regency of Purwakarta.[404] What is interesting is to see the position of the two technical service units at both research sites. The technical service unit in Cibaduyut is under the jurisdiction of the provincial level while the technical service unit in Plered is under the jurisdiction of the regency level. Based on the interview conducted by the researcher, there is no difference in treatment by local governments to the two technical service units as well as the two clusters. However, differences in the position of superior agency can be interpreted that the footwear cluster in Cibaduyut gets more attention from the local government for its economic potential compared to the decorative ceramic industrial cluster in Plered.[405] This certainly brings a new problem which is a long bureaucratic mechanism for the ceramic cluster compared to the footwear cluster. The illustration is as follows: for the ceramic cluster the bureaucracy mechanism should be done first through the technical service unit in the site, continue to the second step to the regency office, then to the provincial office, and last step to the two ministries. As for the footwear cluster the same mechanism is only done through the technical service unit in the site, the provincial agency, and the two ministries.

In the case of developing industrial clusters in both locations, the concept of decentralization is unclear since this policy is made with the *top-down* approach and is implemented by the central government. That means the Ministry of Industry (as a representative of the central government) is responsible for the development of 35 priority industrial clusters

403 Cf. Article 3 Paragraph 13 of Regulation of the West Java Governor No. 113/2009.

404 Cf. Article 2 Paragraph 2 of Regulation of the Purwakarta Regent No. 44/2009.

405 See previous chapter describing the production potential in the footwear cluster in Cibaduyut and the ceramic cluster in Plered. For example, the total production value of the footwear cluster is IDR 529.92 billion compared to IDR 16.26 billion in the ceramic cluster in Plered.

(including footwear and decorative ceramic). Examples on the *top-down* approach in the two clusters are: (a) the granting of ceramic combustion machine by the Ministry of Industry to the UPTD Litbang Keramik Plered,[406] even though the use of this device is not optimal because it uses gas fuel in which its distribution and price do not support the industrial activities in Plered and (b) the issuance of Regulation of the Minister of Industry No. 13/2013 on the Program to Restructure of SMIs' Machinery/Equipment in order to increase the competitiveness of national SMIs in which one of the target recipients is the footwear SMIs. In order to develop these clusters, the ministry is helped by related local government agencies such as the office of industry and trade. Looking at the above explanation, there many agencies involved in developing the two industrial clusters. Not to mention about the difficulty of coordination between offices (governmental, provincial, city, and regency) in Indonesia. Bennet (2010) said that one of the problems of local autonomy in Indonesia is that the government officials at the provincial level sometimes lack the authority to coordinate with local leaders.[407] Recalling that the development of these two clusters is an initiative of the central government (the *top-down* approach) through the Regulation of the President of the Republic of Indonesia and the Regulation of the Minister of Industry, it can be imagined how difficult it is to get attention to further develop these two industrial clusters. Because of the implementation of decentralization as mentioned earlier, the responsibility and the development of the two cluster becomes vague, whether it is in the hands of the central government (in this case the Ministry of Industry and the Ministry of Cooperatives and SMEs) or in the hand of local governments i.e. the provincial level (for footwear cluster) or in the hand of the regency (for ceramic cluster).

The example of this situation can be found in both research sites. In Plered, based on a research conducted by Desy Ariyani, it is found that there are several trainings which are organized by the UPTD Litbang Keramik Plered in collaboration with the Bandung Ceramic Center such as: (a) training on design (in 2010), (b) training on production techniques such as the manufacture and molding of ceramic models (in 2010), combustion techniques (in 2008 and 2011), and training on the basic knowledge and treatment of burning stoves (in 2009), (c) trainings on raw

406 Interview with A.N. from the UPTD Litbang Keramik Plered on March 8, 2012 in Plered, Purwakarta.

407 Cf. Bennet 2010, p. 7.

materials such as the introduction of clay raw materials (in 2008) and the type of fuel for the production of ceramic (in 2009), and (d) training on product innovation (in 2009).[408] Moreover, in 2009 the Plered Technical Service Unit for Research and Development of Ceramic in collaboration with the West Java Office of Industry and Trade has organized training on policy of exporting ceramic.[409] In addition to those trainings mentioned above, the Plered Technical Service Unit regularly conducts training related to production techniques and ceramic burning techniques. Lack of coordination is clearly noticeable as in the last three years there were only three (government) institutions that conduct training for potters in Plered. Moreover, there is almost no training that is undertaken by the Purwakarta Office of Cooperatives, SMEs, Industry, and Trade, the West Java Office of Cooperatives and SMEs, the West Java Office of Industry and Trade, or from the two ministries. Although, if we look at the working program of the offices and ministries as noted in the previous chapter, there are several programs that could be done by these offices and ministries in the ceramic cluster. Looking at working programs of the Purwakarta Office of Cooperatives, SMEs, Industry, and Trade in 2010, 2011, and 2012 below, it is quite clear that there is no program that is aimed particularly at the development of ceramic cluster in Plered. The details of the programs can be seen in the following table.

Table 6.1: Working Program of the Purwakarta Office of Cooperatives, SMEs, Industry, and Trade, 2010-2012

Year	Programs
2010	Program on Developing SMIs
	Program on Regulating Industrial Structure
2011	Program on Developing Entrepreneurial Spirit and Competitive Advantage of SMEs' Products
	Program on Creating a Supportive Business Climate
	Program on Developing Potential Industry
	Program on Increasing and Developing Exports
	Program on Increasing the Capacity of Production System's Technology

408 Cf. Ariyani 2012, pp. 7-8.
409 Cf. ibid.

	Program on Increasing the Ability of Industrial Technology
	Program on Developing SMIs
2012	Program on Creating a Supportive Business Climate
	Program on Developing Entrepreneurial Spirit and Competitive Advantage of SMEs' Products
	Program on Developing Business Support System For SMEs
	Program on Developing SMIs
	Program on Increasing the Ability of Industrial Technology
	Program on Developing Potential Industry

Source: Data modified from Buku Kerja Dinas Koperasi, UMKM, Perindustrian, and Perdagangan Kabupaten Purwakarta Tahun 2010, 2011, and 2012

The researcher tries to read carefully the programs mentioned in the table, unfortunately there is no detailed explanation on each program. Therefore, it is not clear whether those programs are intended for developing the ceramic cluster in Plered or are generally done to various SMEs' sectors in Plered. Moreover, there is no explanation whatsoever in these programs whether to work with other government agencies (such as related offices in the provincial level, related offices in other regencies and cities, research centers, and universities) or not. In fact, the researcher found one document that stated that this office agreed to propose several action program priorities to develop the ceramic cluster in collaboration with other government agencies such as the Directorate General of Small and Medium-sized Industries of the Ministry of Industry, the West Java Office of Industry and Trade, the Bandung Ceramic Center, the West Java Indonesia Chamber of Commerce and Industry, and the Purwakarta Office of Transportation, Culture, Tourism, Post, and Telecommunications.[410] Unfortunately this agreement was not listed in the annual program formulated by the office in 2010-2012. It can be concluded that: *first*, the officer(s) who attended the meeting did not have the authority to make decisions. *Second*, there is lack of coordination between the officer(s) and the office to follow up the results of the meeting. Things like this are very common to happen in the Indonesian bureaucracy.

The same situation also occurs in Cibaduyut. Programs that are designed by the Office of Industry and Trade (as described in the previous

410 Cf. Dinas Koperasi, Usaha Mikro, Kecil, Menengah, Perindustrian dan Perdagangan Kabupaten Purwakarta 2009.

section) in practice are not running well. WD, from the Office for Developing the Small and Medium-sized Shoe Industry in Cibaduyut, found that several trainings conducted in Cibaduyut sometimes are not really needed by the craftsmen.[411] One example of the trainings is on financial management, conducted by the Office of Industry and Trade. According to WD, what is needed most by the craftsmen in Cibaduyut is training on production techniques and designs to improve the quality of their product. There is also a program conducted by the West Java Office of Cooperatives to SMEs in Cibaduyut which is called the Business Group program. The program is designed to provide funding for a business group in the cluster. Unfortunately, the implementation of this program only gives funds to a business group without either supervision or evaluation of the program. Looking at the strategic plans of the West Java Office of Industry and Trade, unfortunately there is no detailed explanation of the programs in terms of related agencies the cooperation should be undertaken. Looking at the two examples above, it is quite clear that there is lack of coordination between the two offices and the technical service unit in Cibaduyut concerning the problems faced by and the needs of craftsmen in Cibaduyut. There is many training conducted for SMEs/SMIs in Cibaduyut, but some of them are either not needed by these SMEs or not implemented well like the above examples.

What happened in the two research sites is similar to what Bhasin and Venkataramany (2010) researched on current policies of SMEs in Indonesia.[412] They said that the main problem that causes loss of competitiveness of SMEs is the lack of coordination among departments responsible for developing SMEs i.e. too many institutions involved but there is no coordination and there is no master plan to develop SMEs. A research conducted by Tulus Tambunan supports this argument.[413] He stated that government efforts to support the existence of SMEs (and SMIs) are sometimes not effective. Another evidence that there is lack of coordination among government agencies in these two clusters is: the lack of official data on the latest number of business units and their production (for instance data showing how many enterprise upgraded its size i.e. micro en-

411 Interview with W.D. from the Office for Developing the Small and Medium-sized Shoe Industry in Cibaduyut in Bandung on September 19, 2012 conducted by Lukas Tambunan.

412 Cf. Bhasin/Venkataramany 2010, pp. 97-100.

413 Cf. Tambunan 2010.

terprise becomes small enterprise, small enterprise becomes medium enterprises, and medium enterprise becomes larger enterprise), there is no data on the number and type of product innovation (for instance data showing the number of patent resulted in the two clusters), and the unavailability of the evaluation that can be used as a parameter whether the designed programs are successful or not. To provide such data, there must be a chain of distribution of information and a line of coordination starts from the technical service unit (in each cluster) to the sub-regional offices (city and regency level) to the offices in the regional level (province) and to other related government agencies (such as the bureau of statistics). The Ministry of Industry once published the Performance Accountability Report 2010 in which there is a section that discusses the results of the performance achievements of industrial cluster development as stated in the Strategic Plan of the Ministry of Industry 2010-2014.[414] Unfortunately, the report is too general and lack of a specific and detail report and evaluation on programs in each (industrial) cluster. Fortunately, the Ministry of Industry conducts annual working meetings in which one of the agendas is the evaluation of industrial cluster development program.[415] Looking at the agenda of the meeting and the resulting output, there are many positive outcomes that unfortunately have not seen implemented in two clusters (research sites) yet.

Furthermore, lack of coordination in Indonesia occurs not only in the SMEs/SMIs' development policy but also occurs in many sectors. For example, a research conducted by Triwibowo and Pakpahan (2012) found that in the handling of corruption cases, there are at least three state agencies in which their duty and authority are almost similar to each other that often caused friction between them.[416] Similarly, a research conducted by Yazid (2012) also found that in handling the problem of Indonesian migrant workers, there are as many as 18 state agencies without a clear coordination line.[417] Sutanto (as cited in Bhasin and Venkataramany, 2010) suggested that the development of SMEs/SMIs should be centralized and coordinated in a single institution.[418] Actually, the idea to create one institution which is responsible for developing the SMEs/SMIs actually al-

414 For further details on the report, please see Kementerian Perindustrian (n.d.c). Laporan Akuntabilitas Kinerja (LAKIP) 2010.

415 Cf. Kementerian Perindustrian (n.d.d.).

416 Cf. Triwibowo/Pakpahan 2012, pp. 246-47.

417 Cf. Yazid 2012, p. 226.

418 Cf. Bhasin/Venkataramany 2010, p. 97.

ready exists at the sub-regional governmental level. The case of the Plered Decorative Ceramic Industrial Cluster for instance, there is only one office that is responsible for developing this industry which is the Office of Co-operatives, SMEs, Industry, and Trade of the Regency of Purwakarta. However, looking back at the decentralization process and the policy of regional development that must be in harmony with the national development plan, the function of this office becomes unclear. The office again has to coordinate its policy with other governmental agencies. As Brown (2000) said, to overcome problem of decentralization, it is important to have a close coordination and appropriate coordination mechanism among different government agencies.[419] Possible forms of coordination to overcome those problems is to hold regular weekly meetings for the sub-regional level (between the technical service unit with local government agencies i.e. related offices in the city/regency level), regular monthly meetings for the sub-regional and the regional level (between the city/regency offices with the provincial offices), and regular coordination meeting (can be monthly or quarterly) in the national level (between offices in the provincial level with the relevant ministries/government agencies). The meeting agenda should also include (weekly and monthly) monitoring and evaluation of the programs. The importance of having program evaluation in the policy implementation is to assess the performance of the program as well as to improve the (current) program.[420] Therefore, should there be a problem; the solution can be given immediately. Furthermore, the advantage of having a weekly (and monthly) meeting is that the aspirations and the needs of SMEs can be absorbed directly and given a way out right away when having problems. This coordination definitely requires a commitment from the entire government officials in supporting the development of SMEs/SMIs in the region.

The *second* point related to the failure of policy implementation at the regional government level. The failure of government programs at the regional level can be interpreted that there is a penetration failure of the central government programs in the region. LaPalombara (1971) described such situation as a crisis of penetration.[421] He described penetration as "[…] the effective presence of a central government throughout a territory

419 Cf. Brown 2000, pp. 7-8.
420 Cf. deLeon/deLeon 2002, p. 475.
421 See LaPalombara 1971, pp. 205-32.

over which it pretends to exercise control".[422] He also stresses that penetration means a compliance with the public policy enunciated by the authority of the central government.[423] However, the problem here is the implementation of the program in a certain region. Van Meter and Van Horn (1975) defined policy implementation as "[...] those actions by public and private individuals (or groups) that are directed at the achievement of objectives set forth in prior policy decisions".[424] Using the two research sites as a case study, it is obvious that the nature of the industrial policy (with regard to the development of footwear and decorative ceramic clusters) refers to the *top-down* approach (see Chapter 3). In this sense, the policy created by the central government is used as operational and coordination guidelines by government officials (both at central and local level) in implementing the policy.

In achieving the fundamental goal of a state which is to increase public welfare, the central government has made a national policy known as the National Medium-term Development Plan 2010-2014. This national development plan is served as a basis for each Ministry's Strategic Plans 2010-2014.[425] This National Medium-term Development Plan along together with the Strategic Plans of the ministries is then used as a guideline for formulating the Regional Medium-term Development Plan 2010-2014.[426] This Regional Medium-term Development Plan is then used as a basis not only for formulating strategic plans of each office (*dinas*) in the provincial level but also for sub-regional governments to formulate their policy and program of development for their respective offices. This is confirmed in the meeting among the Ministry of Industry, Regional Office of Industry, and the Regional Body for Planning and Development (*Badan Perencana Pembangunan Daerah*, Bappeda) in 2010 declared that the National Medium-term Development Plan 2010-2014, the National Industrial Policy, the Strategic Plans of the Ministry of Industry 2010-2014, and the Road Map of the Priority Industrial Cluster Development must be implemented by the whole units and working units under the Ministry of Industry both at central and regional level as well as regional offices that deal

422 Ibid., p. 207.

423 Cf. ibid., p. 208.

424 Van Meter/Van Horn 1975, p. 447.

425 Cf. Article 2 Paragraph 3a of Regulation of the President of the Republic of Indonesia No. 5/2010.

426 Cf. Article 2 Paragraph 3b of Regulation of the President of the Republic of Indonesia No. 5/2010.

with industrial sectors.[427] Therefore, these offices are asked to design and plan their strategic plans according the programs mentioned in the National Medium-term Development Plan 2010-2014, the National Industrial Policy, the Strategic Plans of the Ministry of Industry 2010-2014, and the Road Map of the Priority Industrial Cluster Development. Looking at the above explanations, it can be interpreted that all policies and working programs created by the Office of Cooperatives and SMEs as well as the Office of Industry and Trade of the Province of West Java must be consistent with the national development plans and programs especially in the of sector of SMEs and industry. Similarly, the Office of Cooperatives, SMEs, Industry, and Commerce of the city of Bandung and the regency of Purwakarta should also design their programs according to the national development plan and the regional development plan. In fact, what takes place in the regional and sub-regional level is quite different. In Indonesia, decentralization gives more autonomy to the sub-regional governments (regencies and cities) instead of regional government (Pepinsky/Wihardja, 2011; Hadiz, 2004).[428] This is because the concept of decentralization is also applied to the sub-regional level. In that sense, the sub-regional governments are given the authority to formulate policies to improve the welfare of their people. This authority is usually led to a situation where government programs are not run by the sub-regional (city and regency) government. This is usually related to differences in political orientation between the central government and regional governments. The explanation of this issue will be discussed later on in this chapter.

Related to the development of footwear industrial cluster in Cibaduyut and the development of decorative ceramic industrial cluster in Plered, the researcher has described the strategic plans and working programs of the Ministry of Industry to develop this cluster. Looking at Table 5.2 and Table 5.3 (in Chapter 5), there are many programs that are designed to involve other government agencies. Simply, we can see whether the program that are designed by the central government has been implemented or not by looking at the working programs of the subordinate levels such as the provincial offices (the Office of Cooperatives and SMEs and the Office of Industry and Trade) and the city/regency offices. Looking back at the working programs conducted by the West Java Office of Industry and Trade (in Chapter 4) in developing the footwear industrial cluster, the

427 Cf. Kementerian Perindustrian (n.d.e).

428 Cf. Pepinsky/Wihardja 2011, p. 342, Hadiz 2004, p. 708.

researcher cannot find programs that are designed by the Ministry of Industry in cooperation with the local government such as: program to improve investments for supporting industry by giving facilities and ease of doing business, programs to improve the role of research and development institutions to develop the main and substitution materials, supporting materials, and accessories, program to improve the quality of raw skin in the abattoir, and programs to strengthen the leather tanning industries' UPT by supporting the availability of the raw leather materials to increase services for small industries in order to support the availability of raw materials. One example is the program to improve the human resource skills in designs and production techniques through workshops and internships. This program is designed to involve Ministry of Industry, Ministry of Cooperatives and SMEs, Ministry of Education and Culture, Ministry of Manpower and Transmigration, and related university. Unfortunately, until 2013 there is no such training is ever conducted in Cibaduyut for the craftmen as designed in the Medium-term Plan of the Footwear Cluster Industry Development. Based on interviews with the shoemaker and craftsmen, there are only training on production techniques (provided by the technical service unit) and other training which have mentioned above. This proves that not only did the central government programs failed to be implemented but also this shows lack of coordination by having no supervision to the policy implementation at the lower level.

Similarly, looking at the working programs of the Purwakarta Office of Cooperatives, SMEs, Industry, and Trade (see Table 6.1 above) there is no such programs to develop the ceramic cluster in collaboration with local governments such as: a program to develop a conducive business environment, a program to promote marketing, a program to enhance technology standards and product quality, a program to increase the competency of human resources, a program to provide easy access to raw materials, a program to help access the financial institutions, a program to develop business institution, and a program to improve the capability of research and development. However, there are several programs that are designed by the Purwakarta Office of Cooperatives, SMEs, Industry, and Trade that are in line with the working program of the Ministry of industry. Unfortunately, in practice those programs are not in line with the objectives of the development of ceramic cluster in Plered. For example, a program to develop a conducive business environment by the Ministry of Industry consists of eight action plans in which two of them are supposed to be carried out by the local governments. The two program are programs to provide guidance and ease in handling (business) license and program to provide support to develop institutions/agencies to improve the competency of human resources for industrial pottery and decorative. Looking at the working program of the Purwakarta Office of Cooperatives, SMEs, Industry, and Trade, it is stated that the program to develop of a conducive business environment for SMEs/SMIs is consisted of the facilitation to develop SMEs and the facilitation to make plans in developing SMEs.[429] Looking at the program of the two institutions (with the same title of program), it is obvious that the understanding of conducting a conducive business environment is interpreted and implemented differently. It can be concluded: *First*, there is ambiguity among government agencies over the program. For instance, there are many interpretations about conducting a conducive business environment. Is it about tax and fiscal incentive? Is it about political stability? Or is it about law enforcement? Of course the answer of those questions varies. *Second*, there is a failure of (central) government programs in the region i.e. a penetration crisis. This crisis must be understood as part of the political battle in the regional and sub-regional levels. Referring to Law No. 32/2004 on Regional Development, it is stated that in terms of regional autonomy (decentralization), each region has the right to elect local leader through a direct general election by the people in that area.[430] There are many cases that the elected mayor or regent has different political orientation (political party) with the elected governor. The case of Purwakarta for instance, as a result of regional general election in 2008, the elected regent of Purwakarta and the elected governor of West Java Province have different political party background. Sometimes this results in lack of harmonization of government programs because each level (regional and sub-regional) has the authority to make regional/local development program (although it has been mentioned before that the regional development programs must be aligned with national development program). This is caused by the belief that those elected are responsible to their constituents.[431] Hadiz (2004) found similar situation in North Sumatra and Yogyakarta that there is a tendency that the sub-provincial government level opposes the authority of the provincial government level.[432]

429 Cf. Dinas Koperasi, UMKM, Perindustrian, dan Perdagangan Kabupaten Purwakarta 2011, p. 30.
430 Cf. Article 21 Paragraph b and Article 24 Paragraph 5 of Law No. 32/2004.
431 Cf. Jati 2012, p. 764.
432 Cf. Hadiz 2004, p. 710.

The failure of the government program is also caused by the capability of the human resource. Decentralization requires the extraction of central government employees that are assigned in the region.[433] These people were given the choice whether to continue working as the central government employees (usually member of ministry) or change their status to be a local government employee. The problem is that not all of these people are willing to change their status. This is where the problem occurs. Vacancy positions in the local government offices (provincial offices and town/regency offices) have forced the local government and existing (limited) human resources to fill in the vacant positions without (sometimes) considering a person's background or expertise. With all due respect to existing offices, sometimes vacant positions in local government offices are filled by people who do not have competence. The result is a lack of understanding about the programs that should be their authority.

Another cause of the failure of the central government's programs in the region is usually related to lack of commitment from the local government officials in implementing the (central) government's program due to different political orientation or because of lack of capacity of human resources as mentioned above. Moreover, there is lack of supervision and evaluation by the central government of programs that are run by local governments. Even if there is any kind of supervision and evaluation, it is unclear whether there is a sanction that can be given if there is a violation by not implementing the program. This factor, according to the researcher, is the crucial factor that influences the implementation of business cluster in both clusters.

433 Cf. Bennet 2010, pp. 6-7.

6.2 The Influence of Culture in the Implementation of Business Clusters in Indonesia

Cultural factor becomes one of the findings in this research. Hofstede and Hofstede (2005) stated that almost everybody is bound by the categories and types of culture at the same time, whether it is about national culture, local/regional culture (could be related to ethnicity and religion), gender, or social status.[434] The importance of considering cultural factor in the economic activity is mentioned by Cole (2007) who stated that the structure and the culture of the society influence the entrepreneurial development.[435] The same thought came from Max Weber who mentioned that culture produces forms of economic behavior.[436] Using the Hofstede's categories and types of cultures, there are at least three types of cultures that are embedded in the structure of the society of West Java. They are: the national culture of the spirit of working together (*gotong royong*), the Javanese culture of togetherness (*mangan ora mangan anggere kumpul)*, and the Sundanese culture of comforting, educating, and caring toward each other (*silih asih, silih asah, silih asuh*). According to Adian (2011), *gotong-royong* is "[...] an indigenous ideal of social life rooted in reciprocity, cooperation, mutual aid, and volunteerism".[437] The basic idea of *gotong-royong* is cooperation in doing everything. This concept, according to Muhammad Natsir – the fifth Prime Minister of Indonesia, is used as an ethical principle of Indonesian social life and is the uniqueness of Indonesia that distinguishes from western and eastern philosophy.[438] The Javanese principle of togetherness can be interpreted as an act of harmonization among societies. In Indonesia, as Reisinger and Turner (as cited in Cole, 2007, 466) it is found out that the importance of group harmony and living together in harmony is emphasized. Together in thick and thin is chosen by the Javanese people and is used as a guideline in social life. Common characteristic of the Javanese people that are friendly and tend to avoid conflict (competition) is believed to be the main reason why this concept still exists until now. The Sundanese principle of comforting, educating, and caring toward each other is used to motivate people in pro-

434 Cf. Hofstede/Hofstede 2005, pp. 10-11.
435 Cf. Cole 2007, pp. 461-62.
436 Cf. Fukuyama 1995, pp. 43-44.
437 Adian 2011, p. 6.
438 Cf. ibid., pp. 6-7.

moting a better performance.[439] The combination of those three cultures in the two clusters will be used to analyze the implementation of business clusters in Cibaduyut and Plered. In helping the researcher analyze the relationship between culture and economic activity, the Hofstede's four dimensions of national culture will also be used. The four dimensions of national culture according to Hofstede are: (1) power distance, (2) collectivism versus individualism, (3) femininity versus masculinity, and (4) uncertainty avoidance.[440] Power distance is defined as "the extent to which the less powerful members of institutions and organizations within a country expect and accept that power is distributed unequally".[441] Individualism refers to a loose pattern of individual relationship within a society, while collectivism refers to a strong connection between individual within a society.[442] Masculinity refers to a situation when gender roles are clearly distinct such as men are supposed to be a tough figure while women are supposed to be a modest figure. Meanwhile, femininity refers to a situation when gender roles overlap i.e. that there is no distinction between the role of men and women.[443] Uncertainty avoidance is defined as "the extent to which the members of a culture feel threatened by ambiguous or unknown situations".[444] The four dimensions above will be used to analyze the implementation of business clusters in the two research sites: power distance, collectivism, masculinity, and uncertainty avoidance as a basis to analyze the way people conduct activity in a cluster. In this case study, power distance refers to the situation where there are differences in status, power, and authority within the society. In the business context in Indonesia, this refers to the difference of position between the government and business actors (where the government issues regulations on how business activities should be carried out), between large firms and small firms (where small firms usually depend on large firms for example in the case of subcontracting products), between the owners and the workers (where commonly the workers simply follow order from the owner in producing a product). Collectivism refers to a collective action in a cluster that affects the economic goals of the cluster. Masculinity refers to the dominant position of men in business activity and the assumption that men are the eco-

---

439 Cf. Prasetyo 2005, p. 173.
440 Cf. Hofstede/Hofstede 2005, p. 23.
441 Ibid., p. 46.
442 Cf. ibid., pp. 74-75.
443 Cf. ibid., p. 120.
444 Ibid., p. 167.

nomic backbone of the family (breadwinner). While uncertainty avoidance refers to how business actors (the owners and the workers) try to avoid situations that could lead to instability in the day-to-day economic activity. Reisinger and Turner (as cited in Cole 2007, 264), states that uncertainty avoidance can also be interpreted of an act to avoid conflict and competition that are considered to threaten the stability of the business as well to minimize (business) risks.

Recalling what is mentioned by Porter that business clusters will generate innovation through competition and cooperation, what the researcher found in these two clusters reflects different situations. Business activities in Cibaduyut and Plered reflect the business pattern that commonly occurs in the small (and medium) industrial sector in Indonesia. Referring to the concept of cooperation that is mentioned by Marijan (2005) and Tambunan (2005), a form of joint action and internal-external networks dominate the business pattern in both locations.[445] The following will explain how cooperation is carried out in both locations. In Cibaduyut, business activities are divided into three major activities namely: *first*, between the core industry and supporting industries. In this case, business activities that involve SMEs, raw materials (leather) stores, spare parts industries, packaging industries, and rubber soles stores. *Second*, day-to-day business activity usually happens among SMEs inside a cluster. In this case, what commonly happens in Cibaduyut is the subcontracting method that shares the making of shoe to several SMEs as mentioned in previous chapter (see Chapter 5). *Third*, day-to-day business activity usually happens between large enterprises and SMEs. In this case, to meet the quantity of shoes that will be sold (usually exported); these large companies subcontract the manufacture of shoes to local SMEs. This large enterprise simply gives an example (a model) of the desired shoes to the SMEs, offers a number of target (number of shoes), and proposes work deadlines. The same pattern happens in Plered. In Plered, business activities can be divided into three major activities. They are: (a) business activity between the core industry (SMEs) and supporting industries (mostly raw materials industry); (b) among SMEs in producing ceramic such as the formation of (raw) ceramic, the decoration, the burning process, and the finishing touch and in selling ceramic especially for fulfilling international demand.

Looking at the business activities in Cibaduyut and Plered, it can be concluded that the pattern of business activities does not reflect competi-

445 Cf. Marijan 2005, pp. 221-22, Tambunan 2005, p. 140.

tion among SMEs/SMIs. There are several factors that contribute to the lack of competition in business activities in those locations. Employing the Hofstede's cultural dimensions, we can see how cultures affect business activities and negate competition in the two research sites. *First*, it can be said that the business activities in the two locations highly stress on collectivism. That means that business activities in these two locations stress on a strong connection between individuals within a society. Moreover, collective action taken by SMEs/SMIs in these locations are influenced by the cultures such as the principle of *gotong-royong* (mutual assistance), the principle of *silih asuh* (caring) towards each other, and the principle of *kebersamaan* (togetherness). It is found from the observation that the concept of competition cannot be found (or at least hard to find) because of the influence of the culture. Day-to-day business activities at the Cibaduyut Footwear Industrial Cluster and the Plered Decorative Ceramic Industrial Cluster show that a strong social relationship among the owners and the workers characterizes business activity in these two clusters. The principle of *gotong-royong* (mutual assistance) is obvious in day-to-day business activities especially for micro and small enterprises. For example in the Plered Decorative Ceramic Industrial Cluster, many SMEs/SMIs share the cost of burning ceramic into a final process because they have limited capital to have (buy) a ceramic combustion engine. This can happen in the form of purchasing raw materials (wood) to burn ceramic, in the sense that purchasing wood in bulk will reduce the price. This is due to the close kinship between those enterprises (business owners). Many micro and small enterprises' owner is related (has a family relation) to each other. According to AN, this kinship was created a long time ago where the primary livelihood of the villagers of Anjun (Plered) is a ceramic craftsman.[446] Therefore, the business of making ceramic is done by generations that split into smaller enterprises later on.

In Cibaduyut, shoemaking can be done by two or three enterprises (or two to three sections/divisions in medium and large enterprises). As mentioned in the previous chapter, there is a clear division of jobs (especially in micro and small enterprises) among SMEs such as cutting leather materials into pieces and manufacturing of rubber soles for footwear materials. This semi-finished material will be passed to other SMEs which conduct sewing to combine leather with rubber footwear in the first phase above.

446 Interview with A.N. from the UPTD Litbang Keramik Plered on March 8, 2012 in Plered, Purwakarta.

Then, the finishing process will be carried out either by other SMEs or back to the first SMEs (in the first phase) before being sold to the market. In this process, the payment process from the one enterprise to another enterprise (as illustrated above) is done with the principle of kinship and trust. That means the payment will be paid after the shoes are sold. Another example is the cooperation among small-sized enterprises to meet the demand of large enterprises. For example, there is a large enterprise that would like to export (sell to the international market) 1,000 pairs of shoes. Usually, this large enterprise will sub-contract the making of shoes to several small enterprises. This large enterprise simply gives an example of the desired shoes to the small enterprises, offers a number of target (number of shoes), and proposes work deadlines. This illustration shows a sense of togetherness and compassion among SMEs in conducting their daily business activities.

The same situation happens in Plered. Many (usually micro and small-sized) firms purchase raw materials together. This is because buying raw material (clay) in bulk is cheaper than buying in smaller quantity. Usually there are two or three firms (commonly firms that their owners have family relations) buy clay in large quantity and then divide it among them to be made into decorative ceramics and other ceramic products. The principle of mutual assistance and togetherness are reflected in which there is one party (firm) that covers the full payment of buying the materials and the other companies get the flexibility to pay to the first company later on. Or in some cases, the payment from the buyer (the three firms as an example before) to the seller (the owner of the raw materials) is paid afterwards, based on trust and social relationship. Looking at those examples above, it can be said that the implementation of business clusters is being hampered due to business activity that is based on trust and social relationship. In this case, the competition among firms becomes invisible.

Second, in these two locations, society accepts differences in status, power, and authority within the society. Here, Hofstede's power distance refers to different positions among people. It can be between the owners and the workers, between SMEs/SMIs and large enterprises, or between micro and small-sized enterprises and medium-sized enterprises. Prasetyo (2005) separates the (village) society into two groups: '*the haves*' and '*the have nots*'.[447] Looking at the two research sites in Cibaduyut and Plered, '*the haves*' refer to large (and sometimes medium-sized) enterprises and

447 Cf. Prasetyo 2005, p. 80.

'*the have nots*' refer to (mostly) micro and small-sized enterprises. Differences in the position as mentioned above have a negative implication in business activities in the two research sites. The nature of Indonesian culture emphasizes on obedience, authority, supervision.[448] This culture puts the position of '*the haves*' higher than '*the have nots*'. Looking at this context, those who are in the higher position have authority to regulate things to those who are in the lower level. The division of power distance as mentioned above shows that the owner and large (and sometimes medium-sized) enterprise have higher in rank compare to the worker and micro and small-sized enterprise. This culture according to the researcher slows the innovation process in doing business. The relationship between the owners and the workers for instance, confirms this. In conducting day-to-day business activities, the relationship between owners and workers goes in one direction in which the owner always gives orders to the worker to do something. The workers disincline to provide input to the owner because of hierarchical position. The worker believes that it is the task of the owner to find solutions to most problems and to promote innovation. This is because of the nature of business activities that is done when they were told to do so. The making of shoes, for example, began when buyers (or large firms) purchased shoes to SMEs. There are a few SMEs (or even no) tries to create a new design and model due to limited skills. Usually, they only imitate existing designs/models from magazines or from prospective buyers. It is rarely found that SMEs design a new model of shoes or ceramic in the two locations. Based on the observation in the two research sites, competition occurs mostly in the process of selling shoes and ceramic products in stores in Cibaduyut and Plered. In that sense, competition occurs mainly to attract as many as potential buyers to visit their stores (and websites) and sell the products to the customers. This is done simply by displaying their products in order and as neat as possible.

Third, the dominant position of males that refers to Hofstede's masculinity. Tambunan (2008) stated that there are two reasons to explain that phenomenon[449]: (a) low levels of education. In a traditional culture (especially in rural areas), education belongs to men, and women are in charge of housework and childcare; (b) traditional and Islamic-based norms which put women in second place after her husband. According to these norms, women must comply with their main duty as their husband's part-

448 Cf. Cole 2007, p. 465.
449 Cf. Tambunan 2008a, pp. 155-56.

ner and housewife. Moreover, they are not allowed to establish their own business and if they could start their own business, the decision maker of the company is generally their husband. Here, men are always perceived as the head of the family and therefore men are also perceived as the owner of both family and business assets such as land and buildings. Based on observations and interviews conducted in the two locations, it is found that almost all SMEs/SMIs in Cibaduyut and Plered are run by men. The involvement of women is quite obvious in the process of making decorative ceramic in Plered. This is due to the process of making ceramic that is still using human labor (hand-made) and the belief that women's hands will produce a more beautiful ceramic form. This however, in some way, inhibits the emergence of female entrepreneurs who have the potential to develop (both) business clusters and reduce the chance to wider employment as well as to wider competition among firms. Unfortunately, there is no official data from the local government or the UPT on the number of male and female who owned and run the SMEs/SMIs in Plered.

Fourth, in keeping harmonization in a society, uncertainty is avoided. Employing Hofstede's uncertainty avoidance, harmonious social relations in a society is emphasized. Cole (2007), by using an example of Ngadha society, stated that conflict among people should be avoided.[450] In a traditional culture, there is a belief that wealth is set by God i.e. wealth comes from heaven. There is no need to compete with one another. With this belief, business goals are set only to fulfill daily needs and to send the children to go to school. It is common for the owners and the workers to sit together after the (informal) working hours having a cup of coffee/tea and snacks while sharing tips and information related to new products and market opportunities. This togetherness is done as part of the Javanese (and Sundanese) culture which always prioritizes a harmonious society. A form of togetherness is already mentioned above shows a form of cooperation among small-sized enterprises to meet the demand of large enterprises. This togetherness, according to the researcher, at least resulted in a loss of people feeling to compete with each other.

Regarding the family business ownership, what is found in the two locations can provide the answer on why this factor also influences the implementation of business cluster in Indonesia, especially related to the attribute of firm structure and rivalry. The family management system that is run by most of SMEs/SMIs in Cibaduyut and Plered creates difficulties

450 Cf. Cole 2007, p. 467.

to develop these industrial clusters. The composition of the family members (including spouses, relatives, and children) dominates the structure of the company. This is due to: (a) the need to reduce the cost of production and (b) the convenience of working with family members than with workers who are not members of the family. The recruitment of family members regardless of sufficient ability to produce certain products becomes one of the causes of low quality of product in Cibaduyut and Plered. There are many cases where the owners of small business units put themselves not only as the owner or the leader of the company but also as the workers and the salesman. There is no clear vision, mission, and objectives of their business so usually they run their business for fulfilling their basic objectives: to be able to eat for today and be able to send their children to school. As for the medium business units, even though they notice at the importance of the managerial aspect (characterized by a clear and well-managed division of labor and the recruitment of the worker based on skill), but they do not yet fully run a good enterprise's management system. This can be seen from the absence of the quality control management where many of their products are rejected by potential buyers because the products do not meet with the minimum standard of product required by the potential buyers. Thus, involving family members who do not have the sufficient ability and passion in running the business results a low entrepreneurial spirit in SMEs/SMIs. This, referring to Rosenfeld's factors of a strong cluster, will slow down the development of a strong cluster. However, the cultural factor, according to the researcher, is the additional (supporting) factor that influences the implementation of business clusters in both clusters.

6.3 Additional Attributes to Porter's Diamond Theory Using the Indonesian Context

Recalling Porter's diamond theory, there are six attributes to promote a competitive advantage of a firm: (a) firm strategy, structure, and rivalry, (b) factor conditions, (c) demand conditions, (d) the presence of related and supporting industries, (e) the government, and (f) chance. However, after conducting research in the two business clusters as a case study – the Cibaduyut Footwear Industrial Cluster and the Plered Decorative Ceramic Industrial Cluster, is was found that there are two other attributes that affect the implementation of business cluster in Indonesia, namely: decentralization and cultural factor. Decentralization plays an important role because both clusters are under the authority of a regional government – in this case the government of the West Java Province. The implementation of decentralization (local autonomy) in Indonesia gives broader authority to the local government to organize matters in accordance with the provision of law. Also, the cultural factor is considered to affect the implementation of business cluster (day-to-day business activity) because there is a strong connection between the community (business actors) and cultures. This connection eliminates domestic rivalry and thus hinders innovation in the two research sites. Figure 6.1 describes the connection of the two additional attributes into Porter's diamond theory.

Figure 6.1: The Diamond Theory with Additional Attributes

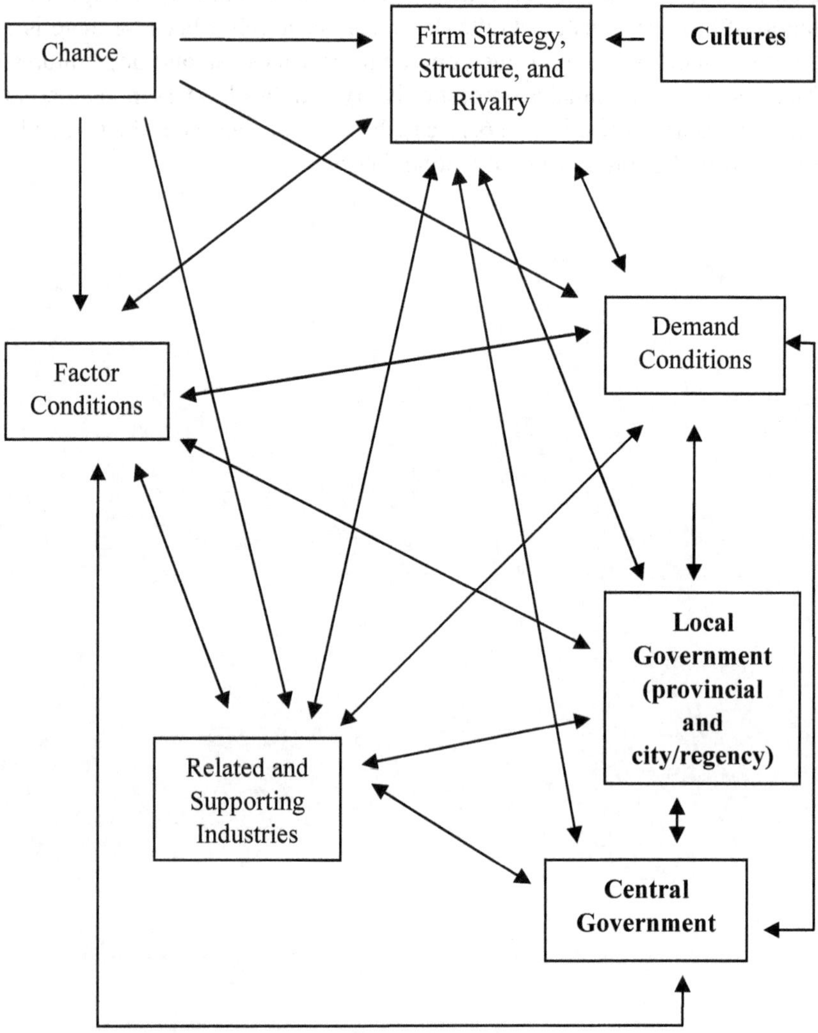

The explanation of the figure is as follows. *First*, in the context of decentralization, the policy to develop business clusters in both locations (the Cibaduyut Footwear Industrial Cluster and the Plered Decorative Ceramic Industrial Cluster) begins with Regulation of the President of the Republic of Indonesia No. 5/2010 on the National Medium-term Development Plan (2010-2014) a guide for ministries or government agencies in preparing strategic plans, which are subsequently taken into consideration for local governments in preparing and adjusting their local development plans to achieve national development goals. Not only that, Regulation of the President of the Republic of Indonesia No. 28/2008 on the National Industrial Policy shapes and strengthen the strategic plans of related government agencies in the national (central) government level to prepare and develop potential business clusters. At this level, there are at least two ministries that are in charge to support the development of business cluster in both locations: the Ministry of Industry and the Ministry of Cooperatives and SMEs. The Ministry of Industry by using the *top-down* and *bottom-up* approaches establishes a roadmap of the priority industrial cluster development, a roadmap of provincial industrial development, and a guide roadmap of industrial districts and a municipality's development. While the Ministry of Cooperatives and SMEs forms several strategic plans to develop and empower SMEs (to increase the capacity of SMEs) in order to strengthen the existence of SMEs in the business cluster. At this point, all policies and plans are well prepared. Then, it comes to the decentralization process. The provincial government of West Java has its main goal (especially related to economic goal) of reducing poverty rate, improving quality of life, expanding employment opportunities, developing strategic and basic infrastructure, and improving the competitiveness of the industrial sector. In order to support the central government program (especially related to the establishment of business cluster in its region), the Government of the West Java Province has assigned two regional offices to support the national program of establishing potential business cluster in West Java. The two regional offices are: the Office of Cooperatives and SMEs and the Office of Industry and Trade. As mentioned in previous chapter, both offices have their mission and programs to develop and empower SMEs in West Java as well as to develop potential industrial sector in West Java. As explained earlier, the Cibaduyut Footwear Industrial Cluster is managed by the West Java Office of Industry and Trade while the Plered Decorative Ceramic Industrial Cluster is managed under the Office of Cooperatives, SMEs, Industry, and Trade of the regency of Purwakarta.

Looking at the arrows in the figure above, both central government and regional governments have their programs in establishing and supporting both clusters in Cibaduyut and Plered (see Chapter 3 and Chapter 4). Both governments (central and local) also have programs to develop both business clusters. The problems actually start at this point. Lack of coordination among government agencies is a common issue in Indonesia. This makes the potential of both business clusters to be not optimal. The goal to increase competitiveness of SMEs and industrial products in order to promote regional economic development fails. This failure is not only because of the problem of coordination among agencies but also internal problems faced by SMEs and the two business clusters (see previous chapter).

Second, in the context of culture, the influence of national and local cultures contributes to the performance of the two business clusters. Based on the principle of *gotong royong*, the principle of togetherness, and the principle of *silih asah, silih asuh, and silih asih* as well as employing the Hofstede's cultural dimensions, day-to-day business activity emphasizes on the harmony among people as a result of a strong social relationship between individuals based on collectivism. Not only that, the importance of harmony within a society makes most business owners (and workers) avoid conflict and competition (uncertainty avoidance). This strong relationship is also influenced by family relations among business people in the two business clusters. The belief that wealth comes from heaven and a modest lifestyle performed by some owners is the reason on the lack of a long-term business plan and strategy. It is not surprised if we hardly see innovation in the two clusters due to a low spirit of competition as one of the conditions to promote innovation and increase the firms' competitiveness.

In short, the two additional attributes as in Figure 6.1 illustrates that the aim of (both central and local) government programs to create a strong industrial structure i.e. to increase competitiveness of SMEs/SMIs in the two business cluster does not happen yet. In order to achieve the main goal of increasing productivity and competitiveness as well as having a strong industrial structure, the government should deal with the two additional attributes as mentioned above.

7. Conclusion

7.1 Introduction

The implementation of the concept of business clusters has attracted many researchers for many decades. There are many researches and studies on the impacts on implementing business clusters. Looking at that phenomenon, this research examines the implementation of business clusters in Indonesia by using the two business clusters which are the Cibaduyut Footwear Industrial Cluster and the Plered Ceramic Cluster. Both locations are located in the Province of West Java, Indonesia. The selection of these two sites is done with the following considerations: *first*, the location of the two clusters is not far from the city of Bandung so that the interview process and observations at the site are easier in order to complete the research process. This is also to ease getting permission from the authorities to be able to conduct research at the site. Spending almost twenty years in this area helps the researcher to collect data and conduct interviews. *Second*, these two industrial clusters have been formed since the 1900s in a form of *sentra* before being formalized into industrial clusters in 2009. *Third*, the government and the Ministry of Industry had chosen these two sites to be developed into a (dynamic) cluster by issuing Regulation of the President of the Republic of Indonesia No. 28/2008 on National Industrial Policy which used as the basis of the issuance of Regulation of the Minister of Industry of the Republic of Indonesia No. 110/M-IND/PER/10/2009 on the Roadmap of the Development of the Footwear Industrial Cluster and Regulation of Minister of Industry of the Republic of Indonesia No. 135/M-IND/PER/10/2009 on the Roadmap of the Development of Pottery and Decorative Ceramic Industrial Cluster.

Given that the phenomenon of business clusters can be widely observed, the researcher would like to examine the governmental roles in developing business clusters and the implementation of business clusters concept in Indonesia (including rural areas). Despite a growing number of studies on the implementation of business cluster in recent years, there are still few researches and studies the micro i.e. rural areas. In Indonesia, there are few researches on the impact of clustering on firms in rural areas for example Tambunan (2009) and Sandee/Andadari/Sulandjari (2000). In this case, it is worth conducting a research on the implementation of business cluster in rural area, in this case in Cibaduyut and Plered, West Java. This research, then, tries to answer the following questions. *First*, what is the role of the Indonesian government in developing business clusters in Cibaduyut and Plered? *Second*, how is business cluster reflected in contemporary regional economic development in the footwear industrial cluster in Cibaduyut and the decorative ceramic cluster in Plered? What are the problems faced by business actors (including SMEs/SMIs) in the two locations that impede the implementation of business cluster concept in Indonesia? *Third*, are there any other factors that influences (and impedes) the implementation of business cluster in the two locations? *Fourth*, how can the implementation of business clusters in the two locations give contribution to Porter's diamond theory especially in understanding the implementation of business clusters in Indonesia?

To address these research questions, the researcher relied on the qualitative analytical method. The researcher will explore the research by focusing on all business actors involving in this research. All actors involving in the business cluster such as individuals, SMEs, business cluster itself, research centers, universities, associations, and government institutions will be subjects of this research to examine the implementation of business cluster in the two research sites. To help collecting and analyzing data, this research will use several techniques: by going into individuals and (central, regional, sub-regional) governmental institutions, by observing interactions and communications of the people and government officials in the two research sites, by examining official documents, by conducting interview with the businessmen, government officials as well as academicians.

The main focus in this research is to emphasize the vital role of the Indonesian government in developing business/industrial clusters. Despite the state's endorsement of a free market economy, the government continues its crucial role in nurturing SMEs, especially in situations where the SMEs are faced with structural weaknesses. The reason behind this is that the government would like: (a) to focus on the three development strategies that are pro-growth, pro-jobs, and pro-poor, (b) to accelerate the economic growth and increase economic competitiveness of the industrial sector by involving SMEs/SMIs as the main driver. Involving SMEs/SMIs is done by considering their potential of offering job opportunities and how they are not easily impacted by a financial crisis (SMEs/SMIs were not impacted during the 1997-1998 financial crisis). Thus, focusing on increasing the competitiveness of SMEs/SMIs, the concept of business clusters is employed to explain the government programs in economic development. The main conceptual framework used in this research is based on Porter's diamond theory. Michael Porter is known as a pioneer of the new theory of economic development when he proposed the concept of clusters in order to increase a nation's competitiveness and boost up regional economic development. There are six attributes that create a competitive advantage of a firm and a nation. The six attributes are: (a) firm strategy, structure, and rivalry, (b) factor conditions, (c) demand conditions, (d) related and supporting industries, (e) the government, and (f) chance. Porter (1998) states there are at least three advantages in doing competition within a cluster.[451] *First*, it will increase the productivity of firms (SMEs). *Second*, it will drive innovations of new products. *Third*, it will stimulate the formation of new firms that support current firms and perhaps extend the cluster itself. By having these advantages, a firm will increase its competitiveness in the midst of global competition.

The main findings, implications for policy, research limitations, and recommendations for further research are discussed in 7.2, 7.3, and 7.4 respectively.

7.2 The Findings

7.2.1 The Governmental Roles in Developing Business Clusters

The governmental roles in developing business clusters in Indonesia are crucial (if not dominant). The dominant role of the government can be seen in the issuance of many regulations that aim to develop business clusters in Indonesia (including at Cibaduyut and Plered). Those regulations are divided into two categories: regulations made by the central government and regulations made by the local government.

First, the regulations made by the central government in developing business clusters are: Law No. 20/2008 on Small and Medium-sized Enterprises (SMEs), Regulation of the President of the Republic of Indonesia No. 5/2010 on the National Medium-term Development Plan 2010-2014, Presidential Instruction No. 1/2010 on Accelerating the Implementation of National Development Priorities 2010, and Regulation of the President of the Republic of Indonesia No. 28/2008 on the National Industrial Policy. These regulations are also supported by other regulations that have been

451 See Porter 1998, p. 213.

issued before such as Government Regulation No. 44/1997 on Partnership, Government Regulation No. 32/1998 on Building and Developing Small Business, Presidential Instruction No. 10/1999 on Empowering Medium Business, Presidential Instruction No. 2/2006 on the Policy Package for Improving the Investment Climate, Regulation of the Minister of State-owned Enterprises No. 236/2006 on the Partnership Program with the Small Business and the Community Development Program, and Regulation of Minister of Cooperatives and SMEs No. 2/2008 on Empowering BDS-P) for the Development of Cooperatives and SMEs. Moreover, the above regulations are followed by policies issued by the two governmental agencies that are responsible with the development of SMEs/SMIs which are the Ministry of Cooperatives and SMEs and the Ministry of Industry. Such policies include: (a) the four major policies in the development and empowerment of SMEs of the Ministry of Cooperatives and SMEs include improving business climate for SMEs, increasing access to productive resources, developing SMEs' product and marketing for SMEs, and improving the competitiveness of human resources of SMEs and (b) the *top-down* and *bottom-up* approaches to implement the seven strategic objectives of the Ministry of Industry. The *top-down* approach is done by determining the priority industrial clusters that are considered able to compete in the domestic and international markets; in this case 35 priority industrial clusters including the Cibaduyut Footwear Industrial Cluster and the Plered Decorative Ceramic Industrial Cluster. While the *bottom-up* approach is done by encouraging regional self-reliance based on the local potentials in order to build and develop an independent economy of the province, city, and district. Through these two approaches, the development and strengthening of the Indonesian industrial sector is done through the clustering approach. The establishment of the two industrial clusters in Cibaduyut and Plered begins with the issuance of Regulation of the Minister of Industry of the Republic of Indonesia No. 110/M-IND/PER/10/2009 on the Roadmap of the Development of the Footwear Industrial Cluster and Regulation of Minister of Industry of the Republic of Indonesia No. 135/M-IND/PER/10/2009 on the Roadmap of the Development of Pottery and Decorative Ceramic Industrial Cluster. These two regulations are based on Presidential Regulation No. 28/2008 on the National Industrial Policy that supports the objective of improving the industrial competitiveness so that the Indonesian national industry has a strong industrial structure. The implementation of the business cluster concept is in line with the argument made by Porter (1998) that a cluster will increase productivity of firms, drive innovations, and stimulate new firms formation. These three advantages are believed to increase competitiveness of firm in the midst of global competition.

Second, the regulation made by the local government in developing SMEs/SMIs is West Java Provincial Regulation No. 10/2010 on the Empowerment and Development of Cooperatives, Micro, Small and Medium-sized Enterprises as the basis for regional economic development. To carry out the purposes of empowerment and development of SMEs, the government of the West Java Province assigned two regional offices in empowering and developing SMEs/SMIs, the West Java Office of Cooperatives and SMEs and the West Java Office of Industry and Trade. The focus of this provincial regulation is divided into two parts, the *first* part is focused on the growth of a friendly business climate and the *second* part is focused on the development of SMEs/SMIs. In supporting the empowerment and development of SMEs, the West Java Office of Cooperatives and SMEs emphasizes on two programs which are: the Development of Entrepreneurship and Competitive Advantage and the Development of Supporting System for SMEs. While the West Java Office of Industry and Trade focuses on several programs such as: Program on Developing SMIs, Program on Strengthening Structure of and Increasing the Capability of Industrial Technology, Program on Developing the Domestic Trading System, Program of Consumer Protection and Protection of Domestic Trade, Program on Improving and Developing Export, and Program on Development Communication, Information, and the Utilization of Information Technology.

Looking at the above regulations, policies, and programs created by both the central government and the local government, there is no denying that there is a dominant role of the government in developing SMEs/SMIs in Indonesia through the clustering approach.

7.2.2 The Implementation of the Business Cluster Concept

The Cibaduyut Footwear Industrial Cluster

The Cibaduyut Footwear Industrial Cluster is located in the southern part of the city of Bandung and has a total area of around 14 km^2. It includes five villages in the city of Bandung and three villages in the regency of Bandung. The importance of this industrial cluster especially to promote regional economic development is significant. *First*, this cluster plays a vital role in the structure of West Java's and the city of Bandung's economic performance in terms of number of existing units, number of employees, number of annual shoe production, total investment, and the production value. *Second*, the presence of SMEs in the region has also led to the birth of several supporting industries such as raw material stores, spare parts industry, packaging industry, and rubber soles industry that contribute to wider employment opportunity through new firms formation. *Third*, this cluster contributes a significant part to the West Java GRDP.

The implementation of the business cluster concept can be seen in the Cibaduyut Footwear Industrial Cluster. Employing Porter's diamond theory, there are four attributes that can be seen in this cluster. *First*, In terms of firm strategy, structure, and rivalry, most of the SMEs/SMIs in Cibaduyut have business goals and objectives. However, even though these SMEs/SMIs have business goal and objective, most of these firms are categorized as a family business and informal business. That means there is no formal management structure of the company and no clear division of work between administrative (the owner) and operational (the employees) levels. Moreover, what was said by Porter about a cluster promoting cooperation and competition at the same time is not clearly seen. Cooperation is more dominant than competition amongst SMEs in Cibaduyut. *Second,* looking at factor conditions in Cibaduyut, this cluster has a pool of (skilled) human resources, raw material sources, the availability of capital or funds, and good infrastructure facilities. *Third*, looking at demand condition i.e. the nature of local market and local demand, this cluster is helped by complicated buyers. There are two types of buyers in nearby area: (a) those that look for a high quality product without questioning the price of the product and (b) those that look for a cheaper price. *Fourth*, the presence of related and supporting industries really helps in developing this cluster. Looking at the area of Cibaduyut, there are at least 249 related and supporting industries exist in Cibaduyut such as showrooms, shopping center, raw materials stores, spare part industries, packaging industries, rubber soles stores, and other industries. The (local) government also established the technical service unit in order to support the development of this cluster. Moreover, there are many universities, research centers, and business associations that support the existence of this cluster.

Problems Faced by SMEs/SMIs in Cibaduyut

The existence of the Cibaduyut Footwear Industrial Cluster is supported by many elements as mentioned above. However, there are still problems faced by the SMEs/SMIs in this cluster. The *first* is related to the aspect of human resources including the worker, the craftsman, and the entrepreneur (owner). There is no formal education or training acquired by the shoemaker and the craftsmen that result in the poor design and poor quality products. Also, these people (including business owner) have a low of entrepreneurial spirit. This is related to the low level of education of the SMEs' owners (entrepreneurs) in Cibaduyut resulting to the low quality of the products. The *second* is related to the managerial aspect. The family management system run by most of the business industry in Cibaduyut makes this industrial cluster difficult to develop. There is no clear vision, mission, and objectives of their business so usually they run their business for fulfilling their basic objectives: to be able to eat for today and be able to send their children to school. The *third* is related to the capital issue. Some of the SMEs/SMIs in Cibaduyut have no legal entity resulting to difficulty in accessing banking facilities. Thus, these SMEs/SMIs have difficulties in financing or even increasing their business activity. The *fourth* is related to the technological aspect. In general, the technology and machinery used by the shoemakers and the craftsmen is an outdated technology that is not economical, requires high maintenance costs, and a decline in the machine's accuracy. The result is low quality of products produced by the SMEs/SMIs. The *fifth* is related to the marketing aspect. The main problem is that these SMEs/SMIs do not have the capacity to locate potential markets due to their low of education level. The *sixth* is related to the infrastructure aspect. There are at least two issues in Cibaduyut: (a) common (daily) traffic jam because of relatively small roads in the region and (b) flooding due to poor drainage systems. These two problems are believed contribute to the declining number of tourist arrivals and prospective buyers.

The Plered Decorative Ceramic Industrial Cluster

The Plered Decorative Industrial Cluster is located at Plered, a district in Purwakarta regency, West Java, with an area of 91.1 ha. This cluster has contributed to the economic structure of the Regency of Purwakarta. There are two positive contributions of this cluster. *First*, there are about 286 business units in the Plered Ceramic Industry that employs around 3,000 workers. *Second*, the Plered ceramic products are usually sold both to local and international markets. The sale of ceramic to various locations at least guarantees the survival of craftsmen in Plered as well as a promotional tool to promote the region of Plered to attract local and international tourists and consumers.

The implementation of the business cluster concept can be seen in the Plered Decorative Industrial Cluster. Employing Porter's diamond theory, there are four attributes that can be seen in this cluster. *First*, in terms of firm strategy, structure, and rivalry, almost all business units (business owners) have business goals and objectives. Similar to the Cibaduyut Footwear Industrial Cluster, most SMEs/SMIs are categorized as a family business and informal business. Similar to SMEs/SMIs in Cibaduyut, they have no formal management structure and thus there is no clear division of work between administrative (the owner) and operational (the employees) levels. Cooperation among SMEs/SMIs is dominant in Plered due to the close relationship among business owners in Plered (most have brotherly ties with each other). This answers why competition is quite rare in Plered. However, a form of competition still occurs in Plered but only in the process of selling ceramic products in stores located in Plered. *Second*, looking at factor conditions in Plered, this cluster has a pool of (skilled) human resources, raw material sources, the availability of capital or funds, and good infrastructure facilities. *Third*, in terms of demand conditions, there are two types of buyer that help the production of decorative ceramic in Plered. They are: local buyers that buy ceramic items for household use and foreign buyers that are concerned with the quality of the product. *Fourth*, related and supporting industries in Plered are not as much as in Cibaduyut. In Plered, there are only four related and supporting industry which are the raw materials (clay) industry, the UPTD Litbang Keramik Plered, production facilities (workshop production) of the UPTD Litbang Keramik Plered, and the Plered Ceramic Gallery. However, there are many supporting industries that are not located in Plered such as the Bandung Institute of Technology, University of Indonesia, the Bandung Ceramic Center, Indonesian Institute of Sciences, and the BPPT.

Problems Faced by SMEs/SMIs in Plered

Looking at the industrial cluster in Plered, there are many problems faced by SMEs/SMIs there. The *first* is related to the aspect of human resource.

A common problem that occurs to the SMEs in Plered is a '*one-man show*' business activity. Most of SMEs/SMIs are managed by individuals who work as an owner as well as an employee of the company. Therefore, sometimes the owner disregards the separation of company and personal affairs. Related to the skill of the worker, there is almost no formal training obtained by these workers that result in the poor design and poor product quality. They acquire the skills to make pottery from: their parents, their fellow crafters, and independent learning. Hence, most of their products have problems with precisions and are difficult to be standardized. Moreover, the involvement of their relatives in running the business is common in Plered. This is because of: (a) these business owners try to reduce the cost of production by recruiting their family members and (b) business owners feel more comfortable and confident in family members than workers who are not members of the family. The recruitment of family members regardless of insufficient ability to make decorative ceramic becomes one of the causes of low quality ceramic products in Plered. The *second* problem is related to the work ethic and technology issues. There are several steps to produce a good decorative ceramic. However, due to the local work ethics and culture issues (to produce fast and cheap), these SMEs tend to ignore such procedures. It is further worsened by the use of traditional combustion engines (using firewood as the primary fuel) that cannot provide an exact measure of the combustion quality that leads to a poor ceramic production. The *third* problem is the increasing number of foreign competitors and imported products. It is undeniable, the flood of Chinese ceramics in Indonesian local market (as well as international markets) put Plered's SMEs/SMIs in danger.

7.2.3 Other Factors Affecting the Implementation of Business Clusters in Cibaduyut and Plered

The implementation of the concept of business clusters in Indonesia does not automatically provide the advantage of increasing a firm's competitiveness and product innovation in the research sites. This is because of two factors that affect the implementation of that concept in Indonesia, namely: decentralization and the influence of culture. The concept of decentralization in Indonesia is actually enacted by Law No. 32/2004 on Regional Government. In this law, the local government is authorized to regulate and manage its own affairs. Cultural factor must be considered in the economic activity because the structure and the culture of the society influence the entrepreneurial development as mentioned by Cole (2007)[452] and culture produces forms of economic behavior as mentioned Max Weber.[453]

Decentralization

The concept of decentralization is important because the implementation of a business cluster concept in the two research sites (Cibaduyut and Plered) firstly came from the central government's initiative. Here, the formation of the two clusters formally outlined in the regulation of the minister of industry (as a representative of the central government) and then implemented locally by the local governments. There are at least two points with regards to decentralization and clustering in West Java. *First*, the lack of coordination among government agencies which happens not only between the central government and local governments but also between local governments and sub-regional governments (in this case the city and regency governments). *Second*, the failure of policy implementation at the regional level i.e. the program that is designed by the central government is sometimes not carried out properly at the level of local and sub-regional governments.

Regarding the coordination among government agencies, it is found that there is almost no coordination among central, local (provincial), and sub-provincial (city and regency). Looking at the development of the two business clusters, there are at least two central government institutions, two provincial offices, and two sub-provincial offices involved in developing the two business clusters. Not to mention that the development of these two clusters also involve other government and non-governmental institutions such as ministries, centers, and universities (see Table 5.2 and Table 5.3). Because of the implementation of decentralization, the responsibility and the development of the two cluster becomes vague, whether it is in the hands of the central government (in this case the Ministry of Industry and the Ministry of Cooperatives and SMEs) or in the hand of local governments i.e. provincial level (for a footwear cluster) or in the hand of the regency (for a ceramic cluster). This creates ambiguity in terms of conducting programs and trainings for instance. Looking at the road map

452 Cf. Cole 2007, pp. 461-62.
453 Cf. Fukuyama 1995, pp. 43-44.

to develop the two industrial clusters by the Ministry of Industry and programs designed by the provincial and sub-provincial offices of the Province of West Java, there are many programs and trainings to prepare, develop, and empower SMEs/SMIs and business clusters. However, most of the programs are either not implemented in the two clusters or needed by SMEs/SMIs in the two locations. Another result of lack of coordination among government agencies is that there is no official data on: (a) the latest number of business units and their production, (b) the number and type of product's innovation, and (c) the evaluation that can be used as a parameter whether the designed programs are successful or not. To overcome such problems, it is important to have a close coordination and appropriate coordination mechanism among different government agencies such as to hold regular meetings for the sub-regional level (between the technical service unit with local government agencies, i.e. related offices in the city/regency level), regular meetings for the sub-regional and the regional level (between the city/regency offices with the provincial offices), and regular coordination meeting in the national level (between offices in the provincial level with the relevant ministries/government agencies).

Regarding the failure of policy implementation of central government at the regional government level, this happened because of decentralization. As mentioned earlier, the program to develop the two industrial clusters refers to the *top-down* approach which initiated by the central government. In this sense, the policy created by the central government is used as operational and coordination guidelines by government officials (both at central and local level) in implementing the policy. It is discovered that there are many programs in the provincial and especially the sub-provincial levels (offices) are not in line with the program designed by the central government. *First*, this is because decentralization gives more autonomy to the sub-regional governments (regencies and cities) instead of regional government. In that sense, the sub-regional governments are given the authority to formulate policies to improve the welfare of their people. This authority usually led to a situation where government programs are not run by the government sub-regional. This is usually related to differences in political orientation between the central government and regional governments. This situation must be understood as part of the political battle in the regional and sub-regional levels. There are many cases that the elected mayor or regent has different political orientation (political party) with the elected governor. The case of Purwakarta for instance, the elected governor of the West Java Province, and the elected regent of Purwakarta has different political party background. This results in lack of harmonization of government programs because each level (regional and sub-regional) has the authority to make regional/local development program (although it has been mentioned before that the regional development programs must be aligned with national development program).

Second, the failure of policy implementation of central government at the regional government level is caused by the capability of human resources. Decentralization requires the extraction of central government employees that are assigned in the region. Vacancy positions in the local government offices (provincial offices and town/regency's offices) have forced the local government and existing (limited) human resources to fill in the vacant positions without (sometimes) considering of a person's background or expertise. With all due respect to existing offices, sometimes vacant positions in local governments offices are filled by people who do not have competence. The result is a lack of understanding about the programs that should be their authority.

Third, the failure of policy implementation of central government at the regional government level is also caused by lack of supervision and evaluation by the central government of programs that are run by local (provincial and sub-provincial) governments. It is common in Indonesia that everything on paper is ideal but once it comes to the implementation, the result is null.

Culture

There are at least three types of cultures that are embedded in the structure of the society of West Java. They are: the national culture of the spirit of working together (*gotong royong*), the Javanese culture of togetherness (*mangan ora mangan anggere kumpul)*, and the Sundanese culture of comforting, educating, and caring toward each other (*silih asih, silih asah, silih asuh*). These three principles are obvious in day-to-day business activities especially for micro and small enterprises/industries. The case of purchasing raw materials by business owners (SMEs/SMIs), covering the (full or down) payment, and fulfilling demand (sub-contract) from large enterprise can be an example. These cultures influence day-to-day business activities in the two clusters. Based on observations and interviews conducted by the researcher, it is found out in the two research sites that a form of cooperation is more dominant that competition. Employing the concept of cooperation from Marijan (2005) and Tambunan (2005), a form of joint action and internal-external networks dominate the business pattern in both locations. Common forms of cooperation in both locations are: (a) between the core industry and supporting industries, (b) among SMEs inside a cluster, and (c) between large enterprises and SMEs.

Employing Hofstede's cultural dimensions, cultural factors influence day-to-day business activities and negate competition in the two research sites because of several reasons. *First*, it can be said that the business activities in the two locations highly stress on collectivism. That means, business activities in these two locations stress on a strong connection between individual within a society. *Second*, using Hofstede's power distance concept, the society in both locations accepts differences in status, power, and authority within the society. The nature of Indonesian culture that emphasizes on obedience, authority, supervision slows the innovation process in doing business. *Third*, the dominant position of males that refers to Hofstede's concept of masculinity. This inhibits the emergence of female entrepreneurs who have the potential to develop (both) business clusters and reduce the chance to wider employment as well as to wider competition among firms. *Fourth*, in keeping harmonization in a society, uncertainty is avoided. In a traditional culture, there is a belief that wealth is set by God (wealth comes from heaven). There is no need to compete with one another. With this belief, business goals are set only to fulfill daily needs and to send the children to go to school. Thus, looking at the four cultural dimensions above, it is not surprising if (new) innovation is not clearly seen in both clusters.

Another feature of business activities in the two clusters is the involvement of family members including spouses, relatives, and (in several cases) children. This, in some cases, results to the lack of clear vision, mission, and objectives of their business. Moreover, the recruitment of family members regardless of sufficient ability to produce certain products becomes one of the causes of low quality of products in both clusters. Therefore, many of their products are rejected by potential buyers because the products do not meet with the minimum standard of product required by the potential buyers. It is not surprising that the development of both clusters is not running as planned.

Looking at current performance and condition in both clusters, it can be said that the implementation of business clusters in Indonesia (by using the two clusters) is '*masih jauh panggang dari api*' or there is a big gap between idea and reality.

7.3 Implications for Policies

The aim to promote a strong industrial structure and to increase an industry's competitiveness should take those findings above as a consideration. Based on a research conducted by Rosenfeld, there at least 12 (twelve) key factors to support a strong cluster: research and development capability, knowledge and skills, human resource development, proximity of suppliers, capital availability, access to specialized services, machine and tools builders, intensity of networking, social infrastructure, entrepreneurial spirit, innovation, and shared vision and leadership.[454] Employing Rosenfeld's factors of a strong cluster and looking at condition at both clusters, the government (both central and local) should focus on at least three factors: human resource development, entrepreneurial spirit, as well as a shared vision and leadership. In terms of human resources, high-skilled workers are crucial to the existence and development of a cluster. For promoting an expected cluster (whether a working cluster or a dynamic cluster), the need to increase its quality of product depends on the capability of its workers. Therefore, conducting training that is aimed to increase the capability of the workers is a must. However, looking at current experiences at both clusters, there is a need to design training that is needed by both clusters (workers). In order to do so, a close coordination among government agencies is important. In terms of entrepreneurial spirit, the government must continue to educate existing entrepreneurs and young generations to have a strong entrepreneurial spirit. This is needed in order to create a strong firm structure that is characterized by the existence of business strategy. Having a strong firm structure will lead to a strong cluster as well as promote competition that at the end will promote more innovation. In terms of shared vision and leadership, the government must ensure to have a policy that is characterized by a clear objective, a clear strategy, and a clear coordination in order to support the development of a cluster. A strong policy as well as an evaluation can be used as a guideline to ensure that this cluster including firms, research centers, and government institutions contribute to their full potential to promote regional economic development.

From the findings, a *one-size-fits-all* policy does not seem to be an appropriate strategy. For example, the development of the footwear industrial cluster as regulated in Regulation of the Minister of Industry of the Re-

454 Cf. Rosenfeld 1997, pp. 12-17.

public of Indonesia No. 110/M-IND/PER/10/2009 and the development of the pottery and decorative industrial cluster as regulated in Regulation of the Minister of Industry of the Republic of Indonesia No. 135/M-IND/PER/10/2009 must consider factors like decentralization and cultures as explained earlier. Moreover, each location as mentioned in that regulation has different characteristics so that a detailed policy and program for each location is needed.

7.4 Research Limitations and Recommendations for Further Research

The current research took the case of the Cibaduyut Footwear Industrial Cluster and the Plered Decorative Ceramic Industrial Cluster to study the im-plementation of the business cluster concept in Indonesia. However, looking at a big number of industrial clusters in Indonesia, there are still several problems which have not been covered in this research. Based on this research, the researcher found that there are some issues that should be considered for future research.

First, the findings in this research do not automatically reflect the situation in all industrial clusters in Indonesia. For example, the finding, that innovation did not occur due to low competition in both clusters, cannot be used alone as a basis to judge the implementation of business clusters in Indonesia. There are many successful industrial clusters in other regions in Indonesia such as the Jepara Furniture Industrial Cluster. Thus, the need for more research using more numbers of clusters and more time in doing observations could give a more accurate analysis about the implementation of business clusters in Indonesia.

Second, due to the limitation in terms of data availability, the current study cannot make an accurate analysis of the performance of a cluster. The lack of data and information about both clusters should take into consideration for future research in order to examine the performance of a cluster especially when dealing with the benefit of a cluster as mentioned by Porter (1998): in terms of productivity of SMEs/SMIs, in terms of innovation, and in terms of new firms formation.[455]

Third, the performance of industrial clusters is not constant overtime. For example, the recent performance of industrial clusters may change in

455 Cf. Porter 1998, p. 213.

the next five years or may change due to the changes in political settings. However, due to limited time to conduct a research and limited data, this research could only examine the implementation of business clusters in a specific period of time.

References

Abdullah, Mohd Yusof Hj/Bakar, Noor Rahamah Hj Abu/Sulehan, Junaenah/Awang, Abd. Hair/Liu, Ong Puay (2012). Participatory Rural Appraisal (PRA): An Analysis of Experience in Darmareja Village, Sukabumi District, West Java, Indonesia. In: Akademika, Vol. 82, No. 1, pp. 15-19.

Adian, Donny Gahral (2011). Multicultural Politics in Indonesia: Dialogue and Gotong Royong. In: Dialogue AND UniversalismE, Vol. 2, No. 2, pp. 1-12.

Altenburg, Tilman/Meter-Stamer, Jorg (1999). How to Promote Clusters: Policy Experiences from Latin America. In: World Development, Vol. 27, No. 9, pp. 1693-713.

Antara, Ngakan Timur (2009). Peranan Pusat Inovasi Keramik Plered. Paper presented at the workshop on Konsinyering Pengembangan Inovasi Teknologi Keramik. Plered, November 30, 2009.

AntaraJawaBarat.com (2012). BJB Siap Fasilitasi Pembiayaan Wirausaha Muda. December 6, 2012. http://www.antarajawabarat.com/lihat/berita/40925/bjb-siap-fas ilitasi-pembiayaan-wirausaha-muda, accessed January 7, 2013.

Antara News (2011). Mendag: Industri Sepatu Cibaduyut Miliki Potensi Internasional. February 12, 2011. http://www.antaranews.com/berita/245873 mendag-industri-sepatu-cibaduyut-miliki-potensi-internasional, accessed September 14, 2012.

Antic, Miljenko (2003). Reexamining Role of the State in Promoting Development. In: Politicka Misao, Vol. XL, pp. 18-29.

Ariyani, Desy (2012). Evaluasi Pelatihan Ketrampilan Bagi Perajin Keramik Plered Tahun 2008-2011. Skripsi, Bandung: Universitas Pendidikan Indonesia.

Aspiranti,Tasya/Nurfahmiyati/Sundaya, Yukha (2008). Analisis 'Quality Function Deployment' Pada Sentra Industri Kecil Sepatu Cibaduyut. Bandung, Mimbar. Jurnal Sosial dan Pembangunan, Vol. 24, No. 1 (2008), pp. 1-11.

Astriani, Yuni (2012). Tingkat Kesejahteraan Pengrajin Industri Keramik di Desa Anjun Kecamatan Plered Kabupaten Purwakarta. Skripsi. Universitas Pendidikan Indonesia.

Badan Pusat Statistik (2010). Profil Industri Mikro dan Kecil 2010. Jakarta: CV Ryan Indah.

Badan Pusat Statistik Kabupaten Purwakarta (2010). Purwakarta Dalam Angka 2009.

Badan Pusat Statistik Kota Bandung (n.d.). Produk Domestik Regional Bruto Kota Bandung Tahun 2006-2009 Menurut Lapangan Usaha.

Baier, Elisabeth/Kroll, Henning/Zenker, Andrea (2013). Regional Autonomy With Regard to Innovation Policy: A Differentiated Illustration of the European Status Quo. Working Papers Firms and Region No. R3/2013. Karlsruhe: Fraunhofer ISI.

Baptista, Rui/Swann, Peter (1998). Do Firms in Cluster Innovate More? Research Policy 27, pp. 525-40.

Barkley, David L./Henry, Mark S. (2001). Advantages and Disadvantages of Targeting Industry Cluster. Clemson University Public Service Activities. REDRL Research Report 09-2001-01. http://cherokee.agecon.clemson.edu/ redrl_rpt3.pdf, accessed January 9, 2014.

Beaudry, Catherine/Breschi, Stefano (2003). Are Firms in Clusters Really More Innovative? In: Economics of Innovation and New Technology, Taylor and Francis Journals, Vol. 12 (4), pp. 325-42.

Belanja Online Lewat Gerai KUMKM. http://diskumkm.jabarprov.go.id/index.php?option=com_content&view=article&id=126:belanja-online-lewat-gerai-kumkm&catid=1:bewara&Itemid=65, accessed June 14, 2013.

Bennet, Richard (2010). Decentralizing Authority After Suharto: Indonesia's 'Big Bang', 1998-2010. Innovations for Successful Societies, Princeton University. http://www.princeton.edu/successfulsocieties, accessed January 9, 2014.

Bhasin, Balbir B/ Venkataramany, Sivakumar (2010). Globalization of Entrepreneurship: Policy Considerations for SME Development in Indonesia. In: International Business and Economics Research Journal: April 2010, Vol. 9, No. 4, pp. 95-104.

Black, Thomas R. (2002). Understanding Social Science Research. 2nd ed. London: Sage Publications.

Boari, Cristina (2001). Industrial Cluster, Focal Firms, and Economic Dynamism: A Perspective from Italy. The International bank for Reconstruction and Development/the World Bank. Stock Number 37186.

Brown, Jason (1993). The Role of the State in Economic Development: Theory, the East Asian Experience, and the Malaysian Case. Asian Development Bank, Economic Staff Paper No. 52. http://www.adb.org/sites/default/files/pub/1993/es52.pdf, accessed January 5, 2014.

Buku Tanya Jawab Seputar Kredit Usaha Rakyat (KUR). http://www.komite-kur.com, accessed September 12, 2013.

Burger, Kees/Kameo, Daniel/Sandee, Henry (2001). Clustering of Small Agro-Processing Firms in Indonesia. In: International Food and Agribusiness Management Review, 2 (3/4), pp. 289-99.

Clark, Gordon L. (1984). A Theory of Local Autonomy. In: Annals of the Association of American Geographers, Vol. 74, No. 2 (June 1984), pp. 195-208.

Cole, Stroma (2007). Entrepreneurship and Empowerment: Considering the Barriers – A Case Study from Indonesia. In: Tourism Review, Vol. 55, No. 4, pp. 461-73.

Creswell, John W. (1994). Research Design: Qualitative and Quantitative Approaches. London: Sage Publications.

Creswell, John W. (2013). Qualitative Inquiry and Research Design: Choosing among Five Approaches. 3rd ed. Los Angeles: Sage Publications.

Corbin, Juliet/Strauss, Anselm (2008). Basics of Qualitative Research. 3rd ed. London: Sage Publications.

Decree of Minister of Cooperatives and SMEs No. 14/2006 on Guideline on Guarantee Credit and Financial Fund for Cooperative and SMEs (Peraturan Menteri Negara Koperasi dan Usaha Kecil Menengah No. 14/2006 tentang Petunjuk Teknis Dana

Penjaminan Kredit dan Pembiayaan Untuk Koperasi dan Usaha Kecil dan Menengah).

deLeon, Peter/deLeon, Linda (2002). What Ever Happened to Policy Implementation? An Alternative Approach. In: Journal of Public Administration Research and Theory: J-PART, Vol. 12, No. 4 (October 2002), pp. 467-92.

Departemen Perindustrian (2009a). Buku I: Peta Panduan (*Road Map*) Pengembangan Klaster Industri Prioritas Basis Industri Manufaktur Tahun 2010-2014.

Departemen Perindustrian (2009b). Buku VI: Peta Panduan (*Road Map*) Pengembangan Klaster Industri Prioritas Industri Kecil dan Menengah Tertentu 2010-2014.

Departemen Perindustrian dan PT INDULEXCO (n.d.). Pengembangan Kompetensi Inti Dalam Rangka Peningkatan Unggulan Daerah: Kabupaten Katingan. http://rocana.kemenperin.go.id/ index.php?option=com_content& view=article&id= 112&Itemid=213, accessed September 15, 2013.

Deputi Bidang Pengkajian Sumberdaya Koperasi dan UKM (2009). Laporan Hasil Kajian Dampak Kredit Usah Rakyat 2009, Kementerian Koperasi dan Usaha Kecil Menengah. http://www.smecda.com/kajian/get8.asp?id=504, accessed January 13, 2014.

Detik Finance (2010). 47,16 Juta Unit UMKM Belum Berbadan Hukum. September 3, 2010. http://us.finance.detik.com/read/2010/09/03/121518/1434289/4/4716-juta-unit-umkm-belum-berbadan-hukum, accessed September 29, 2011.

Dinas Koperasi, Usaha Mikro, Kecil, Menengah, Perindustrian dan Perdagangan Kabupaten Purwakarta (2009). Pengembangan Klaster Keramik Plered – Purwakarta: FGD Tahap ke IV. Unpublished paper.

Dinas Koperasi, UMKM, Perindustrian, dan Perdagangan Kabupaten Purwakarta (2011). Rencana Kerja Tahun 2011.

Dinas Koperasi dan Usaha Mikro, Kecil, dan Menengah Provinsi Jawa Barat (n.d.a). e-Profile. http://diskumkm.jabarprov.go.id/index.php?option=com_wrapper&view= wrapper&Itemid=77, accessed July 2, 2013.

Dinas Koperasi dan Usaha Mikro, Kecil, dan Menengah Provinsi Jawa Barat (n.d.b). e-Profile: Rencana Strategis Tahun 2008-2013. http://diskumkm.jabarprov.go. id/index.php?option=com_wrapper&view=wrapper&Itemid=77, accessed July 2, 2013.

Dinas Koperasi dan Usaha Mikro, Kecil, dan Menengah Provinsi Jawa Barat (n.d.c). Rencana Strategis Dinas Koperasi dan UMKM Provinsi Jawa Barat. http://diskumkm.jabarprov.go.id/index.php?option=com_wrapper&view=wrapper& Itemid=77, accessed July 2, 2013.

Dinas Koperasi dan Usaha Mikro, Kecil, dan Menengah Provinsi Jawa Barat (n.d.d). Sentra Bisnis KUMKM. http://diskumkm.jabarprov.go.id/index.php?option=com_ wrapper&view=wrapper&Itemid=77, accessed July 2, 2013.

Dinas Koperasi dan Usaha Mikro, Kecil, dan Menengah Provinsi Jawa Barat (n.d.e). Belanja Online Lewat Gerai KUMKM. http://diskumkm.jabarprov.go.id/index. php?option=com_content&view=article&id=126:belanja-online-lewat-gerai-kumkm&catid=1:bewara&Itemid=65, accessed July 2, 2013.

Dinas KUKM dan Perindag Kota Bandung (n.d.). Profil Dinas Koperasi UKM dan Perindustrian Perdagangan Kota Bandung. http://diskopukmperindagbdg.blogspot.de/p/profile.html, accessed January 5, 2014.

Dinas Perindustrian dan Perdagangan Pemprov. Jawa Barat dan PT. Nusantara Citra Konsultan (2007). Identifikasi Kebutuhan Pasar Penataan Data Base Industri Alas Kaki: Laporan Akhir. Bandung.

Dinas Perindustrian dan Perdagangan Provinsi Jawa Barat (2009). Rencana Strategis Dinas Perindustrian dan Perdagangan Provinsi Jawa Barat 2009-2013.

Dinas Perindustrian dan Perdagangan Provinsi Jawa Barat (n.d). Data Statistik. http://disperindag.jabarprov.go.id/index.php?mod=manageMenu&idMenuKiri=459&idMenu=463, accessed January 7, 2014.

Dinas Tata Ruang dan Bangunan Pemerintah Kabupaten Purwakarta (2003). Detail Engineering Design (DED) Sentra Keramik Plered: Laporan Pendahuluan.

Dipta, I Wayan (n.d). Strategi Membangun Keunggulan Daya Saing Usaha Mikro, Kecil, Menengah dan Koperasi di Indonesia Dalam Era Perekonomian Baru. Paper presented at the National Conference on Revitalisasi Strategi Pembinaan Usaha Kecil, Menengah dan Koperasi oleh Pemerintah/BUMN Dalam Perekonomian Baru. http://www.smecda.com/ deputi7/file_makalah/era-perekonomian-baru.pdf, accessed January 7, 2014.

El-Mefteh, Muhammad A. (2005). The Economic Role of the State in the Era of Globalization. In: Electronic Journal of the American Association of Behavioral and Social Sciences, Vol. 8, Fall 2005. https://googledrive.com/host/0BwYZA6eD9SMqN0k5QV9YMkhGZ00/Perspectives/Perspectives2005/index.html, accessed January 5, 2014.

Enright, Michael J. and Ffowcs-Williams, Ifor (2000). Local Partnership, Clusters, and SME Globalization. Paper presented in Enhancing the Competitiveness of SMEs in the Global Economy: Strategies and Policies. Conference for Ministers Responsible for SMEs and Industries Ministers. Bologna, Italy, June 14-15, 2000.

Europe INNOVA (2008). The Concept of Clusters and Cluster Policies and Their Role for Competitiveness and Innovation: Main Statistical Results and Lesson Learned. Commission Staff Working Document SEC (2008) 2637. http://ec.europa.eu/enterprise/policies/innovation/files/clusters-working-document-sec-2008-2635_en.pdf, accessed November 3, 2013.

European Commission (n.d). The New SME Definition: User Guide and Model Declaration. Enterprise and Industry Publications. http://ec.europa.eu/enterprise/policies/sme/files/sme_definition/sme_user_guide_en.pdf, accessed September 4, 2013.

Feldman, Maryann P./Francis, Johanna/Bercovitz, Janet (2005). Creating a Cluster While Building a Firm: Entrepreneurs and the Formation of Industrial Clusters. In: Regional Studies, Vol. 39, No. 1 (February 2005), pp. 129-41.

Feser, Edward/Renski, Henry/Glodstein, Harvey (2008). Cluster and Economic Development Outcomes: An Analysis of the Link between Clustering and Industry Growth. In: Economic Development Quarterly, Vol. 22, No. 4, pp. 324-44.

Flick, Uwe (2007). Managing Quality in Qualitative Research. London: Sage Publications.

Fujita, Masahita/Krugman, Paul/Venables, Anthony J. (2001). The Spatial Economy: Cities, Regions, and International Trade. Massachusetts: The MIT Press.

Fukuyama, Francis (1995). Trust: The Social Virtues and the Creation of Prosperity. New York: The Free Press.

Government of the West Java Province (n.d.). Vision and Mission of the Government of the West Java Province. http://www.jabarprov.go.id /index.php/subMenu/79, accessed February 6, 2013.

Government Regulation No. 44/1997 on Partnership (Peraturan Pemerintah No. 44/1997 tentang Kemitraan).

Government Regulation No. 32/1998 on the Development of Small Business (Peraturan Pemerintah No. 32/1998 tentang Pembinaan dan Pengembangan Usaha Kecil).

Government Regulation No. 38/2007 on the Division of Government Affairs among the (Central) Government, the Provincial Government, and the City/Regency Governments (Peraturan Pemerintah No. 38/2007 tentang Pembagian Urusan Pemerintahan antara Pemerintah, Pemerintah Daerah Provinsi, dan Pemerintah Daerah Kabupaten/Kota).

Hadiwinata, Bob Sugeng (2003). The Politics of NGOs in Indonesia: Developing Democracy and Managing a Movement. London: Routledge.

Hadiz, Vedi R. (2004). Decentralization and Democracy in Indonesia: A Critique of Neo-Institutionalist Perspectives. In: Development and Change, Vol. 35, No. 4, pp. 697-718.

Haggard, Stephan (1990). Pathways from the Periphery: The Politics of Growth in the Newly Industrializing Countries. Itacha: Cornell University Press.

Harian Kontan (2012). Pengesahan UU: Akhirnya, DPR Sahkan UU Lembaga Keuangan Mikro, December 11, 2012.

Hill, Hal (2001). Small and Medium Enterprises in Indonesia: Old Policy Challenges for a New Administration. In: Asian Survey, Vol. 41, No. 2, pp. 248-70.

Hofstede, Geert/Hofstede, Gert Jan (2005). Cultures and Organizations: Software of the Mind. New York: McGraw-Hill.

Huggins, Robert/Izushi, Hiro (2011). Competition, Competitive Advantage, and Cluster: The Ideas of Michael Porter. In: Huggins, Robert/Izushi, Hiro (eds). Competition, Competitive Advantage, and Cluster: The Ideas of Michael Porter. Oxford: Oxford University Press, pp. 1-22.

Indonesian Chamber of Commerce and Industry (KADIN) (2010). Key Challenges Faced By Entrepreneur: Indonesia. Paper presented at the Workshop on Reducing Start-Up and Establishment Time of Business. Hiroshima. http://aimp.apec.org/ Documents/2010/EC/WKSP1/10_ec_wksp 1_006.pdf, March 1-2, 2010.

Inkubator Agribisnis dan Agroindustri-Institut Pertanian Bogor. http://inkubator ipb.com/index.php?nama=Home, accessed June 8, 2013.

Instalasi Pengembang Industri Kecil Menengah Alas Kaki/Persepatuan Bandung (2008). Laporan Instalasi Pengembang Industri Kecil Menengah Alas Kaki/Persepatuan Bandung.

Isbasoiu, George-Marian (2006). Industrial Cluster and Regional Development: The Case of Timisoara and Montebelluna. Munich Personal RePEc Archive (MPRA) Paper No. 5037. http://mpra.ub.uni-muenchen.de/5037, accessed January 4, 2014.

Jati, Wasisto Raharjo (2012). Inkonsistensi Paradigma Otonomi Daerah di Indonesia: Dilema Sentralisasi dan Desentralisasi. In: Jurnal Konstitusi, Vol. 9, No. 4 (December 2012), pp. 743-73.

Joint Decree of the Minister of Finance, Minister of Interior, Minister of Cooperatives and SMEs as well as the Governor of Bank Indonesia No. 351.1/KMK.010/2009, No. 900-639A/2009, No. 01/SKB/M.KUKM/ IX/2009, No. 11/43A/Kep. GBI/2009 on Strategic Development of Microfinance Institutions (Keputusan Bersama Menteri Keuangan, Menteri Dalam Negeri, Menteri Negara Koperasi dan Usaha Kecil Menengah, dan Gubernur Bank Indonesia No. 351.1/KMK.010/2009, No. 900-639A/2009, No. 01/SKB/M.KUKM/IX/2009, No. 11/43A/Kep. GBI/2009 tentang Strategi Pengembangan Lembaga Keuangan Mikro).

Kadin Bandung (n.d.). Badan Promosi dan Pengelola Keterkaitan Usaha. http://kadinbandung.org/nonstruktural/divisi/bppku, accessed January 7, 2014.

Kementerian Koperasi dan UKM (2010). Rencana Strategis Kementerian Koperasi dan UKM Republik Indonesia Tahun 2010-2014. http://www.depkop.go.id/index.php?option=com_phocadownload&view=category&id=20&Itemid=82, accessed January 5, 2014.

Kementerian Koperasi dan UKM (n.d.). Visi dan Misi Kementerian Koperasi dan UKM. http://www.depkop.go.id/index.php?option=com_content&view=article&id=5&Itemid=2, accessed January 5, 2014.

Kementerian Perencanaan Pembangunan Nasional/Badan Perencanaan Pembangunan Nasional (2010a). Lampiran Peraturan Presiden Republik Indonesia No. 5/2010 tentang Rencana Pembangunan (RJPMN) Tahun 2010-2014: Buku I Prioritas Nasional.

Kementerian Perencanaan Pembangunan Nasional/Badan Perencanaan Pembangunan Nasional (2010b), Lampiran Peraturan Presiden Republik Indonesia No. 5/2010 tentang Rencana Pembangunan (RJPMN) Tahun 2010-2014: Buku II Memperkuat Sinergi Antar Bidang Pembangunan, Bab III Ekonomi.

Kementerian Perindustrian (2010). Rencana Strategis Kementerian Perindustrian 2010-2014. http://rocana.kemenperin.go.id/index.php?option=com_content&view=article&id=132&Itemid=237, accessed September 8, 2013.

Kementerian Perindustrian (n.d.a). Industri Unggulan Provinsi. http://rocana.kemenperin.go.id/index.php?option=com_content&view=article&id=99&Itemid=201, accessed September 8, 2013.

Kementerian Perindustrian (n.d.b). Pemantauan Ekspor 31 Kelompok Hasil Industri. http://kemenperin.go.id/statistik/kelompok.php?ekspor=1, accessed September 8, 2013.

Kementerian Perindustrian (n.d.c). Laporan Akuntabilitas Kinerja (LAKIP) 2010. http://rocana.kemenperin.go.id/index.php?option=com_content&view=article&id=137&Itemid=256, accessed September 8, 2013.

Kementerian Perindustrian (n.d.d). Working Meeting of the Ministry of Industry. http://rocana.kemenperin.go.id, accessed September 8, 2013.

Kementerian Perindustrian (n.d.e). Rumusan Hasil Rapat Kerja Kementerian Perindustrian dengan Dinas Perindustrian dan Bappeda Provinsi tahun 2010. http://rocana.kemenperin.go.id/index.php?option=com_content&view=article&id=119&Itemid=220, accessed September 8, 2013.

Keputusan Gubernur Jawa Barat No: 561/Kep.1665-Bangsos/2009 tentang Upah Minimum Kabupaten/Kota di Jawa Barat 2010.

Ketels, Christian H.M. (2003). The Development of the Cluster Concept: Present Experiences and Further Development. Paper prepared for NRW Conference on Clusters in Duisburg, Germany. December 5, 2003.

Kuah, Adrian T.H. (2002). Cluster Theory and Practice: Advantages for the Small Business Locating in a Vibrant Cluster. In: Journal of Research in Marketing and Entrepreneurship, Vol. 4, No. 3 (2002), pp. 206-28.

LaPalombara, Joseph (1971). Penetration: A Crisis of Government Capacity. In: Binder, Leonard/Coleman, James S./LaPalombara, Joseph/Pye, Lucian W./Verba, Sidney/Weiner, Myron. Crises and Sequences in Political Development. New Jersey: Princeton University Press, pp. 205-32.

Law No. 5/1984 on Industry (Undang-Undang No. 5/1984 tentang Perindustrian).

Law No. 32/2004 on Regional Government (Undang-Undang No. 32/2004 tentang Pemerintah Daerah).

Law No. 20/2008 on Small and Medium-sized Enterprises (Undang-Undang No. 20/2008 tentang Usaha Mikro, Kecil, dan Menengah).

Marijan, Kacung (2005). Mengembangkan Industri Kecil Menengah Melalui Pendekatan Kluster. In: Jurnal INSAN, Vol. 7, No. 3, pp. 216-25.

Marijan, Kacung (2007). Industrial Policy, Industrialisation and Custer Industries in Indonesia: An Overview. In: UNISIA, Vol. XXX, No. 64, pp. 103-21.

Markusen, Ann (1996). Sticky Places in Slippery Space: A Typology of Industrial Districts. In: Economy Geography, Vol. 72, No. 3 (July 1996), pp. 293-313.

Marshall, Alfred (1966 (1890)). Principles of Economics. 8th ed. London: Macmillan.

Marshall, Alfred (1919). Industry and Trade. London: Macmillan.

Meyer-Stamer, Jörg/Harmes-Liedtke, Ulrich (2005). How to Promote Clusters. Mesopartner Working Paper 08/2005.

Minister of State-Owned Enterprises Decree No. 236/MBU/2003 on the Partnership Program between State-owned Enterprises and Small Businesses (Keputusan Menteri Badan Usaha Milik Negara No. Kep. 236/MBU/2003 tentang Program Kemitraan Badan Usaha Milik Negara dengan Usaha Kecil dan Program Bina Lingkungan.

Ministry of Cooperatives and SMEs (2010). Data of SMEs 2010. (Kementerian Koperasi dan UKM (2010). Data UMKM 2010). http://www.depkop.go.id/in

dex.php?option=com_phocadownload&view=category&id=27:data-umkm&Itemid =93, accessed January 5, 2014.

Ministry of Cooperatives and SMEs (n.d.). Statistics SMEs 2007-2009. (Kemenne-gkop&UKM (n.d.). Statistik Usaha Kecil dan Menengah Tahun 2007-2009).

Möhring, Johanna (2005). Clusters: Definition and Methodology. In: Local Economic and Employment Development OECD. 2005. Business Clusters: Promoting Enterprise in Central and Eastern Europe.

Ontario Association of Trading Houses (n.d). Trading Houses: A Practical Guide. http://www.oath.on.ca/publications/PDF_En/EN_TradingHouses Pra-ctical.pdf, accessed September 12, 2013.

Pakpahan, Aknolt K. (2010). Increasing SMEs' Capacity. In: The Jakarta Post, August 16, 2010, p. 7.

Pakpahan, Aknolt K. (2013). Micro, Small, and Medium-Sized Enterprises in Indonesia: Towards More Coordinated Policies and More Competitive-based SME. In: Heise, Matthias/Rucktäschel, Kathrin (eds.). Indonesia's Search for Democracy: Political, Economic, and Social Developments. Baden-Baden: Nomos, pp. 299-318.

Perry, Martin (2005). Business Cluster: An International Perspective. New York: Routledge.

Pepinsky, Thomas B./Wihardja, Maria M. (2011). Decentralization and Economic Performance in Indonesia. In: Journal of East Asian Studies: September-December 2011, Vol. 11, No. 3, pp. 337-71.

Porter, Michael (1990). The Competitive Advantage of Nations. New York: The Free Press.

Porter, Michael (1998a). On Competition. Harvard: Harvard Business School Press.

Porter, Michael E. (1998b). Clusters and the New Economics of Competition. Harvard Business Review, Reprint Number 98609.

Porter, Michael E. (2003). The Economic Performance of Regions. Regional Studies, Vol. 37, August/October 6-7, 2003, pp. 549-78.

Porter, Michael E. (2008). On Competition: Updated and Expanded Edition. Boson: A Harvard Business Review Book.

Prasetyo, Pius S. (2005). Democracy in the Indonesian Village Society: The Impact of Local Autonomy Policy and the Role of Local Culture toward Democratization in Village Society. Munster: LIT Verlag.

Presidential Instruction No. 10/1999 on the Empowerment of Medium-sized Business (Instruksi Presiden Republik Indonesia No. 10/1999 tentang Pemberdayaan Usaha Menengah).

Presidential Instruction No. 3/2006 on the Policy Package for Improving the Investment Climate (Instruksi Presiden Republik Indonesia No. 3/2006 tentang Paket Kebijakan Perbaikan Iklim Investasi).

Presidential Instruction No. 6/2007 on Acceleration of the Real Sector and Development of Micro, Small and Medium-sized Enterprises (Instruksi Presiden Republik Indonesia No. 6/2007 tentang Kebijakan Percepatan Pengembangan Sektor Riil dan Pemberdayaan Usaha Mikro, Kecil dan Menengah).

Presidential Instruction No. 1/2010 on Accelerating the Implementation of National Development Priorities in 2010 (Instruksi Presiden Republik Indonesia No. 1/2010 tentang Percepatan Pelaksanaan Prioritas Pembangunan Nasional Tahun 2010).

Presidential Instruction No. 3/2010 on the Equitable Development Program (Instruksi Presiden Republik Indonesia No. 3/2010 tentang Program Pembangunan Yang Berkeadilan).

Primont, Diane F. and Domazlicky, Bruce (2008). Industry Cluster Analysis for the Southeast Missouri Region. Center for Economic and Business Research. http://www6.semo.edu/cebr/studies/Southeast_rpc_industry_cluster_study_1.pdf, accessed September 8, 2013.

Regulation of the City of Bandung No. 13/2012 on the Obligation of Implementating Social Responsibility Program (Peraturan Daerah Kota Bandung No. 13/2012 tentang Pelaksanaan Kewajiban Program Tanggung Jawab Sosial dan Lingkungan Perusahaan).

Regulation of the Minister of Home Affairs No. No. 24/2006 on the Guidelines on One Stop System (Peraturan Menteri Dalam Negeri No. 24/2006 tentang Pedoman Penyelenggaraan Pelayanan Terpadu Satu Pintu).

Regulation of the Minister of Home Affairs No. 20/2010 on Community Empowerment through the Appropriate Technology Management (Peraturan Menteri Dalam Negeri No. 20/2010 tentang Pemberdayaan Masyarakat Melalui Pengelolaan Teknologi Tepat Guna).

Regulation of the Minister of Home Affairs No. 64/2012 on Guidelines on Incentives and Investment facilitation in the Region (Peraturan Menteri Dalam Negeri No. 64/2012 tentang Pedoman Pelaksanaan Pemberian Insentif dan Pemberian Kemudahan Penanaman Modal di Daerah).

Regulation of the Minister of Industry No. 78/2007 on the Increasing the Effectiveness of Developing SMIs using the One Village One Product (OVOP) Approach in Business Center (Peraturan Menteri Perindustrian Republik Indonesia No. 78/2007 tentang Peningkatan Efektifitas Pengembangan Industri Kecil dan Menengah Melalui Pendekatan Satu Desa Satu Produk (One Village One Product – OVOP) di Sentra).

Regulation of the Minister of Industry of the Republic of Indonesia No. 110/M-IND/PER/10/2009 on the Roadmap of the Development of the Footwear Industrial Cluster (Peraturan Menteri Perindustrian Republik Indonesia No. 110/M-IND/PER/10/2009 tentang Peta Panduan (Road Map) Pengembangan Klaster Industri Alas Kaki). http://kemenperin.go.id/artikel/19/Kebijakan-Industri-Nasional, accessed July 4, 2013.

Regulation of Minister of Industry of the Republic of Indonesia No. 135/M-IND/PER/10/2009 on the Roadmap of the Development of Pottery and Decorative Ceramic Industrial Cluster (Peraturan Menteri Perindustrian Republik Indonesia No. 135/M-IND/PER/10/2009 tentang Peta Panduan (Road Map) Pengembangan Klaster Industri Keramik dan Keramik Hias). http://kemenperin.go.id/artikel/19/Kebijakan-Industri-Nasional, accessed July 4, 2013.

Regulation of the Minister of Industry No. 105/2010 on the Organization and Administration of the Ministry of Industry (Peraturan Menteri Perindustrian Republik Indonesia No. 105/2010 tentang Organisasi dan Tata Kerja Kementerian Perindustrian).

Regulation of the Minister of Industry No. 98/M-IND/PER/12/2011 on the Restructuring Programs of Machinery and Equipment for Small and Medium-sized Industry (Peraturan Menteri Perindustrian Republik Indonesia No. 98/M-IND/PER/12/2011 tentang Program RestrukturisasiMesin/Pera-latan Industri Kecil dan Menengah).

Regulation of the Minister of Industry No. 13/2013 on the Restructuring Programs of the Machinery and Equipment for Small and Medium-sized Industry (Peraturan Menteri Perindustrian Republik Indonesia No. 13/2013 tentang Program Restrukturisasi Mesin dan/atau Peralatan Industri Kecil dan Menengah (IKM)).

Regulation of the Minister of State-owned Enterprises No. 236/2003 on the Partnership Program with the Small Business and the Community Development Program (Peraturan Menteri BUMN NO. 236/2003 tentang Program Kemitraan Badan Usaha Milik Negara dengan Usaha Kecil dan Program Bina Lingkungan).

Regulation of the President of the Republic of Indonesia No. 28/2008 on the National Industrial Policy (Peraturan Presiden Republik Indonesia No. 28/2008 tentang Kebijakan Industri Nasional).

Regulation of the President of the Republic of Indonesia No. 47/2009 on the Establishment and Organization of State Ministry (Peraturan Presiden Reupblik Indonesia No. 47/2009 tentang Pembentukan dan Organisasi Kemeterian Negara).

Regulation of the President of the Republic of Indonesia No. 5/2010 on the National Medium-term Development Plan 2010-2014 (Peraturan Presiden Republik Indonesia No. 5/2010 tentang Rencana Pembangunan Jangka Menengah Nasional Tahun 2010-2014).

Regulation of the Regent of Purwakarta No. 44/2009 on the Organization, Duties, Functions, and Administration of the Technical Service Unit at the Office of Cooperatives, SMEs, Industry and Trade (Peraturan Bupati Purwakarta No. 22/2009 tentang Organisasi, Tugas, Fungsi dan Tata Kerja Unit Pelayanan Teknis pada Dinas Koperasi, Usaha Mikro, Kecil, Menengah, Perindustrian dan Perdagangan).

Regulation of the Governor of West Java No. 69/2009 on the Main Duties, Functions, Details of Unit's Duties, and Administration of the Office of Industry and Trade of the West Java Province (Peraturan Gubernur Jawa Barat No. 69/2009 tentang Tugas Pokok, Fungsi, Rincian Tugas Unit, dan Tata Kerja di Lingkungan Dinas Perindustrian dan Perdagangan Jawa Barat).

Regulation of the Governor of West Java No. 113/2009 on the Organization and Administrative of the Technical Service Unit and Other Agency in the Province of West Java (Peraturan Gubernur Jawa Barat No. 113/2009 tentang Organisasi dan Tata Kerja Unit Pelaksana Teknis DInas/Badan di Pemerintah Provinsi Jawa Barat).

Reinert, Erick S. (1999). The Role of the State in Economic Growth. In: Journal of Economic Studies, Vol. 26, No. 4/5, pp. 268-326.

Ridwan, Asep M. (n.d.). Potensi Peluang Pasar Keramik di Jawa Barat. Dinas Perindustrian dan Perdagangan Jawa Barat. Unpublished paper.

Ridwan, Asep M. (2009). Kebijakan Ekspor Keramik Jawa Barat. Dinas Perindustrian dan Perdagangan Jawa Barat. Unpublished paper.

Rondinelli, Dennis A./McCullough, James S./Johnson, Ronald W. (1989). Analysing Decentralization Policies in Developing Countries: A Political-Economy Framework. In: Development and Change, Vol. 20, pp. 57-87.

Rosenfeld, Stuart A. (1997). Bringing Business Cluster into the Mainstream of Economic Development. In: European Planning Studies, Vol. 5, No. 1, pp. 3-23.

Sandee, Henry et al. (2000). Small Firm Development During Good Times and Bad: The Jepara Furniture Industy. In: Manning, Cris and van Diermen, Peter (eds.). Indonesia in Transition: Social Aspects of Reformasi and Crisis. London: ZED Books, pp. 184-98.

Satriawan, Bondan/ Oktavianti, Henny (2012). Upaya Pengentasan Kemiskinan Pada Petani Menggunakan Metode Tindakan Kolektif Kelembagaan Pertanian. In: Jurnal Ekonomi Pembangunan, Vol. 13, No. 1 (June 2012), pp. 96-112.

Sentra Bisnis KUMKM. http://diskumkm.jabarprov.go.id/index.php?option= com_ wrapper&view=wrapper&Itemid=77, accessed July 2, 2013.

Sigurdson, Jon (2004). Regional Innovation Systems (RIS) in China. European Institute of Japanese Studies (EIJS) Working Paper No. 195. http://swopec.hhs.se/ eijswp/papers/eijswp0195.pdf, accessed January 5, 2014.

Silverman, David (2001). Interpreting Qualitative Data: Methods for Analysing Talk, Text, and Interaction. 2nd ed. London: Sage Publications.

Soekarni, Muhammad/Suryanto, Joko (2009). Analisis Rantai Nilai UMKM di Jawa Barat: Studi Kasus Sentra Sepatu Cibaduyut Bandung. In: Soekarni, Muhammad (ed.) Peran Value Chain (Rantai Nilai) Dalam Meningkatkan Kinerja Usaha Kecil dan Menengah, Jakarta: LIPI Press.

Soetrisno, Noer (2009). Pengembangan Klaster IKM/UKM di Indonesia: Pengalaman dan Prospek. Paper presented at the Workshop on Developing SMEs' Cluster. Surakarta, October 26-28, 2009.

Solusi Magazine (2012a). Persoalan Gas Industri Keramik Perlu Koordinasi banyak Pihak. In: Solusi Magazine, Vol. 2, No. 1, March 2012.

Solusi Magazine (2012b). Balai Besar Keramik Bandung: Ujung Tombak Kementrian Perindustrian Untuk Mengembangkan Industri Keramik. In: Solusi Magazine, Vol. 2, No. 1, March 2012.

Storper, Michael (1997). The Regional World: Territorial Development in a Global Economy. London: Guildford Press.

Stough, Roger R. et al. (1998). Small Business Entrepreneurship in the High Technology Services Sector: An Assessment for the Edge Cities of the U.S. National Capital Region. In: Small Business Economics, Vol. 10, pp. 61-74.

Subari (2010). Pengembangan Potensi Industri Keramik di Daerah Provinsi Jawa Barat Dengan Memberdayakan Bahan Baku Lokal. Unpublished paper.

Suherman, Agus (2006). Potret Usaha Mikro Kecil (UMK). In: Sosialisasi hasil Sensus 2006: Sensus Sampel (SE06-SS). http://www.bps.go.id/sosialisasi_ SE/SE2006-Potret_UMK-Agus_Suherman.pdf, accessed September 2, 2011.

Sulistyastuti, Dyah Ratih (2004). Dinamika Usaha Kecil dan Menengah (UKM): Analisis Konsentrasi Regional UKM di Indonesia 1999-2001. In: Jurnal Ekonomi Pembangunan: Kajian Ekoomi Negara Berkembang, pp. 143-64.

Tambunan, Tulus (2005). Promoting Small and Medium Enterprises with a Clustering Approach: A Policy Experience from Indonesia. In: Journal of Small Business and Management, Vol. 43, No. 2, pp. 138-54.

Tambunan, Tulus (2007). Entrepreneurship Development: SME in Indonesia. In: Journal of Development Entrepreneurship, Vol. 12, No. 1, pp. 95-118.

Tambunan, Tulus (2008a). SME Development, Economic Growth, and Government Intervention in a Developing Country: The Indonesian Story. In: Journal of International Entrepreneurship, Vol. 6, No. 4, pp. 147-67.

Tambunan, Tulus (2008b). SMEs Development in Indonesia: Do Economic Growth and Government Support Matter? In: International Journal of Asia Pacific Studies, Vol. 4, No. 2, pp. 111-33.

Tambunan, Tulus (2009a). Export-Oriented Small and Medium Industry Clusters in Indonesia. In: Journal of Enterprising Communities: People and Places in the Global Economy, Vol. 3, No. 1, pp. 25-58.

Tambunan, Tulus (2009b). SME in Asian Developing Countries. New York: Palgrave Macmillan.

Tambunan, Tulus TH. (2009c). Productivity in SMEs in Indonesia: Facts and Constraints. Policy Discussion Series 14/10/09.

Tambunan, Tulus (2010). Apakah Kebijakan Pengembangan Usaha Kecil dan Menengah di Indonesia Selama Ini Efektif? Paper presented at the BPPT Workshop, April 8, 2010.

Tambunan, Tulus (2011). The Impact of Trade Liberalization on Indonesian Small and Medium-sized Enterprises. In: Trade Knowledge Network (TKN) Policy Paper.

Tambunan, Tulus (n.d.). Development of Small and Medium Enterprise Clusters in Indonesia: A Review. http://www.eadi.org/fileadmin/WG_Documents/Reg_WG/tambunan.pdf, accessed January 9, 2014.

Tabellini, Guido (2004). The Role of the State in Economic Development. In: Innocenzo Gasparini Institute for Economic Research (IGIER) Working Paper No. 265, July 2004. ftp://ftp.igier.uni-bocconi.it/wp/2004/265.pdf, January 4, 2014.

The Need to Develop SMEs Global Market Network, Purpose: Information, Submitted by: Indonesia, paper presented at the 26th SMEWG Meeting, Kaohsiung, Chinese Taipei, March 30-April 4, 2008. http://www.oath.on.ca/publications/PDF_En/EN_TradingHousesPractical.pdf, accessed January 7, 2014.

Triwibowo, Albert/Pakpahan, Aknolt K. (2012). Fighting Corruption in Indonesia: In Search of Greater Political Will. In: Heise, Matthias/Rucktäschel, Kathrin (eds.). Indonesia's Search for Democracy: Political, Economic, and Social Developments. Baden-Baden: Nomos, pp. 233-58.

United States International Trade Commission (2010). Small and Medium-sized Enterprises: Overview of Participation in the US Exports. Investigation No. 332-508. USITC Publication 4125. http://www.usitc.gov/publications/ 332/pub4125.pdf, accessed January 6, 2014.

UPTD Litbang Keramik Disperindag & PM Kabupaten Purwakarta, Dinas Perindustrian, Perdagangan, dan Penanaman Modal Kabupaten Purwakarta (2006/2007). Profil Industri Keramik Plered. Unpublished paper.

UPTD Litbang Keramik Dinas Koperasi, UMKM, Perindustrian, dan Perdagangan Kabupaten Purwakarta (n.d.). Sejarah Singkat Keramik Plered, Purwakarta. Unpublished paper.

Van Meter, Donald S./Van Horn, Carl E. (1975). The Policy Implementation Process: A Conceptual Framework. In: Administration and Society, Vol. 6, No. 4 (February 1975), pp. 445-88.

Wee, Thee Kian (2006). Policies for Private Sector Development in Indonesia. ADB Institute Discussion Paper No. 46.

West Java Provincial Regulation No. 21/2008 on the Organization and Administration of the Province of the West Java Regional Office (Peraturan Daerah Provinsi Jawa Barat No. 21/2008 tentang Organisasi dan Tata Kerja Dinas Daerah Provinsi Jawa Barat).

West Java Provincial Regulation No. 10/2010 on the Empowerment and Development of SMEs (Peraturan Daerah Provinsi Jawa Barat No. 10/2010 tentang Pemberdayaan dan Pengembangan Usaha Mikro, Kecil dan Menengah).

West Java Provincial Regulation No. 25/2010 on the Amendment of the West Java Province Regional Regulation No. 2/2009 on the Regional Medium Term Development Plan 2008-2013. (Peraturan Daerah Provinsi Jawa Barat No. 25/2010 tentang Perubahan Atas Peraturan Daerah Provinsi Jawa Barat No. 2/2009 tentang Rencana Pembangunan Jangka Menengah (RPJM) Daerah Provinsi Jawa Barat Tahun 2008-2013).

West Java Provincial Regulation No. 21/2011 on (Capital) Investment (Peraturan Daerah Provinsi Jawa Barat No. 21/2011 tentang Penanaman Modal).

Wilson, Dominic/Drysdale, Peter (2000). Perspectives. In: Drysdale, Peter (ed.). Reform and Recovery in East Asia: The Role of the State and Economic Enterprise. London: Routledge, pp. 1-12.

Yang, Hua et al. (2008). A Three-stage Model of Industrial Cluster and an Empirical Analysis. http://ieeexplore.ieee.org/stamp/stamp.jsp?tp=&arn umber=4681223, accessed July 2, 2013.

Yazid, Sylvia (2012). Practicing Democracy in Indonesia: The Involvement of NGO in the Process of Making and Implementing Policies on Labor Migration. In: Heise, Matthias/Rucktäschel, Kathrin (eds.). Indonesia's Search for Democracy: Political, Economic, and Social Developments. Baden-Baden: Nomos, pp. 211-32.